Building Databases
with Approach 3

Building Databases
with Approach 3

Elaine Marmel

John Wiley & Sons, Inc.

New York • Chichester • Brisbane • Toronto • Singapore

Publisher: Katherine Schowalter
Editor: Tim Ryan
Managing Editor: Angela Murphy
Text Design and Composition: Electric Ink, Ltd.

Designations used by companies to distinguish their products are often claimed as trademarks. In all instances where John Wiley & Sons, Inc. is aware of a claim, the product names appear in Initial Capital or all CAPITAL letters. Readers, however, should contact the appropriate companies for more complete information regarding trademarks and registration.

This text is printed on acid-free paper.

Published by John Wiley & Sons, Inc.

This publication is designed to provide accurate and authoritative information in regard to the subject matter covered. It is sold with the understanding that the publisher is not engaged in rendering legal, accounting, or other professional service. If legal advice or other expert assistance is required, the services of a competent professional person should be sought.

Library of Congress Cataloging-in-Publication Data:

Marmel, Elaine J.
    Building databases with Approach 3 / by Elaine Marmel.
        p.   cm.
    Includes index.
    ISBN 0-471-05223-X (acid-free paper)
    1. Database design   2. Lotus Approach for Windows   I. Title.
    QA76.9.D26M38   1995
    005.75'65—dc20   94-31731

Printed in the United States of America
10 9 8 7 6 5 4 3 2 1

Contents

CHAPTER 3

Joining Databases   35

CHAPTER 4

Working in the Design Environment   47

CHAPTER 9

Designing Reports for the Database   147

CHAPTER 10

Creating Form Letters and Mailing Labels   187

CHAPTER 13

Advanced Database Features   233

CHAPTER 14

Exchanging Data in Lotus Approach   265

Preface

In almost every business, tracking some type of information is a daily task. Many software packages specialize in helping you track specific information. For example, you use accounting software to track the money your business earns and the money it spends. On occasion, you identify a need to track information for which you cannot find a specialized software package. In these cases, you can use a database package, such as Lotus Approach, to design your own tracking system.

Throughout this book, as you learn to use Lotus Approach to build a tracking system, you will be following an example based on tracking due dates. Many businesses need to track due dates–lawyers track litigation and court dates, salespeople track dates for calling on customers, and CPAs need to track a variety of due dates related to tax returns for clients. The example throughout the book focuses on a CPA's need to build a system that tracks each client's fiscal year end information, various tax return due dates, when annual reports should be prepared, and when to remind clients to make tax payments.

Use the example in this book as a guideline when you build your own tracking system.

Acknowledgments

Again, I'd like to thank my family and friends for their support during this project. I'd also like to thank the folks at Lotus Approach for their help, and I'd like to thank the other people who made this book possible: Karl Barndt of Electric Ink, Ltd., for an outstanding typesetting job (I really like the look and feel of this book, Karl); Angela Murphy, who kept me sane while I completed this book and moved my home and office; Alison Roarty, for a fine editing job; and Tim Ryan, for giving me this opportunity.

Understanding and Designing Databases

Don't skip this chapter, even though it is the chapter that you will want to skip because it doesn't deal with a lot of hands-on activities. I have included this chapter to try to provide you with tricks, tips, and information that will help you build a better system. Lotus Approach is a flexible program that doesn't require a great deal of advance planning, but the system you build will meet your needs most effectively if you do some planning before you start.

In this chapter, you will learn about database design techniques and become familiar with some terminology that, while not required, might be useful to know. For example, you will learn the difference between relational and flat file databases. (Lotus Approach is a relational database program.) You will also learn how Lotus Approach stores your information, how Lotus Approach displays your data, and how you use different modes to work with your data.

Understanding Relational Databases

Just as you use word processing software to produce letters and documents and spreadsheet software to work intensively with numbers, you use database software to build repositories for information you need to manage. A database is a collection of related information, such as a telephone book, your customer list, or your financial information. In a Lotus Approach database, you also can include graphics, such as logos or pictures of people.

As the information age progresses, the sheer quantity of available information can become difficult to manage without a computer. Therefore, people use database software programs to build electronic databases, which you can search for information or answers to questions.

Database software falls into two different categories: flat file and relational. Flat file database designers face a series of problems that stem from one issue: databases built using flat file software cannot "talk" to each other; that is, you cannot simultaneously access a piece of information in File 1 and a piece of information in File 2. The obvious solution is to store all the information in one database file. However, as flat file database designers know, the database file can become large and therefore will be slow when you try to find information. Sometimes, the amount of information becomes so staggering that designers decide to split the information into two files, to speed things up. But you sacrifice information accessibility to make the database work faster. So, to solve both the accessibility problem and the speed problem, flat file database designers may try to create more than one database, making smaller (and faster) databases, but including the same information in more than one database. Databases built using flat file database software often contain redundant information, and redundant information in more than one database presents two problems:

- If the information is updated in one database and not the other, you lose track of which data is most accurate.

- Carrying the same information in more than one database makes the files bigger, taking up additional storage space on your disk.

Relational database software gives designers the ability to access information in more than one file simultaneously by relating two files. Therefore, when you build a database using a relational database software program, you can store information in several smaller files and relate them by including one common, unique piece of information in each file. Because the files are smaller, searches are faster—and because you relate the files using one piece of information, you can simultaneously access more than one file. Therefore, you don't create redundant data because you don't need to store any information other than the linking information in more than one database. When deciding what information should be stored in a particular database, concentrate on not duplicating information between databases.

Suppose, for example, you wanted to build a customer profile database. In that database, you want to include the customer name, address, phone number, products purchased from you, the sales representative who supports that customer, and some personal information such as the customer's birthday, spouse's name, children's names and birthdays and so on. If you use a flat file software program, you store all the information in one large file. That way, you can find out what the customer buys and offer him a discount for his birthday.

If you use a relational database software program, you break the information into at least two files, one containing work-related information and the other containing personal information. You can still use the files together by including the customer's name (or a similar piece of information) in both files. Thus, you can still find out what he buys and offer him a discount for his birthday.

Lotus Approach is a relational database software program, so you can build databases that require less disk space and run faster. In addition, you can link one database to another by including a common field in each database you want to link.

Using Effective Database Design Techniques

The big question for building a database becomes, "What do I need to put in it?" An easy way to answer this question is to review forms you are already using in your office. You may not be putting the information into a computer, but you probably are putting it into some kind of manual storage system. You may find that you need to make changes to your current forms. Perhaps the current forms contain information that you don't need, or perhaps they ask for information you don't supply because you've found you don't need it. On the other hand, maybe the current forms *don't* ask for information you've decided you want to collect. Review and modify your current data collection forms and design any new forms you think you might need. You don't have to get artistic here; just draw a rough layout that includes the types of information you want to collect.

Since data entry forms don't always describe the whole picture, review the reports you produce and compare them to the data entry forms. Remember that you won't be able to get information out of your database unless you put that information into your database. Although the concept may seem obvious, many designers neglect the question, "What do I need to get out of my database?" Reports you produce serve as the foundation for identifying information you need to include on your data entry forms—and information you *don't* need to include on your data entry forms. Using the reports you currently compile, identify information you have difficulty obtaining. You may need to add items to your data collection forms so that the information will be readily available when you want to produce a report. Also look for information you collect on the data entry forms that doesn't appear on any report; perhaps you don't need to be collecting that information.

Understanding How Lotus Approach Stores Your Data

Like any other database program, Lotus Approach stores your data in records. A *record* contains all the information about one item in your database; in a customer database, each record contains information about one customer. A record is comprised of fields. A *field* represents a specific type of information; in a customer database, the customer's name is a field on each customer's record.

Lotus Approach stores your data in a database file. You can choose one of several different database formats so that other people, using other database software programs, can also access your data. For example, you can create a file in DBASE III+ format so that some-one who uses DBASE III+ can read your database file. Approach can store data in the following formats:

- DBASE III+
- DBASE IV
- Paradox 3.5 and 4.0
- FoxPro 2.1
- Oracle SQL
- Microsoft/Sybase SQL Server
- IBM DB2®-MDI

Tip
Lotus Approach can also read all of the listed formats, so, in using Lotus Approach, you can read and work with the information created by another user in one of the listed database software programs.

If you do not plan to share your database with users of other data-base software, the format you choose is irrelevant.

While Lotus Approach can store and read data in a number of dif-ferent database file formats, you don't actually work with your data in a database file. Instead, you work with your data in a view file. You use view files to store the various ways in which you want to use your data, such as forms and reports.

Comparing How You See Your Data...

When you work with a database in Lotus Approach, you work in a view file with an extension of .APR. (In prior versions of Lotus Approach, these files used an extension of .VEW.) In the view file, you store the various layouts you use to see your data. They are based on the following categories:

- **Forms:** You usually use forms to add information to or change information in your database. A form shows only one record at a time. You can print forms.

- **Reports:** You usually use reports to see specific information for multiple clients. For example, you can use a report to print a name and address list for each customer in the database. You may store other information on each customer's record, but you can print just the names and addresses with a report.

- **Worksheets:** You usually use worksheets to present your data in a grid format (rows and columns). The rows in a worksheet contain one record in your database, and the columns contain one field. You can use worksheets to present a cross-tabulation of your data. In a *crosstab*, you summarize records into two or more categories. In a worksheet for a travel agency, you might look at individual records for each traveler; in a crosstab, you might summarize information by travel agent or destination. In a worksheet for a CPA firm, you might look at individual records showing tax returns, due dates, and the person assigned to prepare the tax return; in a crosstab, you might summarize the information to count the number of tax returns due on a particular date from a particular preparer.

- **Charts:** You use charts to display your data graphically. You can use the data in a crosstab to create a chart, or you can simply create a chart from any set of data in your database. You can create bar charts, line charts, area charts, and pie charts. If you change the data on which a chart is based, Lotus Approach automatically updates the chart.

- **Form Letters:** You use form letters to mix information in your database with static information you type in the letter. For example, if you want to notify only certain clients about estimated tax payments that are due, you can type a form letter that includes the due dates for the tax payments and address the letter to the affected clients only.

- **Mailing Labels:** You use mailing labels to print name and address information onto standard Avery format labels or onto formats that you create.

You can create many different forms, reports, form letters or mailing labels in one database. Each form, report, worksheet, chart, form letter, or mailing label layout you create is called a *view*.

...To How You Work with Your Data

While you work with a view, you work in one of four modes:

- **Design:** You use Design mode to create and edit views (the layouts for forms, reports, form letters, and mailing labels).

- **Browse:** You use Browse mode to see your information in one of the form, report, form letter, or mailing label views you created in Design mode.

- **Find:** You use Find mode and one of the views you created in Design mode to search through your database to find specific information.

- **Preview:** You use Preview mode and one of the views you created in Design mode to see what your information will look like when you print it.

Chapter Summary

In this chapter, you gained an understanding of databases and techniques used when designing them. You learned about the difference between flat file and relational database programs, and that:

- Lotus Approach is a relational database program.

- Lotus Approach stores your information in one of several different database file formats, and you can share data with others who use other database programs.

- You see your data from different *views*, and you can create form views, report views, worksheet views, chart views, form letter views, and mailing label views in Lotus Approach.

- While you work with a view in Lotus Approach, you work in one of four modes: Design, Browse, Find, or Preview.

In the next chapter, you will learn how to set up a database and define fields.

CHAPTER 2

Setting Up a Database

Many software packages are available to help you track information, and many of them are specific to a need. For example, you can use accounting software to track the money your business earns and the money it spends. On occasion, however, you may need to track information for which you cannot find a specialized software package that suits your needs. Perhaps you can't find a package that does what you need done, or perhaps you can't find a package that does what you need done in the way you need to do it. In these cases, you can use a database package, such as Lotus Approach, to design your own tracking system.

You can use Lotus Approach to build many different kinds of databases. Throughout this book, as you learn to use Lotus Approach, you will be following an example based on building a database system for tracking due dates. Many businesses need to track due dates–CPAs need to track a variety of due dates related to tax returns and reports for clients, lawyers track litigation and court dates, and salespeople track dates for calling on customers.

The example throughout the book focuses on a CPA's need for a system that tracks, for each business client, information such as fiscal year end date, various tax return due dates, when annual reports should be prepared, and when to remind clients to make tax payments. We will need to create a series of forms and reports to support the operation of a CPA's office:

- **Client List:** a list of clients and their year end dates.

- **Services Performed Report:** a report that shows each service provided by the CPA and the clients to whom the service is provided.

- **Mailing Lists:** a series of reports that show clients who are to receive specified mailings.

- **Due Dates Report:** a report that shows, by due date, the returns due for each client.

- **Review Dates Report:** a report that shows, by review date, the return due, the client, and the staff person responsible.

In addition, you may want to create form letters to notify clients of various information or events. We will create a form letter and mailing labels you can use to notify your clients of payroll tax law changes. We will also create some worksheet views of the data in the system to display data in a row and column format. We will then use the information to prepare cross-tabulation information and chart information in the database.

Based on the needs identified in these reports, you will set up four databases in this chapter:

- The BUSBACK database, which will store background information for business clients.

- The BUSSERV database, which will store information about services performed for each business client.

- The BUSRETS database, which will store information about the returns and reports required for each client.

- The BUSMAIL database, which will store information about mailings that should be sent to the client.

In Chapter 3, you will learn how to join these databases to take advantage of Lotus Approach's relational capabilities. In Chapter 4, you will learn how to work in the Design environment so that, in subsequent chapters, you can create and modify their appearance, enter information, find information, and prepare reports from these databases.

A Note about Tracking Individual Clients

The examples in this book cover setting up the system to track business clients. There are three ways you can successfully track individual clients. Each way has its own advantages and disadvantages. Regardless of which method you choose, you may want to add another database for individuals to track amounts and due dates for estimated tax payments.

Include Individual Clients in the Business Background Database. If you choose this approach, you should change some of the settings described later in this chapter. For example, you should not set up the Business Name field in the BUSBACK database as a required or unique field. You also should include form 1040 as part of the value list you set up for the Returns field in the BUSRETS database. While this may appear to be the easiest approach, it means that you lose control over data entry verification. You will need to monitor your system carefully for blank records and duplicate records (see Chapter 8).

Create a Separate but Duplicate System for Individual Clients. If you choose this approach, you should create a set of four more databases for Individual clients (you might want to call them PERBACK, PERSERV, PERRETS, and PERMAIL), as well as the additional database mentioned above, PERPMTS. You set up the databases the same way you will find described in this chapter with two exceptions. First, in the PERBACK database, do not set any field options for the Business Name field; instead, make the Last Name field required (but not unique). Second, in the value list you set up for the Required Returns field in the PERRETS database, include only 1040 and 5500. You can create these databases easily by setting up the original set completely and then copying the information to the new files (see Chapter 14). Although the data in your databases will not be redundant, the structure of the databases will be redundant. If you later decide to add a form or report to both databases, you will need to create the form or report twice—once in each database. In addition, if you want to verify that a particular individual is set up both as an Individual client and as a Business client, you will need to switch databases to make the query.

Create a Separate Set of View Files Attached to the Same Set of Databases. You find the instructions for creating a separate set of view files attached to the same database in Chapter 14. Briefly, you use separate view files for the same database when you want to create different data entry forms for the same basic data. If you use this approach, you will need to set up the field definitions as described in the previous option. In addition, you will need to make a few modifications to the designs of your forms and reports. If you later decide to add a form or report to both view files, you will need to create the form or report twice—once in each view file.

Creating a Database

Lotus Approach stores your data in any one of several different database file formats. You can choose the file format so that other people who are using other database software programs, can also access your data. For example, you can create a file in DBASE III+ format so that someone who uses DBASE III+ can read your database file. When you create a new database file, follow DOS naming conventions: assign a name to the file, either a .DB extension for a FoxPro compatible database or a .DBF extension for a DBASE III+, DBASE IV, or Paradox 3.5 compatible database.

Tip

While Lotus Approach can store and read data in a number of different database file formats, you don't actually work with your data in a database file. Instead, you work with your data in a view file. (Usually, this is a file with the same name you used when you created your database and an extension of .APR.) You use view files to store the various ways, in which you want to look at your data, such as forms and reports.

Creating a New Database Using a Model

When you create a new file, you can use the large series of sample databases that Lotus Approach contains to get ideas for building your own database or as the foundation for your database. Appendix A contains a table that lists each of the available databases and a sample of the kind of information you will find in it. You also will find a screen image of the form view of each sample database. Use the Appendix to help you find a sample database that you can use as a model for your own. Many of the databases were designed with the intent of joining them with other sample databases; I have tried to note these cases wherever possible.

We will use the Customer Contacts database to serve as the foundation for the BUSBACK database.

Figure 2.1

The Welcome to Lotus Approach dialog box.

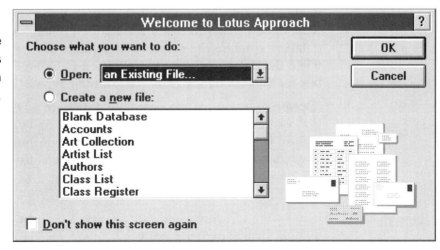

To create the BUSBACK database:

1. Start Lotus Approach. When you first open Lotus Approach, you see the Welcome to Lotus Approach dialog box (see Fig. 2.1).

2. From the Welcome to Lotus Approach dialog box, choose the Create a new file option button. In our example, choose Customer Contacts. Once you make a selection from the list in the Welcome to Lotus Approach dialog box, you see the New dialog box (see Fig. 2.2).

3. In the File name text box, you can use the name suggested or you can supply a different name. If you think you might want to base another database on the same sample, supply a different name. If you don't supply a different name and later discover that you

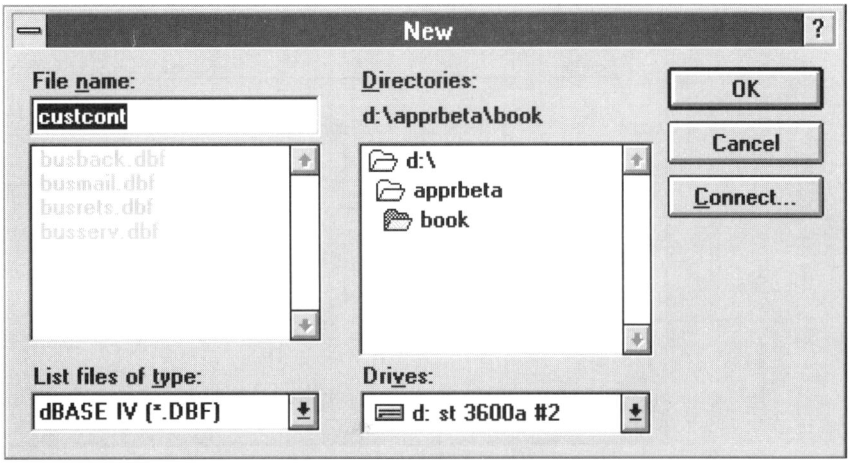

Figure 2.2

The New dialog box.

want to use the same sample database again, Lotus Approach will suggest that you overwrite the first database. If the original database contains data you want to continue to use, do not overwrite the database; supply a different name in the New dialog box for the new database. In the example, type **BUSBACK**.

4. (Optional) If you plan to share the data with a DBASE III+, Fox-Pro, or Paradox user, open the List Files of **T**ype list box and choose the appropriate file type. If you do not plan to share your database with users of other database software, the format you choose is irrelevant. In the next section, you will learn more about the various database formats.

5. Choose the OK command button. Lotus Approach displays the default form shown in Figure 2.3.

Tip

If you are creating a Paradox database, Lotus Approach prompts you to choose a *key field*—a field that you know will be unique in each record of the database. You cannot make any changes to the key field once you select it.

Figure 2.3

The default form contained in the BUSBACK database.

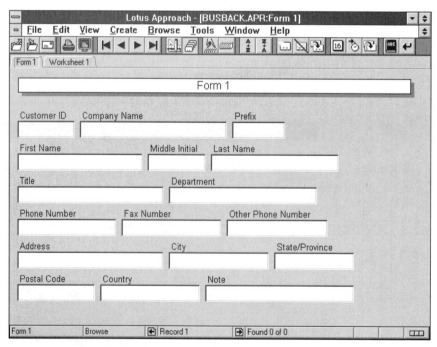

When you finish creating a database, Lotus Approach displays the fields you defined on-screen in Form 1, with the field title appearing above a box that represents the field contents. Notice, at the top of the screen, that the title for the database in the Program Title Bar is BUSBACK.APR:Form 1. When you create a database, Lotus Approach automatically assigns one form and one worksheet to it. You can create additional forms, reports, and worksheets as you need them. Forms display the information in your database one record at a time. Reports typically show information for many records on one page. Worksheets show your data in grid layout. You will learn more about forms in Chapters 5, 6, and 7, you will learn more about reports in Chapter 9 and 10, and you will learn more about worksheets in Chapter 11.

Creating a New Database without Using a Model

If you don't want to use one of the sample databases that Lotus Corporation provides to build your database, you can start with a blank database. In the example system, we will build three other databases to join with BUSBACK; we will not use any sample databases as models. We deliberately did not try to store, in BUSBACK, all the information we want to track. In Chapter 1, you learned some guidelines for determining databases to create and fields they should contain. In this section, we will focus on how to create them. In Chapter 3, you will learn how to join databases.

Tip

You see the Welcome to Lotus Approach dialog box only after starting Lotus Approach, or after opening Lotus Approach but closing any open databases. If you've been following the example, you won't see the Welcome to Lotus Approach dialog box, since we have not yet saved or closed the BUSBACK database. You can leave one database open while creating others; Lotus Approach simply displays each database in a window of its own. If you see the Welcome to Lotus Approach dialog box on-screen, choose the Create a **new** file option button, and select the Blank Database choice from the list below the option button. Then, start with step 2 below.

Figure 2.4

The New dialog box.

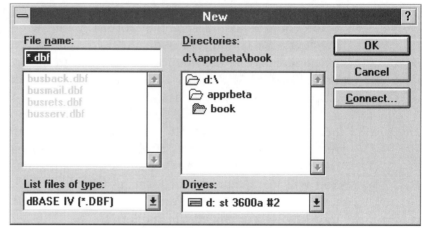

To create a new database without using a model as an example:

1. Open the File menu and choose the New command. Lotus Approach displays the New dialog box (see Fig. 2.4).

2. In the File Name text box, type the name you to assign to the database. For the second database in the due date tracking system, assign the name BUSSERV.

3. If you plan to share the data with a DBASE III+, FoxPro, or Paradox user, open the List Files of Type list box and choose the appropriate file type. If you do not plan to share your database with users of other database software, the format you choose is irrelevant.

4. Choose the OK command button. Lotus Approach displays the Creating New Database dialog box (see Fig. 2.5), which you use to define the fields in your database.

Figure 2.5

The Creating New Database dialog box.

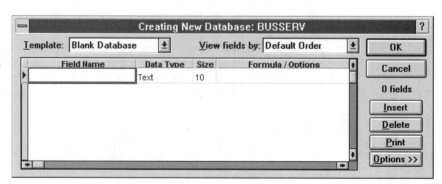

Like any other database program, Lotus Approach stores your data in records. A *record* contains all the information about one item in your database; in a customer database, each record contains information about one customer. A record is comprised of fields. A *field* represents a specific type of information; in a customer database, the customer's name is a field on each customer's record.

When you define a field in Lotus Approach, you specify the name of the field, identify the type and length of information permitted in that field, and specify data entry options. For each field you create, you can set information for Lotus Approach to enter into the field automatically, and you can tell Lotus Approach to check the validity of data automatically as a user enters information into the field. When you define fields, you do not define their appearance or placement on-screen. Instead, you define the field's behavior: how many and what characters Lotus Approach should permit to appear in the field. In Chapter 5, you will learn how to move fields around and change their appearance.

You can create any of the types of fields shown in Table 2.1.

The order in which you add fields is unimportant. Initially, Lotus Approach places the fields in a list that runs across your screen; later, after you define all the fields, you can move fields around on-screen to change both the order of appearance and the location of the field.

To define a field:

1. In the **Name** text box, type a name to represent the field. The name cannot exceed 34 characters.

2. In the **Type** list box, choose the field type.

3. In the **Length** text box, type the number of characters you want Lotus Approach to permit a user to enter when completing this field.

4. Repeat steps 1–4 for each field you want to add to the database.

For the example BUSSERV database, create the fields shown in Table 2.2 with the associated specifications.

Table 2.1   Types of Fields

Field Type	Type of information contained in the field	Possible use for this field type
Text	A combination of not more than 255 alphabetic and numeric characters	Store a mixture of characters and numbers, such as a name, an address, or a phone number.
Numeric	Numbers	Store numbers only; do not permit the user to enter alphabetic characters during data entry.
Calculated	Formula	Store the result of a calculation.
Date	Date	Store a date.
Time	Time	Store the time.
Memo	Text (a combination of alphabetic and numeric characters) that exceeds 255 characters	Store notes or background information about a record.
Boolean	Assign a value of True or False	Answer a yes/no question.
PicturePlus	Picture	Display a graphic or an OLE object from another Windows application on a particular record.
Variable	Based on the field type you assign to the variable field; can be text, numbers, a date or time, or a Boolean value	Store information you use temporarily but don't want to store in the database.

After you define the fields for the BUSSERV database, choose the OK command button to see Form 1 for the BUSSERV database on-screen (see Fig. 2.6).

Repeat the steps above to define the BUSRETS database and the BUSMAIL database. Use the information in Table 2.3 to define the

Table 2.2   Fields for the BUSSERV Database

Field Name	Field Type	Field Length
ID	Numeric	12 (set the decimal place to 0)
Service	Text	40

Figure 2.6

Form 1 of the
BUSSERV
database.

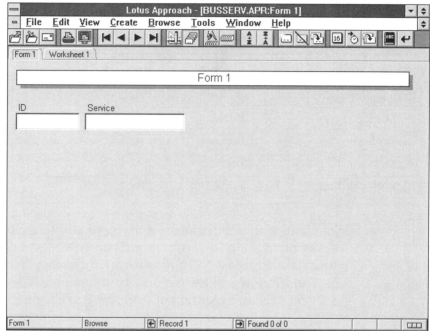

BUSRETS database; use the information in Table 2.4 to define the
BUSMAIL database.

Again, when you finish creating each of these databases, Lotus
Approach displays the fields you defined on-screen in Form 1, with
the field title appearing above a box that represents the field contents.
Just like when you created a database using a model, Lotus Approach
automatically assigns one form and one worksheet to a database you
created without using a model. Again, you can create additional
forms, reports, and worksheets as you need them. Forms display the

Table 2.3   Fields for the BUSRETS Database

Field Name	Field Type	Field Length
ID	Numeric	12 (set the decimal place to 0)
Required Return	Text	15
Due Date	Date	Fixed
Review Date	Date	Fixed
Extension	Boolean	Fixed
Extension Date	Date	Fixed

Table 2.4 Fields for the BUSMAIL Database

Field Name	Field Type	Field Length
ID	Numeric	12 (set the decimal place to 0)
Monthly Newsletter	Boolean	Fixed
Tax Law Changes	Boolean	Fixed
Holiday List	Boolean	Fixed
Annual Payroll Summary	Boolean	Fixed
11 Month Planning	Boolean	Fixed

information in your database one record at a time. Reports typically show information for many records on one page. Worksheets show your data in grid layout. You will learn more about forms in Chapters 5, 6, and 7, you will learn more about reports in Chapters 9 and 10, and you will learn more about worksheets in Chapter 11.

Changing Working Modes

After creating the example database, Lotus Approach left you in Browse mode; you can identify the mode in which you are working from the second box on the status bar at the bottom of the Lotus Approach screen. You can change the mode by clicking on the appropriate SmartIcon in the SmartIcon bar.

Tip

You can identify the function of any icon on the SmartIcon bar by pointing at it. The purpose of the SmartIcon appears next to the icon.

You can also change modes by clicking on the View portion of the status bar; Lotus Approach opens a list box from which you can choose (see Fig. 2.7).

To change modes, click on the mode in which you want to work:

- **Design:** Use Design mode to create and edit views (the layouts for forms, worksheets, reports, form letters, and mailing labels).

Figure 2.7

The Status Bar with the Mode list open.

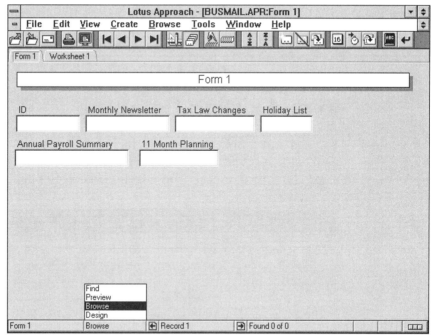

- **Browse:** Use Browse mode to see your information in one of the form, worksheet, report, form letter, or mailing label views you created in Design mode.

- **Find:** Use Find mode and one of the views you created in Design mode to search through your database to find specific information.

- **Preview:** Use Preview mode and one of the views you created in Design mode to see what your information will look like when you print it.

Adding, Modifying, and Deleting Fields in a Database

In the example system, you will never use BUSSERV, BUSRETS, or BUSMAIL as a main database; you will use them only to store information, and you will join them to the BUSBACK database. Use the **W**indow command to switch to the BUSBACK database.

After you create fields initially for a database, you can modify them, delete them, or add new fields to the database.

Adding a Field to an Existing Database

You can add a field at any time to your database. After adding the new field, you will need to enter information into that field for each record in your database. You use the SmartIcon bar to add a field.

Tip
You can identify the function of any icon on the SmartIcon bar by pointing at it. The purpose of the SmartIcon appears next to the icon.

In the BUSBACK database, we will add five fields:

- The Responsible Partner field, which will contain information concerning the responsible partner. It will be a 15-character text field.

- The Address 2 field, which will contain second-line address information. It will be a 30-character text field.

- The Yearend Date field, which will contain the client's year end date. It will be a date field.

- The Prepare Additional Returns? field, which will be a Boolean field that we will use to indicate whether we also prepare individual returns (1040s) for the business client.

- The Staff Person Assigned field, which we will use to indicate the staff member assigned to work on the client's information. This will be a 15-character text field.

To add fields, you reopen the Field Definition dialog box.

To add fields to the BUSBACK database:

1. Open the Create menu and choose the Field Definition command. The Field Definition dialog box appears.

2. Move the insertion point to the bottom of the dialog box, where you see a blank line.

Tip

In earlier versions of Lotus Approach, you could add fields (regular fields, check box fields, option button fields) by drawing them. Although the tools to draw fields remain on the Drawing SmartIcon bar in Lotus Approach 3.0, it is more efficient to add fields by opening the Field Definition dialog box directly as you will learn below.

3. Type the information for the field's name, type, and size (if appropriate).

4. Repeat step 3 for each field you want to add.

5. Choose the OK command button. Lotus Approach switches to Design mode and displays the Add field window (see Fig. 2.8)

6. Drag each field from the Add Field window anyplace onto the form.

7. Repeat step 6 for each field.

8. After you drag the last field onto the form, close the Add Field window.

Figure 2.8

The Add Field window.

The fields you added to BUSBACK don't look the same as the fields that were originally stored in the model for BUSBACK. In Chapter 5, you will learn how to change the style and formatting of the fields.

Changing Field Definitions

To can change a field name, type, or length:

1. Open the **C**reate menu and choose the Field **D**efinition command. Lotus Approach displays the Field Definition dialog box.

2. Highlight the field you want to change.

3. Make the change in the appropriate text or list box. In the example, change the Customer ID field to the Client ID field and make the field 12 digits long.

4. Repeat step 3 for each change you want to make. In the example, also change the State/Province field to the State field and make it two characters long.

5. When you finish making changes, choose the OK command button. Because you shortened the length of the State field, Lotus Approach warns you that you might be truncating data in the database. Since the database currently contains no data, don't worry about this warning message.

Tip
Note that changing a field name does not change the label that appears on the form. In Chapter 5, you will learn how to change the field label.

Deleting a Field

You can delete a field at any time, but if you have already entered data into the database, any data in that field will be lost. You may want to back up your database before deleting a field. Deleting a field from a database does *not* remove the field from any forms on which it appeared; instead, the field will display no information. After deleting a field from a database, you may also want to remove the field from the form.

To delete a field from a database:

1. Open the **C**reate menu and choose the Field **D**efinition command. Lotus Approach displays the Field Definition dialog box.

2. Highlight the field you want to delete. In the example BUS-BACK database, highlight the Department field.

3. Choose the **D**elete command button. Lotus Approach displays a warning dialog box.

4. Choose the OK command button to delete the field.

5. Repeat steps 2–4 for each field you want to delete. In the example, delete the Title field, the Middle Initial field, the Other Phone Number field, the Country field, and the Note field.

6. Choose the OK command button to close the Field Definition dialog box.

Tip

You can remove a field from a form without deleting it from the database. You may, for example, want to create a form that contains only some of the fields in your database. To remove a field from a form without deleting it from the database, switch to Design mode and select the field by clicking on it. Then, press either the **Backspace** key or the **Del** key. The field disappears from the form, but still appears in the Field Definition dialog box (and therefore in your database). Note that if you remove a required field from a form, Lotus Approach will still prompt you to enter data into the required field that does not appear on your form. In the example BUSBACK database, remove the Department field, the Title field, the Other Phone Number field, the Note field, and the Country field.

Setting Field Options

You can define options for each field either as you create the field or after you have defined the field. You also can change field options at any time, which you will learn how to do later in this chapter. The options you can set vary, depending on the type of field. Because you will use the BUSSERV, BUSRETS, and BUSMAIL databases only to store data, you do not need to set field options for the fields in those databases.

Figure 2.9

The Field
Definition
dialog box.

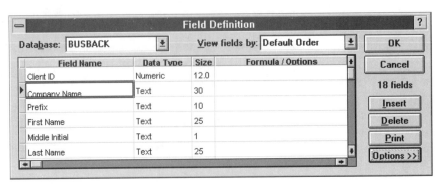

To set options for the fields you have created in BUSBACK, you work from the Field Definition dialog box (see Fig. 2.9). Open the **C**reate menu and choose the Field **D**efinition command.

In the Field Definition dialog box, highlight (in the list box) the field for which you want to set options, and choose the **O**ptions command button. You see the Options dialog box. The appearance of the Options dialog box varies, depending on the type of field for which you are setting options. Set the necessary options for the selected field. Select the next field and repeat the process.

Even though we didn't set up fields for each of the field types, in the following sections you will learn how to set options for all of the field types except the calculated field. You will learn how to set up options for a calculated field in Chapter 7, when we actually define a calculated field in one of the other databases we will create.

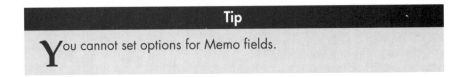

Tip

You cannot set options for Memo fields.

Setting Options for Text, Numeric, Boolean, Date, and Time Fields

You can set the same options for Text, Numeric, Boolean, Date, and Time fields. When you highlight one of these fields and choose the Options command button in the Field Definition dialog box, you see the dialog box shown in Figure 2.10. Note that for some field types, not all options are available.

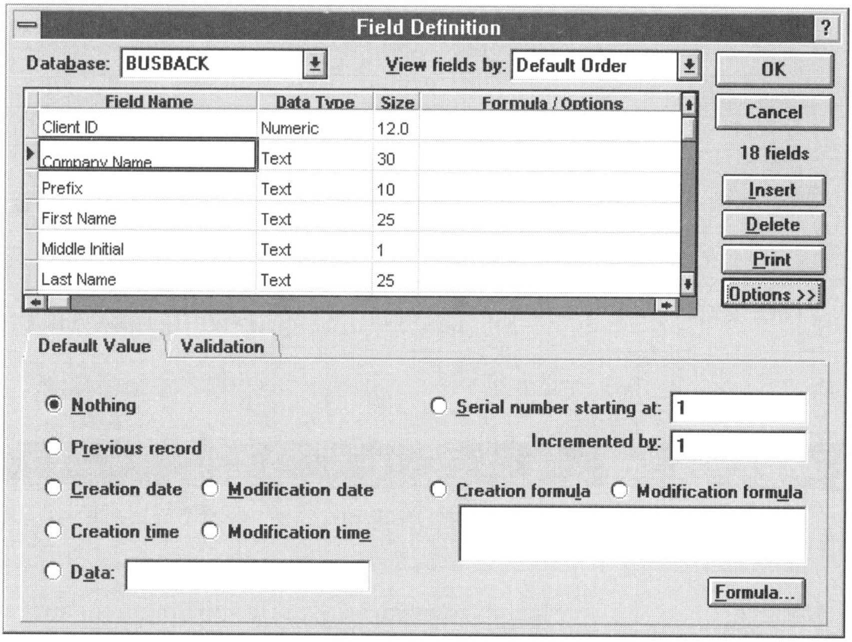

Figure 2.10

The Default Values tab of the Options dialog box for Text, Numeric, Boolean, Date, and Time fields.

You can use the options on the Default Value tab box to help make data entry easier and faster. Using the choices on the Validation tab, you can verify the accuracy of data as you enter it (see Fig. 2.11).

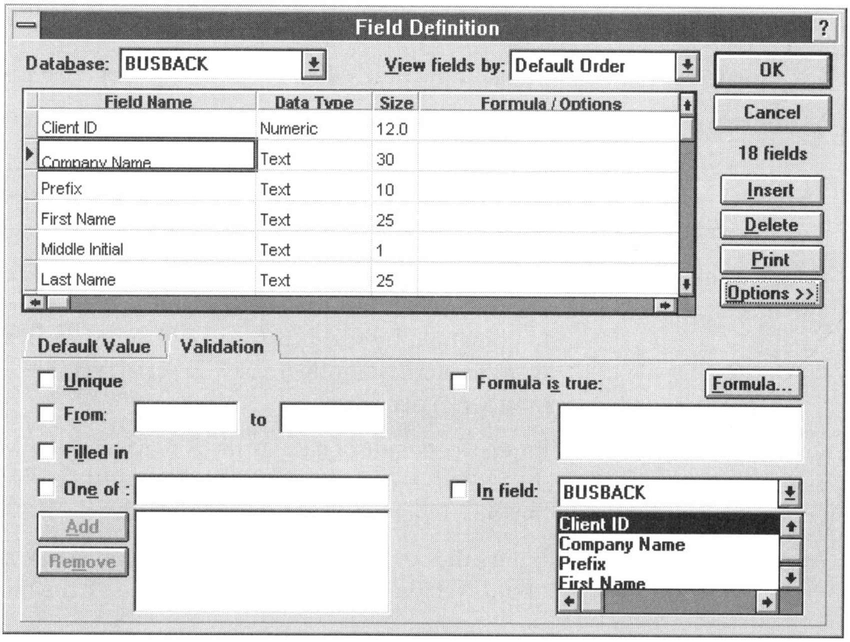

Figure 2.11

The Validation tab of the Options dialog box for Text, Numeric, Boolean, Date, and Time fields.

Use the choices on the Default Value and Validation tabs as shown in Tables 2.5 and 2.6.

In the BUSBACK database, use the Default Value tab to set the following options:

- For the State field, use the Data text box so that, by default, FL appears in the field.
- For the Client ID field, use the Serial Number starting at text box to start the ID numbers at 101, Incremented by 1.

Table 2.5	Default Value Tab Choices
Default Value tab option	**Affects each record in the following way:**
Nothing	Removes a previously selected option for automatic data entry.
Previous Record	Enters the information that appeared in the same field of the previous record. *Note: This option only works if both records were created during the same session.*
Creation Date	Displays the date when the database (not the record) was created.
Modification Date	Displays the date when the database (not the current record) was modified.
Creation time	Displays the time when the database (not the record) was created.
Modification time	Displays the time when the database (not the current record) was modified.
Data	Stores some specific default information in a field on every record. Type the default information in the text box.
Serial Number	Enters a different, sequential number on each record. Use the Starting at text box to specify a starting number; use the Incremented by text box to specify an interval by which you want to increase or decrease the serial number (use a negative number to decrease).
Creation formula	Enters the result of a formula as it appeared when you created the record. Lotus Approach will not update the information in the field when you modify the record.
Modification formula	Enters the result of a formula when you create a record, but updates the result whenever you modify the record.

Table 2.6   Validation Tab Choices

Validation tab options	Affects records in the following way:
Unique	Verifies that the value entered in the field is unique among all records.
From...to	Ensures that the information in the field falls within an alphabetic or numeric range.
Filled in	Verifies that the field was completed during data entry.
One of	Confirms that the value entered in the field matches one of a set of values you define using the Add command button. Use the Remove command button to eliminate a value from the list.
Formula is True	Confirms, using a formula you set up either in the text box or by choosing the Formula command button, that the information entered in the field is true. For example, if you were to type >=10 in the text box, Lotus Approach would ensure that any value entered into the field would be greater than or equal to ten.
In field	Ensures that the value in the current field matches the value in a different field in the same database or a joined database.

Use the Validation tab options in Table 2.6 to set up the Company Name field so that Lotus Approach checks to verify that it is Filled in and Unique.

Setting Options for Variable Fields and PicturePlus Fields

For variable fields, you can set only two options: the type of field and any initial value that should appear in the field when you open the view file. You can define a variable field as a text, numeric, date, time, or Boolean type field.

For PicturePlus fields, which hold graphics for a specific record, you can tell Lotus Approach to permit you to use OLE objects, and then you can define the default program you use to create objects you might incorporate into a Lotus Approach file.

When you select a PicturePlus field and choose the Options command button in the Field Definition dialog box, you see the screen shown in Figure 2.12.

Figure 2.12

The Options dialog box for a PicturePlus field.

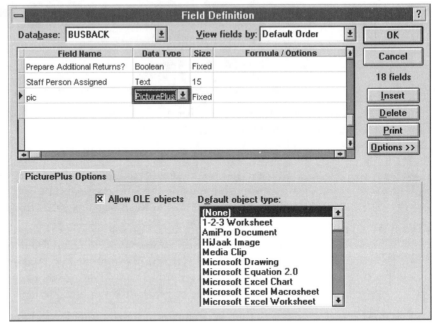

If you remove the "X" from the Allow OLE objects check box, you cannot choose a program from the Default object type list box.

Saving Your Work

As you recall, Lotus Approach stores your data in a database file and the various forms and reports you define in a view file. Later, when you add data to any database (including those we created in this chapter), Lotus Approach will automatically save your data to the database file. When you create, change, or delete forms or reports, however, you must save the view file to save the changes.

Tip

When you reopen the database later, after closing, you open the view file. Typically, the view file will have the same name that you defined when you initially created the database, but the file will have an .APR extension.

To save the BUSBACK database, open the File menu and choose the Save Approach File command. Lotus Approach displays the

Figure 2.13

The Save
Approach File
dialog box.

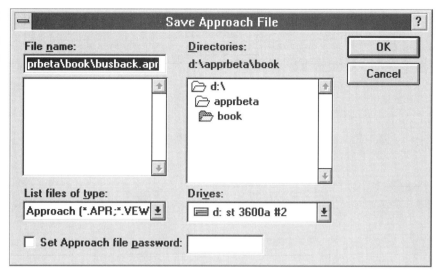

Save Approach File dialog box (see Fig. 2.13) and suggests the same name you supplied when you created the file, but the extension is .APR. Choose the OK command button.

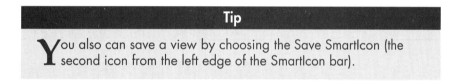

Tip

You also can save a view by choosing the Save SmartIcon (the second icon from the left edge of the SmartIcon bar).

Use the **W**indow command to switch to the other databases you created and save them, assigning the same name to the .APR file as you supplied when you created the file.

Closing and Reopening a Database

When you finish working with a database in Lotus Approach, you need to close it. To close a database, open the File menu and choose the **C**lose command. If you have made changes to a view and need to save them, Lotus Approach will prompt you by asking whether you want to save the changes to the view. Choose the **Y**es command button. If you have not made changes to a view, Lotus Approach won't prompt you; instead, it will close the database.

Figure 2.14

The Open
dialog box.

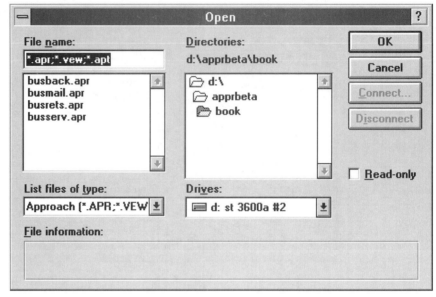

To open a closed database:

1. Choose the Open SmartIcon (the first icon on the left edge of
   the SmartIcon bar), or open the File menu and choose the **O**pen
   command. The Open dialog box appears (see Fig. 2.14).

Tip

You can use a shortcut to open one of the previous five databases
you opened. Open the **F**ile menu and choose the database from
the list that appears at the bottom of the **F**ile menu. Also, if you are
viewing the Welcome to Lotus Approach dialog box, you can open
the list box for the Open an Existing File option button and choose
from the previous five databases you opened.

You can set a default data directory so that you don't have to look
for the database you want to open. To set a default directory, exit to
the Windows Program Manager. Highlight the Approach icon, then
open the **F**ile menu and choose the **P**roperties command. The Program Item Properties dialog box appears. Add the name of the directory containing your databases to the path that appears in the
Working Directory text box and choose OK. When you restart Lotus
Approach and display the Open dialog box, you will see the files in
the default directory you set.

2. Navigate to the drive and directory containing the database you want to open.

3. Highlight the .APR file of the database you want to open and choose the OK command button.

Chapter Summary

In this chapter, you learned how to create databases and define fields for them. You learned how to set options for text, numeric, Boolean, date, time, variable, and PicturePlus fields. You learned how to modify field definitions, delete fields, and add a field to a database after you have already created the database. You learned how to save your work and switch to other modes in Lotus Approach.

In the next chapter, you will learn more about working in Design mode. You will also learn how to modify the appearance of forms in your database and make data entry easier.

CHAPTER 3

Joining Databases

One of the strengths of a relational database package like Lotus Approach lies in your ability to store different kinds of information in different databases and then link the databases together by *joining* them. Using this technique, you can minimize the amount of redundant information that you store—that is, you don't have to store the exact same information in two different databases to have access to it in both databases. Instead, you create one common unique field in each database that you want to join. Typically, you use an ID number field, because ID numbers are usually unique. Incorporating an ID number in a database does *not* mean that you must enter an ID number to add information to your database. The ID number can simply be tied to the name field during data entry. You'll learn how to do this in Chapter 5.

In Chapter 2, we created four databases: the BUSBACK database, which stores background information on business clients; the BUSSERV database, which stores information on the types of services performed by a CPA firm for each client; the BUSRETS database, which helps the CPA office track various dates associated with a client's work so that deadlines can be met when preparing work; and the BUSMAIL database, which identifies the mailing lists on which a client appears. In this chapter, you will learn about joining databases. In Chapter 4, you learn how to work in the Design environment so that, in Chapter 5, you can create a data entry form based on one of the joined relationships.

To join databases, each database you want to join should contain one common unique field. In this section, we will join the databases in the CPA system using the ID number field in each of them. Before we join databases, however, let's examine the possible relationships you can create when using joined databases.

Understanding the Relationship between Joined Databases

As you learned in Chapter 1, you use a joined relationship between two databases to help you access information in both databases simultaneously. For example, in a customer profile database system, you include the customer name, address, phone number, the sales representative who supports that customer, products purchased from you, and some personal information such as the customer's birthday, spouse's name, and anniversary. You break the information into three databases: the Work database, containing work-related information; the Products database, containing the products you sell (and therefore the products a customer buys); and the Personal database, containing personal information. You include the customer's ID number (or a similar piece of information) in both databases so that you can join the two databases together and still find out what he buys to offer him a discount for his birthday.

You can create one of four different types of relationships between information in databases:

One-to-One   In a one-to-one relationship, one record in Database A is related to only one record in Database B. In the example above, each customer in the Work database would have (hopefully!) only one spouse in the Personal database.

One-to-Many   In a one-to-many relationship, one record in Database A is related to many records in Database B. In the example above, each customer in the Work database can buy more than one product from you.

Many-to-One   In a many-to-one relationship, many records in Database A are related to only one record in Database B. This relationship is the opposite of a one-to-many relationship. In the example above, many customers in the Work database can buy one product in the Products database.

Many-to-Many   In a many-to-many relationship, many records in Database A are related to many records in Database B. To understand the many-to-many relationship, think about orders and the items that appear on them. Each order can contain many items, and one item can appear on many orders.

When you create views for joined databases, you use a common unique field, called a *join field*, to link the databases together. In this joined relationship, one of the databases acts as the *main database* and the other acts as the *detail database*. This relationship between the joined databases controls the way your database behaves when you retrieve information. You must decide, when you create forms and reports for joined databases, which database should be the main database and which should be the detail database.

Before you decide, first understand that just like you can have many different views within one database, you also can have many different views within a joined database. Also, the relationship between the databases (that is, which one is the main database and which one is the detail database) can change from view to view. The relationship between the joined databases is established at the time you create a view within them. Therefore, each view you create may have a different set of main and detail databases. The only exception is the one form that exists when you first create a join— the relationship for that form is determined by the way you join the databases (which you will learn to do in the next section).

To decide which database is the main database and which database is the detail database for a particular view, you first must determine the relationship between records in the databases. For each form or report you intend to create, you must decide if the relationship between the databases will be a one-to-one relationship, a one-to-many relationship, or a many-to-one relationship.

To help you decide, ask yourself these questions about each view you want to create:

1. What is the join field in the databases?

2. For this view, how many records will contain the same data in the join field in Database A—one or many?

3. For this view, how many records will contain the same data in the join field in Database B—one or many?

See Table 3.1 for a summary of the answers to the questions.

One-to-one relationships between databases are used as look-ups, and you don't usually need them because you can usually store all the necessary information in one database. However, if you want to establish a view for a one-to-one relationship, you designate the database from which the information will be pulled as the detail database. The main database is the one into which you are pulling the information. In the example databases, we won't be creating any one-to-one relationships.

Generally, when you find that you are creating a one-to-many relationship, you are creating a form; the main database should be the database in which the join field is unique. In the example CPA system, we will create a one-to-many relationship between the BUS-BACK database and the BUSSERV database, indicating that for one customer, the CPA performs many services. In this relationship, main database will be the BUSBACK database, because the Client ID number will be unique in the BUSBACK database, but can appear several times in the BUSSERV database (once for each service the CPA performs for the client).

Table 3.1 Database Relationships		
If You Answered Question 2	**And You Answered Question 3**	**Relationship**
One	One	One-to-One
One	Many	One-to-Many
Many	One	Many to One

Usually, when you find you are creating a many-to-one relationship, you are creating a report; the main database should be the database in which the join field is *not* unique. In the CPA system, we will create a report that shows, for each due date, the return due and the client's name. In this relationship, the main database will be the BUSRETS database, because the Client ID number will not necessarily be unique in the database—it will appear once for each return the CPA must prepare for that client.

While we won't be creating any many-to-many relationships in the example CPA system, you may need one for the system you are building. If you need to establish a many-to-many relationship, remember that you cannot establish a many-to-many relationship directly between two databases in Lotus Approach. To create a many-to-many relationship, you use an intermediate database. For example, in the orders and products scenario, you would have trouble joining them directly using either the order number or the product number. If you use the order number, then each product can appear on only one order. If you use the product number, then each order can contain only one product. To solve this problem, you usually establish an intermediate Items database that contains both the order number and the product number. Then, you can establish a one-to-many relationship with each of the other two databases.

Strange as it may sound, under certain conditions, you may have reason to join a database to itself. Suppose, in the customer profile system, you want to identify the customers for whom a sales person is responsible. You could join the Work database of the customer profile system to itself by creating an alias for the Work database. An alias is not a complete copy of the database; it is just another listing of the database. Once you have created an alias, you can join one field in the database to another field in the same database—you could join the Salesperson field to the Customer field.

Joining Databases

When you join two databases, you use a field contained in both databases as the join field to create the join. In our example databases, we defined the ID number field in all the databases. We will use the ID number field to join the example databases.

To join the BUSBACK database to the BUSSERV database:

1. Open or switch to the BUSBACK database.

2. Open the **C**reate menu and choose the **J**oin command. The Join dialog box appears, showing the BUSBACK database and a list of its fields (see Fig. 3.1).

3. Choose the **O**pen command button. The Open dialog box appears, showing the available databases in the current directory. If necessary, navigate to the directory containing the BUSSERV database, choose the BUSSERV database, and then choose the OK command button. You see the Join dialog box now containing two databases: BUSBACK and BUSSERV.

4. From the list in the database on the left, choose the join field. In the example, from the BUSBACK database, choose the Client ID field.

5. From the list in the database on the right, choose the join field. In the example, from BUSSERV database, choose the ID field.

6. Choose the **J**oin command button. Lotus Approach draws a line between the two fields in the databases (see Fig. 3.2).

7. Choose the OK command button.

Figure 3.1

The Join dialog box.

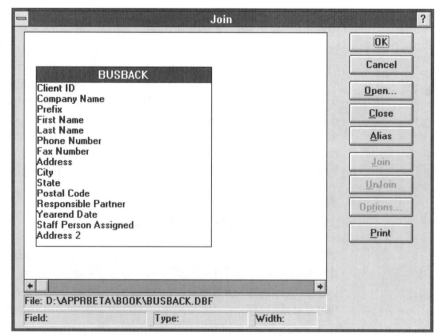

Figure 3.2

The Join dialog box after joining BUSBACK and BUSSERV.

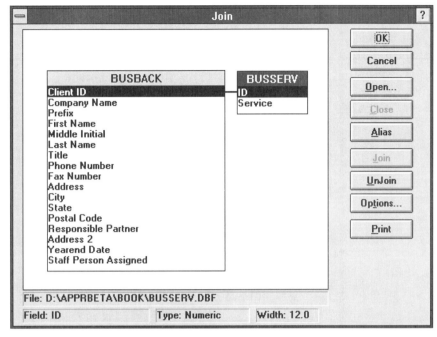

Repeat steps 3–7 above, using the ID number field, to make the following joins:

• The BUSBACK database to the BUSRETS database.

• The BUSBACK database to the BUSMAIL database.

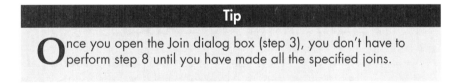

Tip

Once you open the Join dialog box (step 3), you don't have to perform step 8 until you have made all the specified joins.

After joining the BUSBACK database to each of the other databases, the Join dialog box should look similar to the one in Figure 3.3.

The database that appears farthest to the left side of the dialog box is the main database for the current form; in the example, BUSBACK is the main database for Form 1. For all future views you create, you will identify the main database.

Figure 3.3

The Join dialog box after making the specified joins.

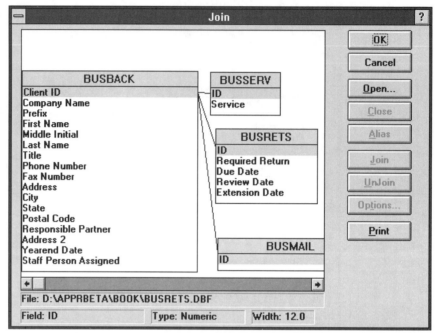

> To create an alias join, follow steps 1 and 2 above. Then, click the **A**lias command button to create a copy of the database in the Join dialog box. Continue with steps 4–7.

Unjoining Databases

You can unjoin databases after joining them. When you unjoin databases, Lotus Approach deletes any forms or reports you created using the joined relationship. If you have not created any joined forms or reports, you may see a warning message that implies that Lotus Approach will delete your database. In fact, Lotus Approach will simply unjoin the databases.

To unjoin two databases:

1. Open the Create menu and choose the Join command. Lotus Approach displays the Join dialog box.

2. Click on the line that connects the two databases you want to unjoin. Lotus Approach displays the line in bold.

3. Choose the Unjoin command. Lotus Approach may display a warning telling you that all the forms and reports you created in the joined database will be deleted. If you are testing this now on one of the sample databases, you won't see this warning since you haven't created any joined forms or reports yet.

4. Click on the detail database you just unjoined and choose the Close command. The detail database disappears from the Join dialog box.

5. Choose the OK command button to close the Join dialog box.

Specifying Joined Database Functioning for Data Entry

Now that we have joined databases, before we start entering and deleting data, we should look at the way in which Lotus Approach will handle the data we enter and delete.

To set options for joined databases:

1. Make sure you are viewing the Form 1 in the BUSBACK database.

2. Open the Create menu and choose the Join command. The Join dialog box appears (see Fig. 3.4).

3. Click on the line joining BUSBACK and BUSMAIL to select it. The line appears bolder than the other join lines. If necessary, drag the database title bars so that you can see the line.

4. Choose the Options command button. The Relational Options dialog box appears (see Fig. 3.5), showing you the options for inserting and deleting records in the joined databases.

5. The first insertion option implies that when we enter a record into a joined form and complete a field that originated in the BUSMAIL database, we want Lotus Approach to enter a record into the BUSMAIL database. Since this case is true, leave the "X" in the first insertion option.

Figure 3.4

The Join
dialog box
showing the
sample
databases.

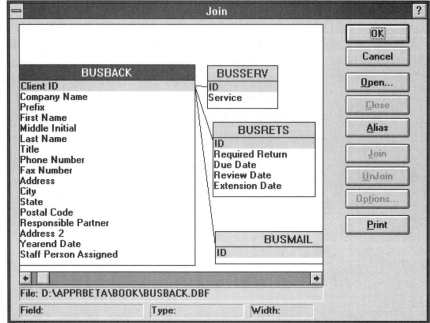

6. The first deletion option implies that we would want to delete a matching record from BUSMAIL if we delete a record from BUSBACK. Since we wouldn't want to send mailings to clients we don't work for anymore, you should place an "X" in the first deletion option.

7. The second insertion and deletion options imply that we would want to insert or delete clients from the main database if we change a detail database by inserting or deleting a record. Leave these two boxes as they appear, with the Insert check box selected but the Delete check box not selected.

Figure 3.5

The Relational
Options dialog
box.

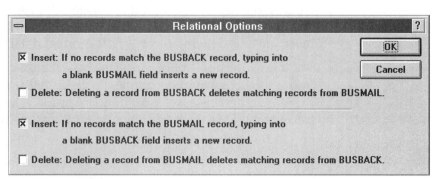

8. Choose the OK command button to return to the Join dialog box.

9. Repeat Steps 3–8 for each of the joins in the Join dialog box, setting up the options for each of the other joins the same as the options for BUSMAIL.

10. Choose the OK command button to return to the Background Data Entry form in BUSBACK.

Don't forget to save before you close so that you don't lose your work.

Chapter Summary

In this chapter you learned how to join databases. You learned to understand the types of relationships you can create between databases (one-to-one, one-to-many, many-to-one, and many-to-many), and you learned to distinguish which database should be the main database for a particular form or report and which database should be the detail database.

In the next chapter, you learn about working in the Design environment so that you can prepare to create additional views for your database.

Working in the Design Environment

In Lotus Approach, you work in one of four modes:

- **Design:** You use Design mode to create and edit views (the layouts for forms, worksheets, reports, form letters, and mailing labels).

- **Browse:** You use Browse mode to see your information in one of the form, worksheet, report, form letter, or mailing label views you created in Design mode.

- **Find:** You use Find mode and one of the views you created in Design mode to search through your database to find specific information.

- **Preview:** You use Preview mode and one of the views you created in Design mode to see what your information will look like when you print it.

After defining the fields in a database, Approach leaves you in Browse mode in a form showing all the fields you defined listed across your screen. By default, Lotus Approach names the form Form 1, and places this name at the top of the form. In addition, if you look at the leftmost portion of the status bar, you see the name of the form in which you are currently working, Form 1. When you use Form 1 to look at data entered into the database, you see one record at a time.

When you create a database, Lotus Approach actually defines one default form, Form 1, and one default worksheet, Worksheet 1. You can switch to Worksheet 1 by clicking on Form 1 in the status bar. Lotus Approach opens the Views list and displays all the views defined in the current view file. If you choose Worksheet 1, Lotus Approach displays the fields in your database in grid format, with one row at the top of the screen. When you use Worksheet 1 to look at data entered into the database, you see many records at one time.

Tip
You also can switch between views using the tabs that appear just below the SmartIcon bar. Just click on the tab of the view you want to see.

You can identify the mode in which you are working by checking the second box on the status bar at the bottom of the Lotus Approach screen. You use Design mode to modify the appearance of various views of your data: forms, worksheets, reports, form letters, and mailing labels. In Design mode, you add fields and objects to a form, you move fields, text and objects around on the screen to suit your purposes, and you change the appearance of fields.

Understanding the Design Area

You can switch to Design mode using the Mode list on the Status bar, using the SmartIcon bar or by opening the View menu and choosing the Design command. Once you switch to Design mode, the screen changes. At the top of the screen, just below the menus, you see the Design SmartIcon bar for forms (the Design SmartIcon Bar changes, depending on the type of view). To see a description of a particular SmartIcon's purpose, point at the SmartIcon. The description of the SmartIcon's function appears next to the SmartIcon. In addition, in Design mode, certain additional SmartIcons become available to help you work—these are found in the Drawing SmartIcon palette.

When you work in Design mode, you see information in the status bar at the bottom of the screen that describes the current view file.

Figure 4.1

The components of the status bar in Design mode for forms.

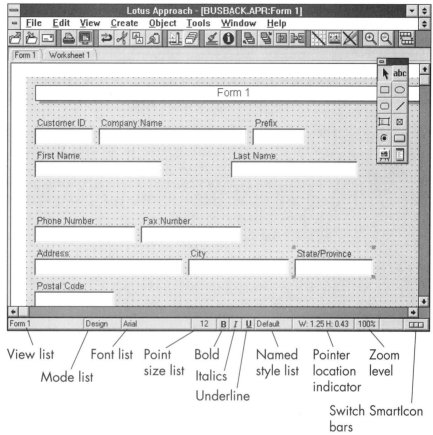

In Figure 4.1, you see the components of the status bar while in Design mode.

Use the status bar to determine the current view, working environment, font, point size, display dimensions, and zoom setting. The status bar is an active status bar—you can use it to control the environment. Working from the left edge of the status bar, use the first pop-up list box on the status bar to switch to a different view in the view file. Use the second pop-up list from the left edge of the status bar to switch to a different working environment. When you select a field, you can use the third and fourth sections to change the font and point size. Use the buttons next to the point size to apply boldface, italics, or underlining to selected text. Use the next section of the status bar to apply a named style to an object or to the background of a view. If you click on the seventh section of the status bar, you change the way in which the current location of the pointer is displayed—you toggle between displaying width and height locations and displaying distances from the left edge and the top edge of the screen. Use the eighth section of the status bar to change the zoom setting, and use the pop-up menu at the right edge of the status bar to change to a different SmartIcon bar.

The menu bar and the SmartIcon bar change while you work in Design mode, depending on the type of view and whether you have selected an object. If you select an object, you will see a menu reflecting the type of object you selected; for example, if you select a text object, you will see the Text menu next to the **Create** menu. If you do not select anything on-screen, you will see a menu reflecting the type of view on-screen; for example, if you are viewing a form, you will see the Form menu next to the **Create** menu. As you change views, the SmartIcon bar changes to reflect icons appropriate for working in the selected type of view.

Selecting Objects

To select any object, switch to Design mode and click on the object. Four selection handles appear on the object, indicating that the object is selected. To deselect an object, click on any blank location on the screen. The selection handles disappear.

You can select more than one object at a time to make the same set of changes to several objects simultaneously. Hold down the **Shift** key and click each object you want to select. Selection handles appear on each object you select.

Determining Object Size and Location

You can determine precisely the size and location of objects. When an object on-screen (a field, for example) is selected, the dimensions you see show the following measurements:

W: Shows the width of the selected object.

H: Shows the height of the selected object.

If you toggle the display, you see the following two measurements for a selected item:

L: Shows the horizontal distance from the left edge of the page to the left edge of the selected object.

T: Shows the vertical distance from the top edge of the page to the top edge of the selected object.

If no object on-screen is selected, then W: and H: represent the relative position of the mouse pointer from the right and bottom margins, and L: and T: represent the relative position of the mouse pointer from the left and top margins.

Showing Field Names or Data

You can view either the data in your database (right now, we don't have any) or you can view the field names. Open the **V**iew menu and choose the S**h**ow Data command to remove the check mark that appears before that command. Field names appear inside each field (see Fig. 4.2). When you show field names instead of data, object

Figure 4.2

The screen while displaying field names instead of data.

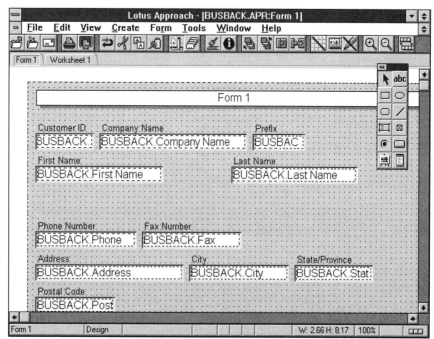

borders (the dotted lines outlining the field name) also appear. Also, if the current database is joined to another database, as ours is, you also see the database name included as part of the field name. Notice that each the field name on Form 1 for BUSBACK is preceded by the database name and a period. Later, when we create some forms and reports based on the joined database, you will see that you can use fields from both databases, and you can identify the database from which a field came by the prefix in the field name.

Turning the Grid On and Off

While you are working in Design mode, the Grid of dotted lines appears by default (see Fig. 4.2). The Grid acts like a magnet and attracts objects while you are moving them. Using the Grid can make aligning objects easier.

To turn off the Grid, open the **View** menu. If you see a check mark next to the Show Grid command, the Grid is on; you can choose it to turn the Grid off (see Fig. 4.3).

Figure 4.3

The screen not showing the grid.

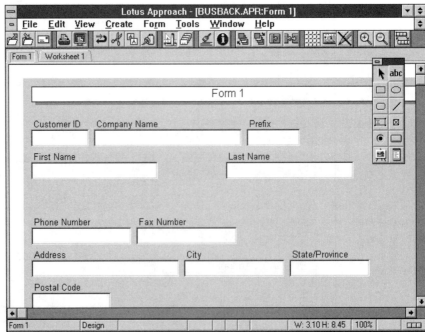

You also can place a check mark before the Snap to **Grid** command so that when you draw objects, you can align them easily to the grid.

Displaying and Hiding the Rulers

Lotus Approach contains horizontal and vertical rulers that you can use to size an object to a specific dimension. To display the rulers, open the **View** menu. If you see a check next to the Show **R**uler command, the rulers already appear on-screen. If you don't see a check mark next to the Show **R**uler command, choose it to display the rulers.

When the rulers are on and you move the mouse pointer, you see markers on the rulers that move with the mouse pointer. You can click at a specific spot (for example, at the intersection of the horizontal 3-inch mark and the vertical 2-inch mark) by aligning the markers on the ruler.

Zooming

While you are working, you can zoom in to take a closer look at an area, or you can zoom out to get a better look at the overall layout of a view.

To zoom in or out, you can use the two SmartIcons near the right edge of the SmartIcon bar. Alternatively, you can open the **V**iew menu and choose the **Z**oom In command or the Zoom **O**ut command. Each time you choose one of these SmartIcons or commands, you zoom by 25 percent. If you prefer, you can open the Zoom list on the status bar and select a percentage. Choosing a higher percentage lets you zoom in; choosing a lower percentage lets you zoom out.

Changing the Margins

You can change the margins of the area in which you design. Be aware, however, that all printers have areas on paper where information won't print. Laser printers, for example, typically will not print any information that appears within the first half-inch on any edge of the paper.

Figure 4.4

A form with
the Page
Margin border
displayed.

Page Margin

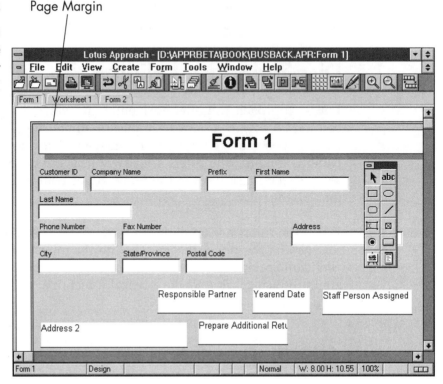

To change margins:

1. Hold down the **Ctrl** key and click anywhere inside the current margins. The Page Margin border appears around all edges of the view (see Fig. 4.4).

2. Drag the Page Margin border to change the margin.

Chapter Summary

In this chapter, you learned about working in the Design environment to set up forms. You learned to understand the Design area on-screen and you learned how to select objects and determine their size and location. You also learned how to turn on the grid and the rulers, how to enlarge the view, and how to change the margins of the view.

In the next chapter, you will learn how to work with fields on your forms to modify their appearance and operation.

5

Working with Fields on Forms

In Chapter 3, we joined the databases in the CPA system. In Chapter 4, you learned how to work in the Design environment. In this chapter, you will create a form based on one of the joined relationships. After creating the form, you will learn how to work in the Design environment to make forms easier to use for data entry. You will learn to:

- Modify the appearance and functioning of your form.
- Make data entry easier by creating list fields and option button fields.
- Change the labels for fields to identify them more easily.
- Move fields around on a form.
- Add borders to a field.

A form is only one view you create of your data—you also can create reports, worksheets, form letters, and mailing labels, all of which you learn about later in the book. You can use the techniques you learn here to modify the appearance of other views of your data as needed.

Creating Forms for Joined Databases

We can take advantage of Lotus Approach's relational nature to make data entry easier and more efficient. We can create a data entry form for two or more joined databases, letting the person who enters data update more than one database simultaneously.

Tip

Remember that your database will not function properly if you forget to maintain the main–detail relationships discussed in Chapter 3 when you create forms and reports. In the steps that follow, you will be opening the Form Assistant dialog box to select fields from various databases to include on your form. The database from which you select the first field becomes the main database. When you finish selecting fields, the Select Main Database dialog box appears, giving you a chance to change the main database. Lotus Approach will treat whatever database you select from this dialog box as the main database. Be sure you have the correct database selected before you close the dialog box.

Let's create a data entry form that contains the information in the BUSBACK database and the information in the BUSMAIL database. The relationship between the two databases is a one-to-many relationship, and the main database will be BUSBACK.

Follow these steps:

1. Open the BUSBACK database.

2. Switch to Design mode if necessary.

3. Open the **Create** menu and choose the **Form** command. The Form Assistant dialog box appears (see Fig. 5.1).

4. In the **Name** field, you see the name that Lotus Approach will assign to the form. You can change this name now or later. Type **Background Data Entry**.

5. From the SmartMaster style list box, choose a style for the form. Watch the Sample Form box to see what your form will look

Figure 5.1

The Form
Assistant
dialog box.

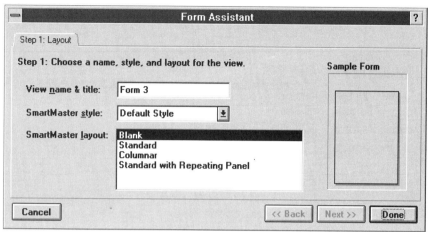

like. For the example, choose Chisel2. (You may want to experiment with these styles some—several of them are quite nice-looking.)

6. From the SmartMaster layout list, choose a layout style. If you choose Blank, Lotus Approach will create a blank form with no fields on it. If you choose Standard, Lotus Approach will place fields on the form in rows running from left to right. If you choose Columnar, Lotus Approach will arrange fields in the form in columns starting at the left side of the screen. You can choose Standard with Repeating Panel if you have joined databases and want to see many detail records for each main record. For the example, choose Standard.

7. The Next command button becomes available and you see the Step 2: Fields tab at the top of the dialog box. Click on either one. The Form Assistant dialog box changes to display the fields available to place on your form (see Fig. 5.2).

8. The first database from which you add a field becomes the default main database. We want to add all the fields in the BUSBACK database and we want that database to be the main database, so highlight each field in the list and choose the **Add** command button.

Figure 5.2

The Form
Assistant
dialog box
displaying
fields
available for
the form.

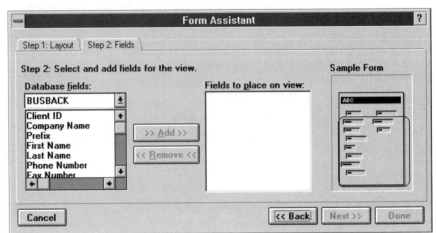

Tip

You can select all the fields by clicking on the first field in the list and holding down the **Shift** key while you click on the last field in the list. You can select individual fields and add them simultaneously by pressing **Ctrl** while clicking on each field you want to add.

---

9. Open the Database fields list box and choose the BUSMAIL database. The fields in the BUSMAIL database appear.

10. In the Database Fields list box, you now see the fields available in the BUSMAIL database. Highlight all the fields *except* the ID field and choose the **A**dd command button.

11. Choose the Done command button. You see the Define Main Database dialog box, asking you to select a main database. In the example, Lotus Approach suggests BUSBACK, since we selected fields from it first.

12. Choose the OK command button. The dialog box disappears and all the fields you selected appear in rows across the screen (see Fig. 5.3).

About the Info Box

Throughout the rest of this chapter, you will learn how to change the appearance and functioning of the fields on this form. You will use the Info box extensively (see Fig. 5.4).

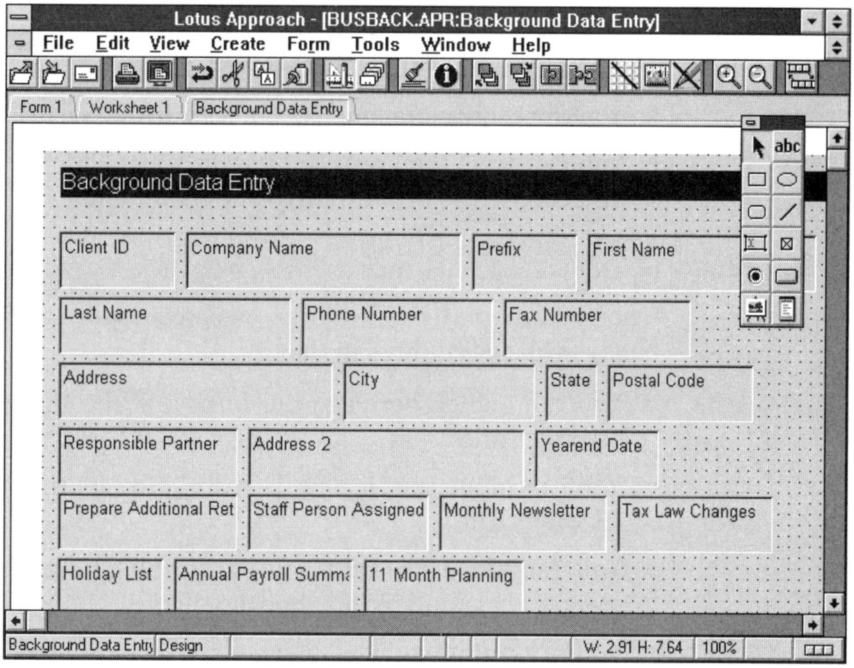

Figure 5.3

The Background Data Entry form.

The Info box consists of a series of panels, to which you switch by clicking on the tab for the panel. Each panel contains options for making different kinds of changes to fields and data within the field.

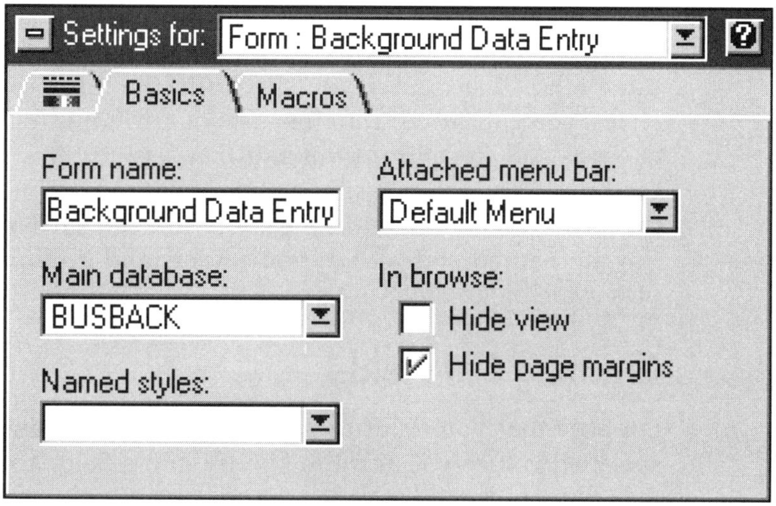

Figure 5.4

The Info box.

You can open the Info box in a number of ways:

- You can double-click on any field on-screen.
- You can click on the Info box SmartIcon (a lowercase "i" in a circle).
- You can open the Form or Object menu (whichever one appears) and choose the Style & Properties command.
- You can press **Ctrl+E**.

Once you display the Info box on-screen, you can leave it there. It behaves like a window, in that

- You can switch between the form and the Info box by clicking on either one.
- You can move the Info box by dragging its title bar, which says "Settings for."
- You can close the Info box by double-clicking on the control menu or opening it and choosing Close.
- You can minimize its size by clicking on the tab of the currently displayed panel of the Info box.
- You can access Help from the Info box by clicking on the question mark in the upper right corner of the Info box title bar.

In the following sections, you will use the Info box to create list fields, option button fields, check boxes, and change the style, appearance and functioning of fields. You learn about the functions available on each panel of the Info box. Then, at the end of the chapter, you learn how to create named styles, which store the same kind of attributes you specify in the Info box. Using named styles, you can set up different sets of attributes for different kinds of fields and the entire form and then assign the style to a field or the form. When you assign a style to a field, the field takes on all the attributes contained in the style. You can save a lot of time setting up named styles once you understand how to set the attributes available in the Info box.

Creating List Fields

Suppose that you want to make sure that users enter only certain specified values you want to specify into a field. You can make the field a drop-down list field and create a list of values, from which users select a choice while entering data. You also can create a field box and list, where users can either select a choice from a list or type in a choice that does not appear in the list.

When you create a list field, you can set up the values that appear in the list. Alternatively, you can tell Lotus Approach to display, in the list for one field, the values stored in another field that appears in the database. You would use the second type of list field, for example, to avoid typing Client ID numbers while searching for data. You would use, instead, a list created from data in the ID number field to tell Lotus Approach to display a list of client names instead of numbers while a user is searching. When the user selects a client name, Lotus Approach actually enters the client ID number in the ID number field. This type of field is particularly valuable because a user can choose a business name instead of having to remember an ID number.

The Staff Person Assigned field should be changed to a drop-down list field—one where you define the items that appear in the list.

To create a drop-down list field:

1. In the Background Data Entry form of the BUSBACK database, make sure you're working in Design mode.

2. Double-click the field for which you want to create a list. In the example, double-click on the Staff Person Assigned field. The Info box appears, displaying the Basics panel (see Fig. 5.5). The Info box contains several panels for making changes to various attributes of a field.

Tip
You also can open the Info box by clicking on the Info box SmartIcon or by opening the Object menu and choosing the Style & Properties command.

3. Open the Data entry type list box and choose Drop-down list or Field box & list. The Drop-down list choice lets the user type text into the field and offers no list of options. The Field box & list choice both displays a list of choices and also lets the user type in a value that doesn't appear on the list. In the example,

Figure 5.5

The Basics panel of the Info box.

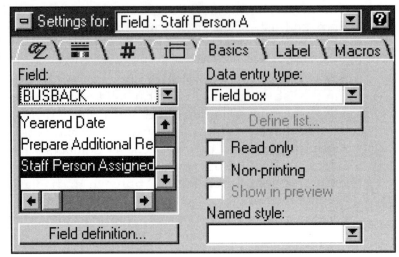

choose Drop-down list. The Drop-Down List dialog box appears (see Fig. 5.6).

4. In the Type in list items list box, type the first choice you want to appear in the list and move the insertion point to the next line in the list.

5. Repeat step 5 for each value you want to appear in the list. For the example, use the list below. If you make a mistake, highlight the mistake and choose the Delete command button.

    • Jeff

    • Tim

    • Kelly

Figure 5.6

The Drop-Down List dialog box.

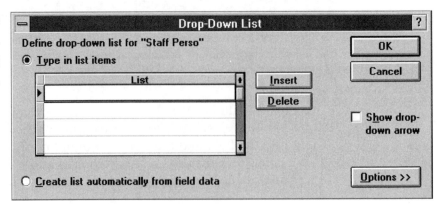

- Jim
- Harvey
- George
- Mary

6. Click on the **Sh**ow drop-down arrow check box so that a drop-down arrow will appear when the insertion point moves into the field.

7. When you finish adding values to the list, choose the OK command button to return to the Info box.

Tip

You can reorder the values in the list. From the Basics panel of the Info box, make sure the list field is highlighted in the list on the left side of the box. Then, click on the Define List command button to reopen the Drop-Down List dialog box. **D**elete the choice that you want to move. Then, highlight the choice that you want to appear below the removed value. Choose the **I**nsert command button and retype the choice.

To create a list field using the values that appear in another field in the database (like the example mentioned earlier, where you can tell Lotus Approach to display names when the insertion point rests in the ID number field):

1. Make sure you are viewing the BUSBACK database.

2. If necessary, switch to Design mode by clicking on the Mode list in the status bar or by clicking on the Design SmartIcon.

3. Double-click the field for which you want to create a list containing database values. In the example, double-click the ID number field. The Info box appears, displaying the Basics panel (see Fig. 5.7). The Info box contains several tabs for making changes to various attributes of a field.

Tip

You also can open the Info box by clicking on the Info box SmartIcon or by opening the Object menu and choosing the Style & Properties command.

Figure 5.7

The Info dialog box displaying the Basics panel.

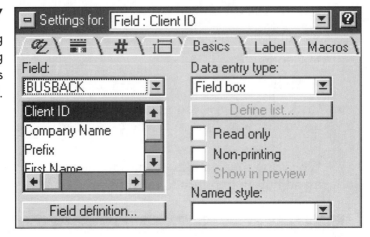

4. Open the Data entry type list box and choose Field box & list. The Field Box and List dialog box appears. Choose the **O**ptions command button. The Field Box and List dialog box expands to include additional options (see Fig. 5.8).

Figure 5.8

The expanded Field Box and List dialog box.

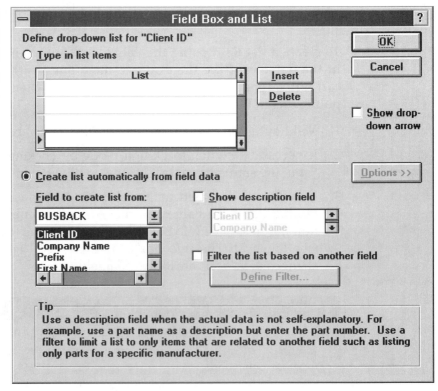

5. Choose the **C**reate list automatically from field data option button.

6. From the Field to create list from list box, choose the field whose values you want to appear in the list. In the example, choose the Company Name field.

7. Click on the **S**how descriptions field check box.

8. Click on the **S**how drop-down arrow check box so that a drop-down arrow will appear when the insertion point moves into the field.

9. Choose the OK command button.

To see how your list boxes work, switch to Browse mode and click in either field. A list box arrow appears in the field, letting you open the list and see the available values. You won't see any values when you open the list box for the Client ID number field because we haven't yet entered any records in the database. Lotus Approach will, however, increment the ID number by one, as we specified in Chapter 2. Press **Esc** to stop editing the record—we'll reset the ID number value later, when we are ready to start entering data.

You might want to save your work at this time. Remember to save your work before you close a database or Lotus Approach.

Creating Option Button Fields

You can use use option buttons to make data entry easier when you have only a few alternatives from which you want the user to choose while entering data. The alternatives must be mutually exclusive; that is, you want the user to choose only one of the available choices. In the BUSBACK database, the Responsible Partner field can be set up using option buttons (since you usually don't have a large number of partners in the firm).

To create an option button field:

1. Switch to Design mode by opening the Mode list or by clicking on the Design SmartIcon. In the example, make sure you are viewing the Background Data Entry form in the BUSBACK database.

2. Double-click on the field for which you want to create option buttons. In the example, double-click on the Responsible Part-

Figure 5.9

The Basics
panel of the
Info Box.

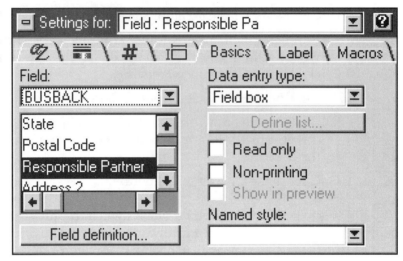

ner field. The Info Box appears with the Basics panel selected
(see Fig. 5.9).

3. Open the Data entry type list box and choose Radio buttons.
You see the Define Radio Buttons dialog box (see Fig. 5.10).

4. In the Clicked Value column, type the information you want to
store in the field when the button is selected. In the example,
type **Harvey**.

5. In the Button Label column, type the label you want to appear
next to the button. In the example, type **Harvey**. *Hint: If you*

Figure 5.10

The Define
Radio Buttons
dialog box.

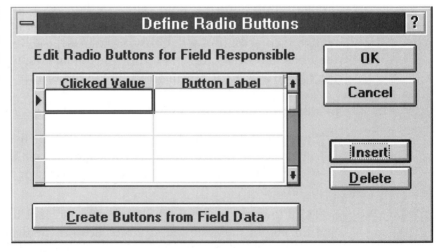

precede the label by a space, you will separate the label from the option button by a space.

6. Repeat the above steps for the other choices you want to appear. In the example, type one more choice, supplying a Clicked Value and a Button Label of **Jim**.

7. Choose the OK command button. Lotus Approach places an option button field on the form at the location you chose.

Creating Check Box Fields

You can create check box fields to make data entry easier. You use check box fields when the answer to a question is either yes or no. On the Background Data Entry form in the BUSBACK database, the Prepare Individual Return? field and the various mailing lists can be set up as check box fields. Note that the fields are defined as Boolean fields; if you don't set up the field as a check box, the user will type Y or N (for Yes or No) during data entry. Lotus Approach will display either Yes or No in the field. To see the difference, we will leave the Prepare Individual Return? field as a simple Boolean field, but we will set up all the mailing list fields as check boxes. You create one check box for each field.

To change an existing field to a check box style:

1. Switch to Design mode by opening the Mode list or by clicking on the Design SmartIcon. In the example, make sure you are viewing the Background Data Entry form.

2. Double-click on the field for which you want to create option buttons. In the example, double-click on Monthly Newsletter. The Info box appears with the Basics panel selected.

3. Open the Data entry type list box and choose Checkboxes. You see the Define Checkbox dialog box (see Fig. 5.11).

4. In the Checked Value column, type the information you want to store in the field when the check box is selected. In the example, type **Yes**.

5. In the Uncheck Value column, type the information you want to store in the field when the check box is not selected. In the example, type **No**.

6. In the Checkbox Label column, type the label you want to appear next to the button. In the example, type **Monthly Newsletter**.

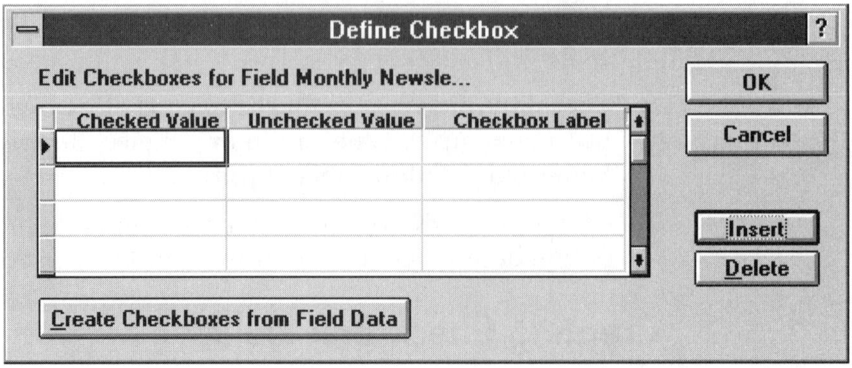

Figure 5.11

The Define
Checkbox
dialog box.

Hint: If you precede the label by a space, you will separate the label from the check box by a space.

7. Choose the OK command button. Lotus Approach replaces the field with a check box on the form at the location you chose.

Repeat these steps for each of the other mailing lists:

*   Tax law changes
*   Annual payroll summaries
*   11 month planning
*   Holiday

In Chapter 6, you will learn how to align the check boxes and make a fancier looking screen by grouping the check boxes, drawing a box around them, and placing a text object title in the box—something like "Mailing Lists." After creating check boxes for each of the mailing list fields, the Background Data Entry form might look similar to the one in Figure 5.12.

Using Field Labels

Sometimes, the names you assign to a field when you define it are abbreviated to fit within the requirements for field name lengths; therefore, the field names that appear on-screen can seem rather cryptic.

To change the name that appears on-screen to identify a field, you modify the label that appears on-screen. You also can change the position and the attributes of a label.

Figure 5.12

The Background Data Entry form after setting up check boxes.

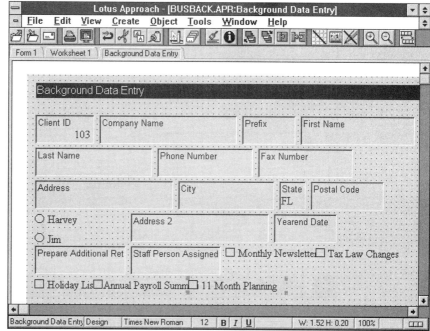

To modify a field label:

1. If necessary, change to Design mode by opening the Mode list on the status bar or by choosing the Design SmartIcon.

2. Double-click on the field to which you want to assign a label. The Info box appears showing the options on the Basics panel.

3. Click on the Label panel to see the options available for field labels (see Fig. 5.13).

4. In the Label text box, type the label you want to appear on-screen for the field.

5. From the Label position list box, choose a placement for the label: Above, Below, Left, or Right. To display no label for a field, choose No label.

6. If you want to change the font style, select a font from the Label font list box.

7. If you want to change the point size of the font, open the Size list box.

8. If you want to change the alignment for the selected label, use the alignment buttons.

Figure 5.13

The Label
panel of the
Info box.

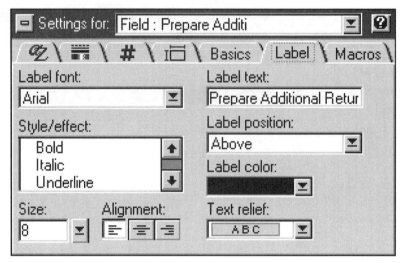

Tip

You can use the Label panel to make changes to the color of a field's title as it appears on-screen. You use the Text panel to change the color of *data* that appears in a field (during and after data entry). You use the Lines and Colors panel to change the color and appearance of the field's background.

---

9. If you want to add bold, italics, underline, or strikethrough to a label, use the Style/effect list box.

10. If you want to change the color of the label text, open the Label color list box.

11. If you want to make the label text appear raised or indented, use the Text relief list box.

Repeat these steps for each field for which you want to set up a label.

Tip

With the exception of Label text, you can change all the attributes mentioned above for multiple fields simultaneously. Select all the fields you want to change by clicking on the first field and then holding down the Shift key while you click on the others. Then, make your changes in the Info box.

Table 5.1 Label Text for the BUSBACK Database	
Current Field Name	**New Field Label**
Address	1st Street Address Line
Address 2	2nd Street Address Line
Postal Code	Zip Code

In the example BUSBACK database, change the label text as shown in Table 5.1.

You might want to save your work at this time. Remember to save your work before you close a database or Lotus Approach.

Setting the Data Entry Format for Fields

You can format fields to make data entry easier. For example, you can set a format for phone number fields so that you can type ten numbers and Lotus Approach will format the phone number with parentheses around the area code and a hyphen between the first three digits and the last four digits of the number. Similarly, you can set formats for date and zip codes.

To set the format for the Phone Number field:

1. Double-click on the Phone Number field. If you've been following along in the book, the Info box displays label information for the Phone Number field. If you haven't been following along, the Info box appears, showing the Basics panel.

2. Click on the Format panel. The Info box changes to display field formatting information (see Fig. 5.14).

3. Open the Format type list box and choose a format for your data. In the example, choose Numeric.

4. Open the Current format list box and choose Telephone. When you enter data into the Phone Number field, Lotus Approach will display the data in the format shown at the very bottom of the Info box: (123) 456-7890.

Repeat the steps above for the Fax Number field and the Zip Code field. For the Zip Code field, select Zip Code in step 4.

Figure 5.14

The Info box
showing the
Format panel.

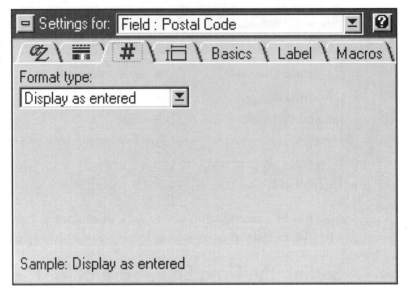

Modifying the Appearance of Fields

You can modify the appearance a field by changing the text attributes of the data that appears in the field or by adding color to the data that appears in the field. In addition, you can change the appearance of a field by adding a border to the field.

Changing the Location of a Field

You can move a field by simply dragging it while in Design mode. If you want to specify a precise location, you can use the Dimensions panel of the Info box (see Fig. 5.15).

Type a different set of coordinates for the top and left measurement.

In the example, rearrange the fields on the Background Data Entry form so that they appear in some semblance of order; for example, you might want to put City, State, and Zip Code on the same line. Turn on the snap-to-grid feature (open the **View** menu and choos the Snap to Grid command) to help with alignment, but don't worry about aligning them—you'll learn how to do that next chapter. When you finish, your form might look something like the one in Figure 5.16.

Figure 5.15

The Dimensions panel of the Info box.

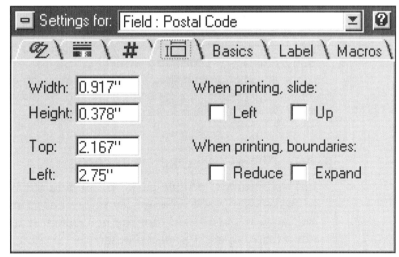

Changing the Way Data Appears in a Field

You can change the way your data looks on the form when it appears in a field. You can change the font, point size, alignment, and color of the data, and you can add boldface, italics, underlining, or strikethrough to the data in a field.

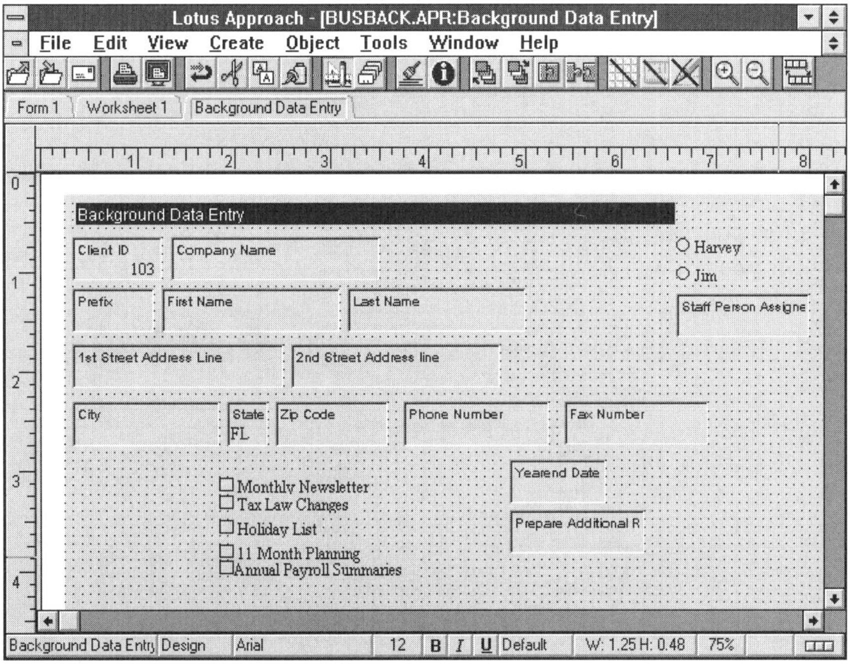

Figure 5.16

The Background Data Entry form after rearranging fields.

Tip

You can use the Label panel to make changes to the color of a field's title as it appears on-screen. You use the Text panel to change the color of *data* that appears in a field (during and after data entry). You use the Lines and Colors panel to change the color and appearance of the field's background.

To change the way data appears in a field:

1. In Design mode, double-click on the field for which you want to make changes. Remember, you are changing the data that will appear in the field, not the field itself. If the Info box was not already open, it appears; otherwise, it changes to reflect the settings for the field you double-clicked on.

2. Click on the Text panel, which is the last panel on the left. The Info box shows text settings for the data of the current field (see Fig. 5.17)

3. Use the Font name list box to change the font of the data that will appear in the field.

4. Use the Style/effect list box to add bold, italics, underlining, or strikethrough to the data that will appear in the field.

5. Use the Size list box to change the point size of the data that will appear in the field.

Figure 5.17

The Text panel of the Info box.

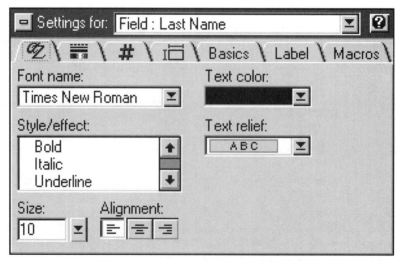

6. Use the Alignment buttons to change the alignment of the data that will appear in the field.

7. Use the Text color list box to change the color of the data that will appear in the field.

8. Use the Text relief list box to make the data that will appear in the field appear raised or indented.

Tip

You can change all the attributes mentioned above for multiple fields simultaneously. Select all the fields you want to change by clicking on the first field and then holding down the Shift key while you click on the others. Then, make your changes in the Info box.

Changing the Color of a Field

You can use borders to help you separate one field from another on a form or report. You can change the sides on which a border appears or the line width and color of the field border, and you can add a shadow to the field. You also can change the color of the inside of the field.

To add borders to or change the color of a field:

1. To practice, switch to Form 1 in the BUSBACK database.

2. In Design mode, select the field to which you want to add a border. You can select more than one field at a time by holding down the **Shift** key and clicking on the fields you want to select. Or, you can select all the fields on your form by opening the **Edit** menu and choosing the Select **A**ll command. In the example, on the Background Data Entry form, select all the new fields you added to the form: Responsible Partner, 2nd Street Address, Yearend Date, Staff Person Assigned, and Prepare Additional Returns?

3. If the Info Box is not on-screen, click on the Info box SmartIcon or open the **O**bject menu and choose the **S**tyle & Properties command. The Info box appears, showing the Basics panel.

4. Click on the Lines and Colors panel (the second panel from the left edge of the Info box) to see the Lines and Colors settings for the current field (see Fig. 5.18).

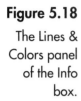

Figure 5.18

The Lines & Colors panel of the Info box.

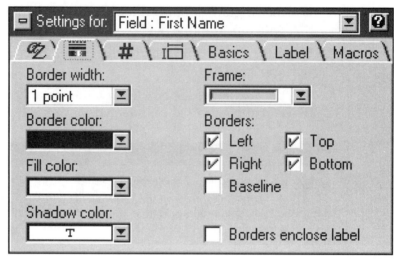

5. Use the Border width list box to change the thickness of the border surrounding the field. In the example, don't make any changes to the border width.

6. Use the Border color list box to change the color of the border surrounding the field. In the example, don't make any changes to the border color.

7. Use the Fill color list box to change the color of the inside of the field. In the example, change the fill color to gray (the first color on the second row of the palette).

8. Use the Shadow color list box to change the color of the inside of the field. To see a shadow, you must choose a different color than the Fill color. In the example, don't change the Shadow color.

9. Use the Frame list box to change the outer appearance of the field. In the example, choose the third frame down in the list box. Note that the frame does *not* appear on the Responsible Partner field, which contains options buttons.

10. Use the Borders check boxes to change sides on which a border appears. Use the Baseline check box to provide the user with a guide for typing in the field. In the example, all the check boxes except the Baseline check box appear gray, because more than one field is selected and the selected fields do not all have the

same attributes for borders. Place checks in all the check boxes except the Baseline check box.

11. Use the Borders enclose label check box to include the label inside the field. In the example, the check box appears gray because more than one field is selected and the selected fields do not all have the same attributes with respect to where labels should appear. Place a check in the check box.

12. Switch back to the Background Data Entry form.

Including Read-Only and Nonprinting Information on Forms

If you don't want the information in certain fields to print or to be updated, you can designate the fields *read-only*, which won't allow updating, or *nonprinting*.

Follow these steps:

1. Select the fields.

2. If the Info box does not appear on-screen, click the Info box Smart-Icon. Display the Basics panel of the Info box (see Fig. 5.19).

3. Place a check in the Read only or Non-printing check boxes, as appropriate.

Figure 5.19

The Info box showing the Basics panel.

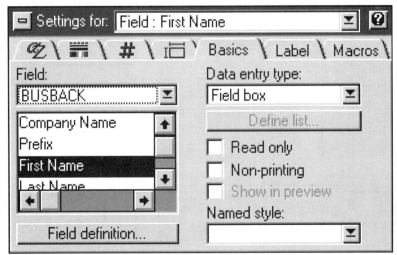

Using Named Styles

When you want to assign the same attributes to a large number of fields, you can create a named style that you can then assign to each field. Using named styles, you can save considerable time making all your fields look the same way. You can store, in a named style, most of the attributes you can set in the Info box. To apply the attributes contained in a named style to a field, you assign the named style to the field.

You can create a named style either using an existing style as a model or starting from scratch. Once you create the style, you can modify it or you can delete it.

To create or modify a named style:

1. Open the **T**ools menu and choose the **N**amed Styles command. You see the Named Styles dialog box (see Fig. 5.20).

2. Choose the **N**ew command button. You see the Define Style dialog box (see Fig. 5.21).

3. In the Style **n**ame box, type a name for the style. If you want to edit a named style, choose it from the list.

4. Use the **B**ased on list box to identify a style you want to use as a starting point while defining your style.

Figure 5.20

The Named Styles dialog box.

Figure 5.21

The Define
Style dialog
box.

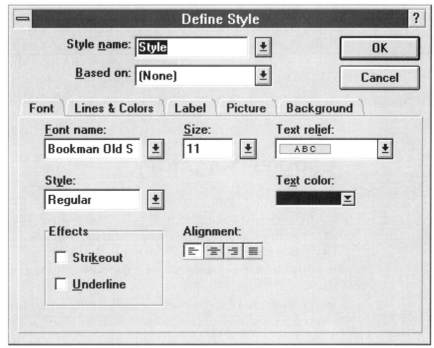

5. Use the Font panel to set the text color and attributes associated with the data that will appear in fields on the form.

6. Use the Lines & Colors panel to set the color of fields and the lines that surround them, as well as to determine which sides of a field should contain a border and how thick the border should be. Also specify here if you want the field to which you apply the style to be a read-only field.

7. Use the Label panel to set the text color and attributes associated with the field label.

8. Use the Picture panel to set the attributes for PicturePlus fields (you will learn more about PicturePlus fields in Chapter 6).

9. Use the Background panel to set the color and line attributes for the background of the form.

10. Choose the OK command button.

If you are unsure about the purpose or function of a particular attribute, refer to the section in this chapter where that function was discussed in relation to the Info box.

To assign a named style to a field, double-click on the field to open the Info box showing the Basics panel for that field. Open the Named styles list box and select the appropriate named style. To assign a named style to the form, open the Info box and then click on any place on the form. In the Info box you see the Basics panel for the form. Open the Named styles list box and select the appropriate named style.

Chapter Summary

In this chapter, you learned how to make data entry easier—you learned how to use the Info box to create labels for your fields and to create list fields, option button fields, and check box fields. You learned how to move fields around on a form and how to modify the appearance of fields on your form by adding colors or borders.

In the next chapter, you will learn to add objects other than fields to your forms, and you will learn how to work with those objects.

Working with Objects on Forms

In Chapter 3, we joined the databases in the CPA system. In Chapter 4, you learned how to work in the Design environment. In Chapter 5, you learned how to create a form based on one of the joined relationships and work with fields, one type of object available in Lotus Approach. In this chapter, you will learn to how to work with the other types of objects available in Lotus Approach: text objects, geometric shapes, and pictures. You will learn how to:

- Add objects to a form.
- Select and manipulate objects on a form.
- Add color to an object.

Working with Objects on a Form

A field is just one kind of object you can place on a form. In addition to fields, you can add objects that fall into four other categories:

- Text
- Geometric shapes

- Graphics
- Macro buttons

In this chapter, you will learn about the first three categories of objects; you will learn about macro buttons in Chapter 13.

In Chapter 2, you learned how to add a field to a form. In this section, you will learn how to add the other types of objects to a form and how to tell Lotus Approach not to print a particular object, even though it appears on the form.

Tip

In earlier versions of Lotus Approach, you added fields (regular fields, check box fields, and option button fields) by drawing them. Although the tools to draw fields remain on the Drawing SmartIcon bar in Lotus Approach 3.0, it is more efficient to add fields using the Field Definition dialog box, as you learned in Chapter 2.

Renaming a Form

In the last chapter, you learned how to create another form and you supplied a name for the form when you created it. You don't need to supply a final name for a form when you create it—you can change the name of a form at any time. Let's change the name of Form 1 to "Original Form" so that you can see how to rename a form.

To change the name of a form:

1. Switch to the form you want to rename. In the example, switch to Form 1.

2. If necessary, switch to Design mode. Click on any blank spot on the form (not on a field or any other object).

3. Click on the Info box SmartIcon or open the Form menu and choose the **Style & Properties** command. The Info box appears (see Fig. 6.1), displaying the Basics tab.

Tip

You can open the Info box by double-clicking on any blank place on the form.

Figure 6.1

The Basics tab
of the Info
box.

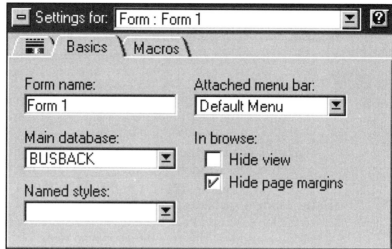

4. In the Form name text box, type the name you want to appear in the View list box at the left edge of the status bar. In the example, type **Original Form** and press **Enter**.

5. The name you gave the form appears in the View list box at the left edge of the status bar instead of Form 1.

To change the title that appears at the top of the screen in the Design area, you must edit that text object. See the next section.

Adding Text to a View

Suppose you want to add data entry instructions to a form or report. Data entry instructions are not fields, because they don't contain data you add to the database; instead, they contain information that shouldn't change as you look at different records in your database. To store this kind of information, you use text objects.

1. Switch to the form to which you want to add a text object. In the example, switch to Background Data Entry in the BUS-BACK database.

2. (Optional) If necessary, switch to Design mode and scroll so that you can see the place where you want to put a text object. In the example, make sure you can see blank areas underneath the fields on the form.

3. Open the **View** menu and choose the Show **Ruler** command.

4. Open the **View** menu and choose the Snap to **Grid** command.

5. Click on the Text Block SmartIcon (the one that says ABC on the button).

6. Position the mouse pointer where you want to the top and left margins of the text block to appear. As you move the mouse pointer, you can see that it has taken the shape of an I-bar. In the example, position the mouse pointer at approximately the intersection of the 1¼-inch horizontal mark and the 4¼-inch vertical mark. The exact placement is not important, because you can move the object later, when we realign objects on the form. Just make sure that no field appears at the spot where you place the pointer, and that the area below is also clear.

7. Drag down and to the right, drawing a text block approximately 3 inches across and 1½ inches down. When you release the mouse button, an insertion point appears inside the text block (see Fig. 6.2).

8. Type the text you want to appear. Don't press **Enter** while you type; Lotus Approach will automatically wrap text at the end of the line. In the example, type **Use this form to enter background information for clients.**

9. When you finish typing text, click anywhere else on-screen. Later in this chapter, you will learn how to set the attributes for a text block.

Tip
When you create a text block, you can paste text from the Clipboard into it instead of typing. Simply open the Edit menu and choose the Paste command.

Add a text object containing the words "Responsible Partner" and place it to the left of the option buttons Jim and Harvey.

Adding a Geometric Shape to a Form

You can draw lines, rectangles, squares, circles, rounded rectangles, rounded squares, and ovals in Lotus Approach using four SmartIcons. Suppose, for example, you want to draw a rectangle

Figure 6.2

A text block in the process of being added.

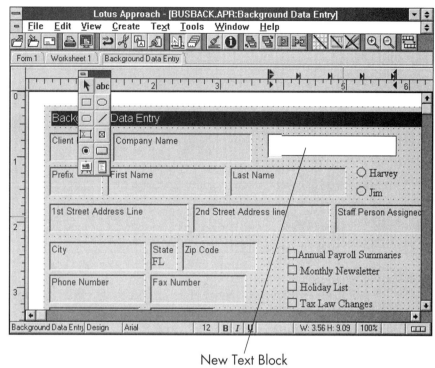

New Text Block

around the group of mailing lists on the Background Data Entry form in the BUSBACK database.

To draw a geometric shape:

1. From Design mode, click on the appropriate SmartIcon. In the example, click on the Rectangle SmartIcon.

Tip

If you can't remember the function of a SmartIcon, point at it.

2. Position the mouse pointer where you want the upper left corner of the geometric shape to appear. As you position the mouse pointer, it changes to the shape of a plus sign. In the example, position the mouse pointer above and to the left of the mailing lists.

3. Drag down and to the right until the geometric shape reaches the size you want. In the example, make the rectangle. When you release the mouse button, Lotus Approach places a rectan-

gle over the text object, which seems to disappear. In fact, the text object is "behind" the rectangle—later in this chapter, you will learn how to make it reappear. After inserting the geometric shape, Lotus Approach selects the geometric shape—handles appear on the edge of the shape.

Tip

To draw a straight line, click the Line SmartIcon and Shift+Drag. To draw a square or rounded square, click on the Rectangle or Rounded Rectangle SmartIcon and Shift+Drag. To draw a circle, click on the Circle SmartIcon and Shift+Drag. To use a tool repeatedly (so that you can draw several objects of the same type), double-click the SmartIcon. On color monitors, the SmartIcon becomes blue when you double-click it.

You can select a geometric shape by clicking on one of its borders. You can delete the rectangle you just drew by pressing the **Del** key while the rectangle is selected.

Later in this chapter, you will learn to set the attributes for this rectangle, such as how thick the rectangle should be.

Adding a Logo to a Form

You can add a graphic image that might serve as a logo to a form. Adding graphic images to a form differs from using a PicturePlus field: when you add a graphic to a form, the graphic appears on every record in the database. When you use a PicturePlus field to add a graphic, you add the graphic only to a specific record. To add a graphic to a form, you need a file containing a graphic.

Follow these steps:

1. Switch to Design mode if necessary.

2. Click in the form where you want the upper left corner of the graphic to appear.

3. Open the Edit menu and choose the Paste from **File** command. The Paste from File dialog box appears (see Fig. 6.3).

4. Navigate to the drive and directory containing the graphic you want to place in the form.

Figure 6.3

The Paste from
File dialog
box.

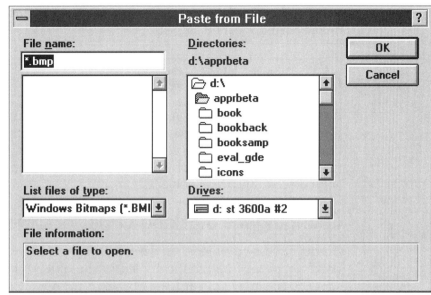

5. Highlight the file in the File Name list box and choose the OK
   command button. The graphic appears in your Lotus Approach
   form (see Fig. 6.4).

Figure 6.4

A Windows
metafile on a
Lotus
Approach
form.

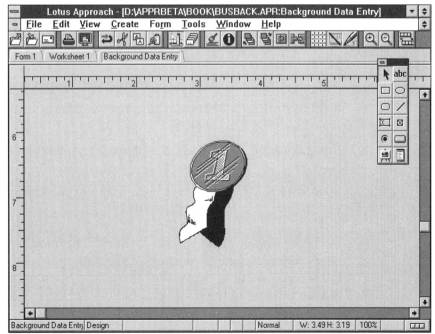

Later in this chapter, you will learn how to set attributes for graphic images that appear on forms.

Manipulating Objects

If you have two objects on-screen in the same place, typically you can see only the top object. You can, however, change the stacking order of objects. You also can change the size of objects, group and ungroup objects, move objects to different locations on the form, align objects, and delete objects.

Changing the Stacking Order of Objects

If you have two objects on-screen in the same place on-screen, Lotus Approach automatically *stacks* the objects. For this reason, some objects may appear to be obscured from view by one or more other objects. For example, the rectangle you drew to surround the mailing lists appears "on top" of them, instead.

If you want the objects on top of each other, like the mailing lists and the rectangle, you can change the stacking order of the objects. Select one of the objects in question, then open the **O**bject menu and choose the Arrange command. From the submenu that appears, choose one of the four following commands:

Command	Purpose
Command	*Purpose*
Bring to Front	Moves the object to the top of a stack of objects.
Send to **B**ack	Moves the object to the bottom of a stack of objects.
Bring Forward	Moves the object one layer closer to the top of the stack.
Send Backward	Moves the objects one layer closer to the bottom of the stack.

In the example, choose Send to **B**ack. The mailing lists reappear inside the rectangle. A portion of the rectangle may be obscured—in the next section, when you learn how to size objects, you can reduce the size of the check box field or increase the size of the rectangle so that you can see all of both objects.

Changing the Size of Objects

You can change the size of an object. Suppose you would like to enlarge a field to see its entire field label. You resize an object from Design mode by selecting it and dragging on one of the sizing handles that appears. As you pass the mouse pointer over the sizing handle, the mouse pointer shape changes to a two-headed arrow pointing diagonally. If the mouse pointer shape changes to a hand, *do not* drag—you will move the object.

Tip

To select a geometric shape, click on one of its borders. To select a graphic image, pass the mouse pointer anywhere over it and click.

On the Background Data Entry form, you may need to resize the one of the mailing list check boxes that you previously surrounded with a rectangle to make it smaller so that all the text fits inside the rectangle. Or, you may want to resize the rectangle to make it larger. You may also need to resize some other fields.

Moving Objects Around on a Form

When you initially define fields on a form using a standard layout, Lotus Approach places them in rows across your screen. You can move the fields around on-screen, changing the order in which fields appear or the location of a field; you did this in Chapter 5.

You move objects the same way you move fields. We will move all the fields on the Background Data Entry form down so that we can place the text object containing data entry instructions near the top of the form. You can move more than one object at a time by selecting each object you want to move.

To move an object:

1. Switch to Design mode by opening the Mode list on the status bar and choosing Design.

2. (Optional) You can use the grid to position objects easily. Open the **View** menu and choose the Show Grid command. Make

sure the Snap to **G**rid command has a check before it. Also, if the rulers don't appear on-screen, open the **V**iew menu and choose the Show **R**uler command.

3. Select the object you want to move by placing the mouse pointer over the field you want to move and clicking. Four gray handles appear around the edges of the field. In the example, click on the Client ID field. For the example, select all the rest of the objects on-screen except the text object containing the title "Background Data Entry."

Tip

You can select all the objects on-screen by opening the Edit menu and choosing the Select All command. Then, hold down the Shift key and click on the title text object that you don't want to select.

---

4. Drag the object to the location where you want it to appear. Use the ruler to help identify location. When the text object is positioned where you want it, release the mouse button. In the example, drag all the selected objects down about one inch.

5. Click on any blank spot on-screen to unselect all the objects.

6. Select the text object containing the data entry instructions.

7. Move the text object up under the title of the form and to the right side of the form.

You may want to make some other cosmetic moves, like moving the Client ID and Company Name fields up into the empty space next to the data entry instructions text object. I made the text object smaller in the example you see in Figure 6.5.

Tip

As you move objects, if you want more precise positioning, use the arrow keys on the keyboard to move a selected object.

Aligning Objects

While you move or resize objects, you may find that things just don't line up the way you want anymore. Using the grid helps, but you can align objects more precisely.

Figure 6.5

The BUSBACK database after moving objects.

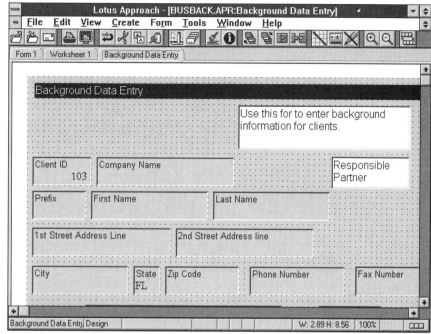

You can align objects vertically, horizontally, or in both directions. You can align objects to each other or to the nearest grid. You can align objects using any of their boundaries: top, bottom, sides, or centers. You can also place an equal amount of space between objects.

Let's start by aligning the left edges of the mailing lists and evenly distributing the distance between them.

The align and distribute objects:

1. Switch to Design mode.

2. Select the option buttons and the text object.

3. Open the Object menu and choose the Align command. The Align dialog box appears (see Fig. 6.6).

4. Make sure the To Each Other option is selected in the Align objects box. Choose Left in the Horizontal Alignment box. Choose Distribute vertically in the Vertical Alignment box.

5. Choose the OK command button. The dialog box closes and you see the check boxes aligned on their left edges with an equal amount of space between them.

Figure 6.6

The Align
dialog box.

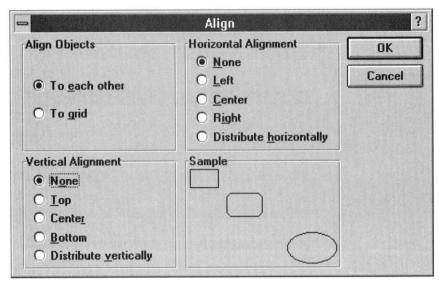

Tip

You can group objects so that you can easily move them simultaneously.

To align all the objects that appear in the left column of the form,
select just those objects, open the **Object** menu and choose the **Align**
command. Set the Horizontal Alignment to Left and the Vertical
Alignment to None. Align the objects to each other and choose the
OK command button. If you don't like the results of your alignment, open the Edit menu and choose the **Undo** command.

For each set of fields that appear on the same line, select just those
fields. Open the **Object** menu and choose the **Align** command. Set
the Horizontal Alignment to None. Set the Vertical Alignment to
Top.

After you align the objects, your screen should look similar to the
one in Figure 6.7.

Grouping and Ungrouping Objects

You can group several objects. When you group objects, they act as
one object. Any changes you make are made to all the objects in the

Figure 6.7

The
Background
Data Entry
form after
fields have
been aligned.

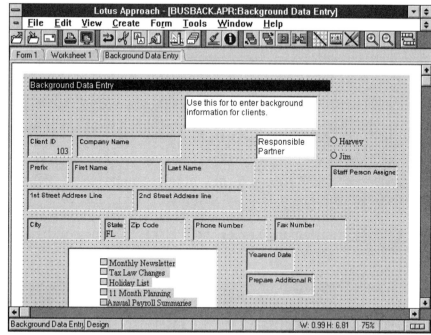

group. When you move a grouped object, all objects in the group move and maintain the same relative position they had before you moved them.

To group objects:

1. If necessary, switch to Design mode.

2. Select all of the objects you want in the group by holding down the **Shift** key and clicking on each object. Handles appear around each object as you select it. In the example, select the rectangle and each of the mailing list check boxes.

3. Open the **O**bject menu and choose the **G**roup command. Only one set of handles now appears around the group.

To make the objects stop operating as a group, select the group by clicking on it, open the **O**bject menu and choose the **U**ngroup command.

In the example, group the mailing list check boxes and the rectangle you placed around them. Note that if you chose to resize the rectangle so that you could see all of both the rectangle and the mailing list check boxes, you may need to move or size the rectangle so that it appears centered around the check boxes. If you need to move or size the rectangle, take these actions before you group the check boxes and the rectangle. See the previous section for sizing instructions; see the next section for moving instructions.

Deleting Objects

In Chapter 2, you learned how to delete a field and how to remove a field from a form without actually deleting the field. You delete other objects the same way you remove a field. From Design mode, select the object you want to delete and press either the **Backspace** key or the **Del** key. The object disappears from your screen.

Tip

When you delete the object, you can place a copy of the object on the Clipboard by selecting it and opening the Edit menu and choosing the Cut command. If you want to copy the object to the Clipboard, you can open the Edit menu and choose the Copy command. You can use the Paste command to put the object in a different place on the form or into another form.

Modifying the Appearance of Objects

You can modify the appearance of objects in basically the same way you modified the appearance of fields. You use the Info box to make changes to the appearance of objects.

Changing the Appearance of a Text Object

You can change the appearance and functioning of that object just like you changed the appearance and functioning of a field. You can change the text object's color and borders, and you can can change the font style, size, alignment, and special effects of a text object. You also can change the actual text that appears in the text object; for example, you may want to change the words of the title that appears on the top of a form.

To change any attibute besides the actual text that appears in a text block:

1. Click on the text object you want to change to select it. In the example, make sure the text object containing data entry instructions is selected.

2. Open the Info box by clicking on the Info box SmartIcon. You see the Text panel of the Info box (see Fig. 6.8).

3. Use the Text panel to change the font, point size, alignment, spacing, or color of the text in the text object. You also can apply bold, italics, underlining, or strikethrough to the text object.

4. Use the Lines and Colors panel to change the width and color of the text object's border and the fill color, shadow color, and frame of the object. In the example, change the fill color to gray to match the rest of the form. You may also want to make this change for the Responsible Partner text object.

5. Use the Dimensions panel to specify a precise location for the text object.

6. Use the Basics panel to specify that you don't want to print the text object or to assign a named style to the text object.

7. Use the Macros panel to attach a macro to the text object (see Chapter 13 for more information).

Figure 6.8

The Text panel of the Info box.

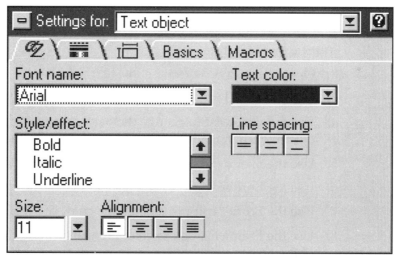

To change the text that appears in a text object:

1. Click anywhere on the text object to select it.

2. Click on the Text SmartIcon.

3. Click on the text within the text object at the location where you want to begin editing. The insertion point appears in the text at the location you clicked.

4. (Optional) If necessary, select text by dragging.

5. Make the changes you want to make.

6. Click outside the text object anyplace on the form to tell Lotus Approach you have finished editing.

Changing the Appearance of an Object

You can change the appearance of an object by filling its background with color or by giving it a shadowed effect.

For example, suppose you want the background of the title text object of the example database to appear in color instead of black.

Tip
If you want to change the color of the text that appears in the text object, see the previous section.

To set colors for an object:

1. Click on the object to select it. In the example, click once on the title text object.

2. Open the Info Box. You see the Text panel.

3. Switch to the Lines and Colors panel (see Fig. 6.9).

4. Use Fill Color list to change the background of the object. In the example, change the color from black to any other color.

5. Use the Shadow color list box to add a shadow to the object.

6. Use the Border width to change the size of the object's border.

7. Use the Border color to change the color of the object's border.

8. Use the Frame list box to change raise or indent the appearance of the object.

Figure 6.9

The Lines and Colors panel of the Info box.

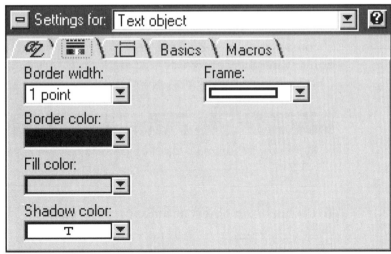

Tip

If you want to change the colors of grouped objects, be aware that Lotus Approach changes the attributes for the group. If you only want to affect part of the group, ungroup the objects first by selecting the grouped object, then opening the Object menu and choosing the Ungroup command.

Copying Properties from One Object to Another

To copy text attributes and line and color properties from one object to another using the Fast Format SmartIcon:

1. Select the object that has the properties you want to copy.

2. Click on the Fast Format SmartIcon or press the right mouse button and choose Fast Format from the shortcut menu. The mouse pointer changes shapes to look like a paint brush.

3. Click on the object to which you want to copy properties. Lotus Approach applies the properties of the first object to the second object.

4. Continue clicking on objects until you finish copying.

5. Click on the Fast Format SmartIcon again to indicate that you are finished copying properties.

Including Nonprinting Objects on a Form

If you want to include data entry instructions on a form and you don't want the data entry instructions to print, you can include them as a nonprinting text object.

Tip

You can set up any type of object as a nonprinting object.

To designate an object as a nonprinting object:

1. Add the object.

2. Select the object and open the Info box.

3. If necessary, switch to the Basics panel.

4. Choose the Non-Printing check box. The object will not print when you print the form.

Tip

To change the object back to a printing object, repeat the steps just listed. Choosing Non-Printing again removes the check mark and permits Lotus Approach to print the object.

Chapter Summary

In this chapter, you learned how to add objects to a form, how to select and manipulate objects on a form, and how to modify the appearance of objects on your form by adding color. You worked with text objects, geometric objects, and graphic objects.

In the next chapter, you will learn how to use the relational capabilities of Lotus Approach to create repeating panels, which display many records from one database on a form for one record in another database.

Customizing Forms

In Chapter 5, you learned how to work with fields on forms, and how to create list fields, check box fields, and option button fields. You also learned how to modify the appearance of fields. In Chapter 6, you learned how to work with objects, such as geometric shapes and graphics, on forms.

One of the strengths of a relational database package like Lotus Approach lies in your ability to store different kinds of information in different databases and then link the databases together by *joining* them. Using this technique, you can minimize the amount of redundant information that you store—that is, you don't have to store the exact same information in two different databases to have access to it in both databases. Instead, you create one common field in each database that you want to join.

Sometimes you need to see, on one form, one record from one database and many records from a joined database. For example, if you were working with a customer order system, you would need to see the customer's name, shipping address, billing address, and terms on the same form as all the items the customer ordered. The customer's name, address, and terms would be stored in one database (the main database), while the items ordered would be in another database (the detail database). Since one order can contain many items, you would need to see one record from the main database and many records from the detail database.

You accomplish this task in Lotus Approach by creating a form that contains a repeating panel. On a form, a repeating panel displays many records from a detail database that are related to one record in the main database. In this chapter, you will learn how to work with repeating panels and forms. You will also learn how to use information in your database to perform calculations on forms.

Creating Repeating Panels

When you want to display a one-to-many relationship on a form, you use a repeating panel. A repeating panel lets you show, on one form, many records from a detail database that are related to the current record in the main database. Lotus Approach uses the value in the join field to determine which records in the detail database are related to a record in the main database. You can add repeating panels to existing forms, or you can create new forms that initially contain repeating panels.

Adding a Repeating Panel to an Existing Form

We can set up a repeating panel on the Background Data Entry form for the services performed for each client. We will be able to enter as many services as we want. When you enter data for a new client, you will be able to specify the services you perform for that client on the same form where you enter the background information for the client.

To add a repeating panel to the Background Data Entry form to show the services performed for each client:

1. If necessary, switch to the Background Data Entry form in the BUSBACK database and switch to Design mode.

2. Click at the location on the form where you want the upper left corner of the repeating panel to appear. In the example, click near the left margin just below the check boxes for the mailing lists.

3. Open the **Create** menu and choose the Repeating **P**anel command. The Add Repeating Panel dialog box appears (see Fig. 7.1).

4. If you open the Database fields list box, you will notice that only the detail databases that you joined appear—you cannot

Figure 7.1

The Add
Repeating
Panel dialog
box.

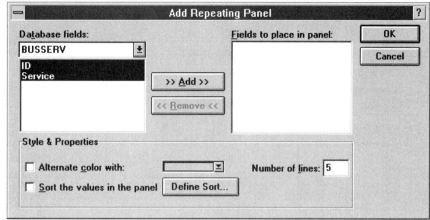

add, as repeating panels, fields from a main database. In the example, make sure that the BUSSERV database appears.

5. From the Database fields list box, choose the SERVICE field and click the Add command button.

6. In the Number of lines text box, type the number of lines you want to appear in the repeating panel. In the example, type **8**. You can create a repeating panel that shows up to 30 lines.

7. (Optional) If you want the rows in the repeating panel to alternate colors, place an "X" in the Alternate color with check box and then open the list box to the right of the words to display a color panel. Click on the color you want as the alternating color.

8. (Optional) If you want the data in repeating panel to appear in a particular order, choose the Define Sort command button to display the Sort dialog box. Select the field(s) by which you want to sort and the sort order (ascending or descending).

9. Choose the OK command button. The repeating panel appears in the form where you clicked (see Fig. 7.2).

Tip

When you add a repeating panel to a form, Lotus Approach does not display any field labels for the fields in the repeating panel. You may want to add titles to the repeating panel to make data entry easier. Use text objects and align the tops or bottoms of the objects vertically.

Figure 7.2

The Background Data Entry form after adding a repeating panel.

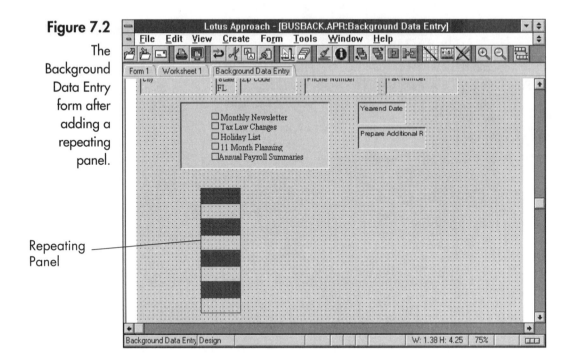

Repeating Panel

Creating a Form Containing a Repeating Panel

In subsequent sections of this chapter, you will learn to move and resize repeating panels. But first, in the example system, we need to create one more form for joined databases—a form that lets us enter the returns prepared for a client and all the relevant due date information. Since more than one return can be prepared for one client, this form will also contain a repeating panel. In Chapter 13, you will learn how to set up the forms so that when a user enters data and completes the first form, Lotus Approach automatically displays the second form.

To create a form that initially contains a repeating panel:

1. Make sure you are in the BUSBACK database. Switch to Design mode if necessary.

2. Open the **Create** menu and choose the Form command. You will see the Form Assistant dialog box (see Fig. 7.3).

3. In the View **name** & title text box, type the name you want for the new form. In the example, change the title of the form to **Returns Data Entry**.

Figure 7.3

The Form Assistant dialog box.

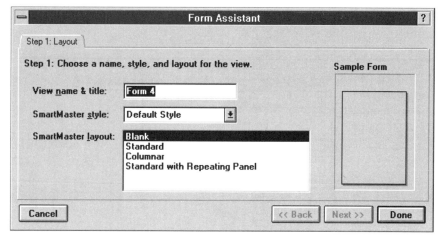

4. From the SmartMaster style list box, choose a style. In the example, choose Default Style.

5. From the SmartMaster layout list box, choose Standard with Repeating Panel.

6. Switch to the Step 2:Fields tab.

7. Make sure the main database appears in the Database fields list box. Highlight the fields you want to appear on the main part of the form and choose the Add command button. In the example, add the Company Name field and the Yearend Date field.

Tip

Lotus Approach identifies the main database for the form as the first database from which you add a field.

---

8. Switch to the Step 3:Panel tab. You see the choices for adding a repeating panel (see Fig. 7.4).

9. Open the Database list box and choose the detail database from which you want to create a repeating panel. In the example, choose the BUSRETS database. The fields for that database appear in the Database Fields list box.

10. Select the fields you want to appear in the repeating panel. In the example, select all the fields in the Database Fields list box *except* the ID field and choose the Add command button. Lotus

Figure 7.4

The Form
Assistant
dialog box
displaying the
Step 3:Panel
tab.

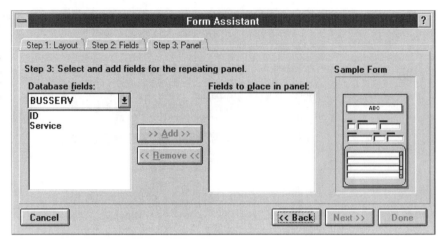

Approach adds the fields to the panel in the order in which you add them to this dialog box.

11. Choose the Done command button. You see a new form containing fields from the main database and a repeating panel.

So that you can identify each field in the repeating panel more effectively, create text objects that appear above each of the fields using the list below:

BUSRETS.Required Return   Required Return

BUSRETS.Due Date   Due By

BUSRETS.Review Date   Review By

BUSRETS.Extension?   Extension?

BUSRETS.Extension Date   Ext. Date

Tip

If you're not sure which field is which, you can double-click on the field to open the Info box. The field that appears selected in the list at the left is the field you double-clicked.

To create a text object, click on the Text Object SmartIcon on the Drawing SmartIcon bar. The mouse pointer shape changes to an I-bar when you move it into the form. Place the middle of the I-bar at the place where you want the upper left corner of the text object to appear. Click and drag in the form to create the text object. When you release the mouse button, type the text. When you finish typing, click outside the text object. Do *not* press **Enter**—you will enlarge the size of the text object.

Repeat the process above until you have created a label for each field in the repeating panel. Don't worry about placing the text objects precisely; later, we will resize the repeating panel so that it will fit below the labels. When you finish creating labels, resize them if necessary, align them, and then group them so that you can move them just above the repeating panel.

In the example, you see the Returns Data Entry form, with only two fields on it from the BUSBACK database and a repeating panel based on the BUSRETS database (see Fig. 7.5).

Double-click on the Company Name field to open the Info box. From the Data entry type list box, choose Drop-down list. When the Drop-Down List dialog box appears (see Fig. 7.6), place an "X" in the **Sh**ow drop-down arrow check box and choose the **C**reate list automatically from field data option button. Lotus Approach will

Figure 7.5

The Returns Data Entry form after adding and labeling a repeating panel.

Repeating Panel Labels

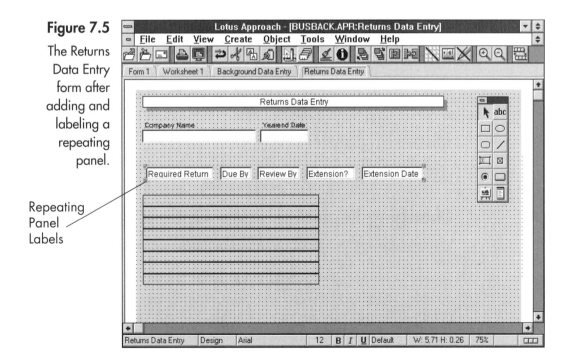

Figure 7.6

The Drop-
Down List
dialog box.

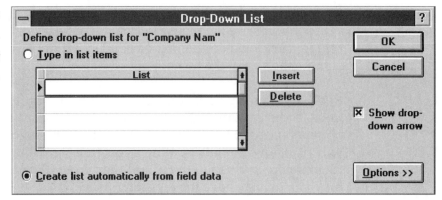

assume that you want to use the data stored in the Company Name field, so choose the OK command button.

Working with Repeating Panels

After you create a repeating panel, you can change its size, its appearance, and its basic characteristics. You also can move a repeating panel to a different location, rearrange the order of fields in a repeating panel, or add fields to the repeating panel. Also, you can summarize data in a repeating panel and delete a repeating panel.

To work with a repeating panel, you may find it easier to show field names rather than data. Open the **View** menu and, if a check mark appears to the left of the **Show Data** command, choose the command to remove the check and display field names on-screen.

To select a repeating panel, click on any border of the panel, or click anywhere inside the panel other than on a field name. A heavy border appears around the panel.

Changing Repeating Panel Options

You can change the database on which a panel is based, the number of lines in the panel, the order in which data appears in the panel, or the named style for the panel. To change any of these options, switch to Design mode and double-click on the repeating panel. The Info box appears (see Fig. 7.7), displaying the Basics panel.

Figure 7.7

The Basics
panel of the
Info box for a
repeating
panel.

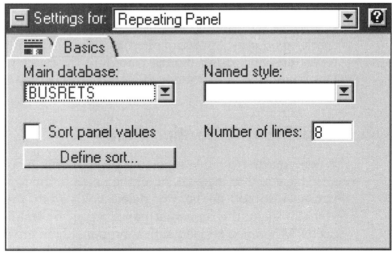

Make your changes accordingly. If you change the database on the which the panel is based, you may get unexpected results during data entry.

You also can change the alternating colors for the panel or the line and border options. Click on the Lines and colors tab of the Info box to display the Lines and colors panel for a repeating panel (see Fig. 7.8).

Use the Border color list box to change the color of the lines between and outside of the panel. Use the fill color to specify the color of the

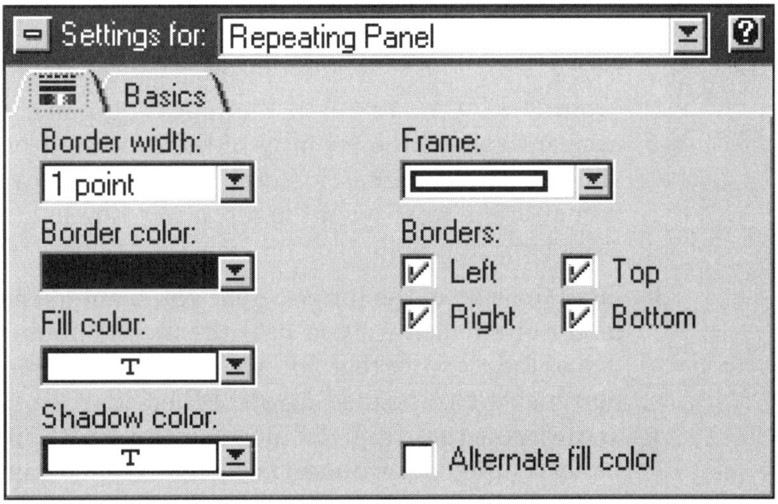

Figure 7.8

The Lines &
Colors panel
of the Info box
for a
repeating
panel.

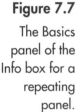

body of the panel. Use the Shadow color to specify a color for the shadow of the panel. If you place a check in the Alternate fill color check box, Lotus Approach alternates the colors of the rows in the repeating panel using the Fill color and the Shadow color. Use the Left, Right, Top, and Bottom check boxes to display lines around the sides of each row.

Resizing a Repeating Panel

When you first create a repeating panel, Lotus Approach creates it at a size equal to the sizes of all the fields in the repeating panel. If you need to add fields to or delete fields from a repeating panel, you can make the repeating panel bigger or smaller to suit your needs. When you resize a repeating panel, you are not resizing the fields in the panel; you are resizing the panel itself. If you make a panel narrower, make sure that the borders of the fields remain inside the boundaries of the panel. If you make a panel longer, you won't affect the number of lines in the panel; instead, each row will become larger. If you want, you can then rearrange fields within the row; see "Moving Fields in a Repeating Panel" later in this chapter.

We will resize the repeating panel we added to the Background Data Entry form to make it fill up the screen horizontally.

To resize a repeating panel:

1. Switch to the form containing the repeating panel you want to resize. In the example, switch to the Background Data Entry form.

2. From Design mode, select the repeating panel. A thick border appears around the top row of the repeating panel. If you are showing field names instead of data, you can see the field names in the top row of the repeating panel surrounded by the thick border.

3. Drag the side of the top row that you want to change to make it larger or smaller. As you pass the mouse pointer over the border of the top row that you want to change, the mouse pointer becomes a two-headed arrow. When you see the two-headed arrow, you can drag. To increase the width of the repeating panel on the Background Data Entry form, drag the right edge

of the top row to the right side of the screen. When you release the mouse button, Lotus Approach resizes the repeating panel.

Note that these steps resize the repeating panel only, not the field that appears in it. Repeat these steps to make the repeating panel on the Returns Data Entry form wider.

Resizing Fields in a Repeating Panel

In addition to resizing a repeating panel, you also can resize the fields that appear in a repeating panel. In the example, we need to resize the Services field because, later in this chapter, we will make this field a list field from which a user can select choices while entering data. When you enter data, the field will need to be bigger so that you can see those choices.

To resize a field:

1. Make sure you are in Design mode, viewing the repeating panel containing the field you want to resize. Also make sure you are viewing field names, not data.

2. Select the repeating panel.

3. Click on the field that you want to resize in the top row of the panel. Sizing handles appear around the field. In the example, click on the BUSSERV.Service field. (You may not be able to see the entire field name; you may only be able to see BUSSERV.)

4. Pass the mouse pointer over a sizing handle; the mouse pointer changes to a two-headed arrow pointing diagonally.

5. Drag the sizing handle to resize the field. In the example, drag one of the handles on the right side of the field until the field fills approximately half of the repeating panel.

In the example, repeat the above steps on the repeating panel in the Returns Data Entry form so that the fields appear underneath the text block titles you created earlier in this chapter.

Moving Fields in a Repeating Panel

You can rearrange the way fields appear in a repeating panel. You can even set up a repeating panel so that one record from the detail database seems to appear on two rows in the repeating panel. As you learned in the earlier section entitled, "Resizing a Repeating Panel," if you make a repeating panel longer, you enlarge the size of each row, making it wider. Then, within the first row, you can move fields around as long as they remain on the wider first row.

Caution
It is important, when you move fields within a repeating panel, that the field remain entirely inside the first row of the repeating panel; otherwise, the repeating panel will not function properly when you enter and view data.

To move fields in a repeating panel, click on the field to select it. You will see four handles on the field. Drag the field to its new location. In the example, spread out the fields on the first row of the Returns Data Entry form repeating panel (see Fig. 7.9).

Tip
If you rearrange fields within a repeating panel, you may want to use the field labels. Simply select the fields in the first row and use the Label panel of the Info box to turn on field labels. You may not see the field labels when you initially switch to Browse mode, however, you will see the field labels once you enter a record. Figure 7.10 demonstrates the concept: I rearranged the fields in the Returns Data Entry form, switched to Design mode, and displayed the form with field names showing.

Adding Fields to a Repeating Panel

You can add fields to a repeating panel if you later decide that you need a field that you didn't include originally.

To add a field you defined previously to a repeating panel:

1. Switch to Design mode on the form containing the repeating panel to which you want to add a field.

2. (Optional) If necessary, make the repeating panel wider to accommodate the additional field.

Figure 7.9

The Returns Data Entry form after spreading out the fields.

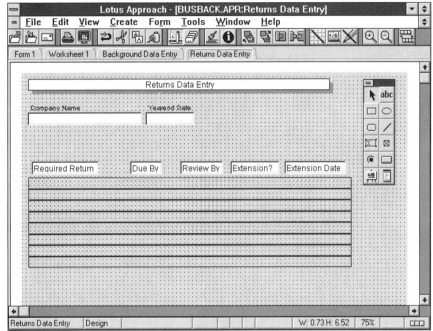

Figure 7.10

The Returns Data Entry form after rearranging the fields in the repeating panel.

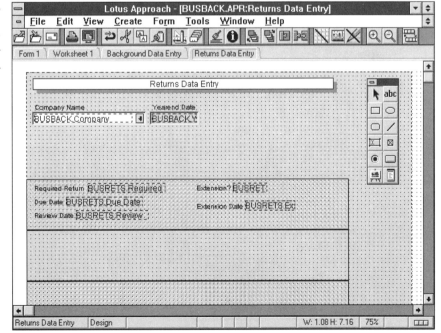

3. Click anywhere on the form other than on an existing field or object. If you click on an empty space on the form, you should see the Form menu; if you click on an empty spot on the repeating panel, you should see the Panel menu.

4. Open the appropriate menu and choose the **Add** Field command. The Add Field window appears (see Fig. 7.11).

5. Drag the appropriate field to an empty place on the first row of the repeating panel. The field must be placed inside the boundaries of the repeating panel. You may need to move or resize the field to make it fit in the top row.

Tip

If you set up the repeating panel options so that the rows alternate with a color, you may need to adjust the colors for the field you add to maintain a uniform look in the repeating panel. Use the Lines and colors panel of the Info box to make your adjustments.

If you want to create an entirely new field, use the Field Definition dialog box (either open the **C**reate menu and choose the Field **D**efi-

Figure 7.11

The Add Field window.

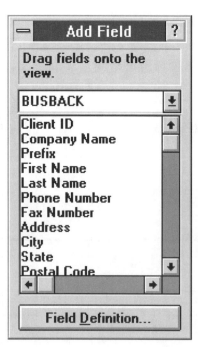

nition command or, from the Add Fields dialog box, click on the Field Definition command button) to define the field, then drag the field to a blank spot in the first row of the repeating panel.

Creating List Fields in Repeating Panels

You can create list fields in repeating panels so that users can choose from a list when creating records. You create a list field in a repeating panel the same way you created a list field outside a repeating panel. The Service field in the BUSSERV database should be set up as a list field.

To create a list field:

1. Switch to the form containing the repeating panel and switch to Design mode mode by clicking on the Mode list in the status bar and choosing Design. In the example, switch to the Background Data Entry form.

2. Click the field for which you want to create a list. In the example, click on the Services field in the repeating panel.

3. Open the Info box and display the Basics panel (see Fig. 7.12).

4. From the Data entry type list box, choose either Drop-down list or Field box & list. Drop-down list lets the user choose from a list of options. Field box & list lets the user choose from a list of options, but also allows the user to type text that doesn't appear

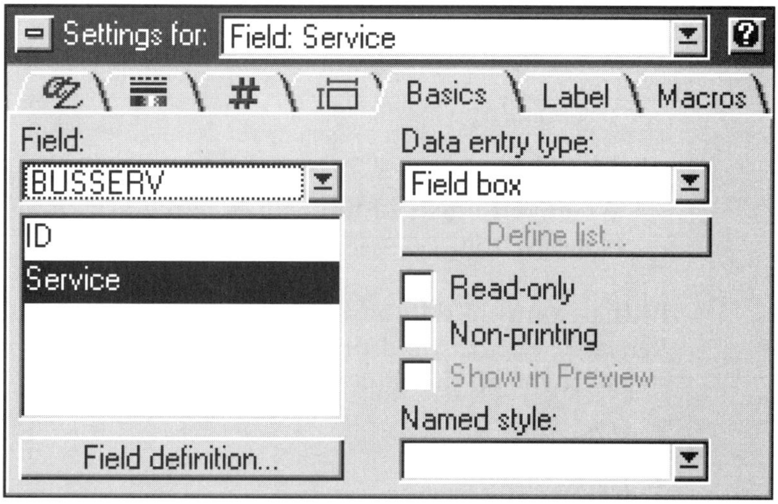

Figure 7.12

The Basics panel of the Info box.

Figure 7.13

The Drop-
Down List
dialog box.

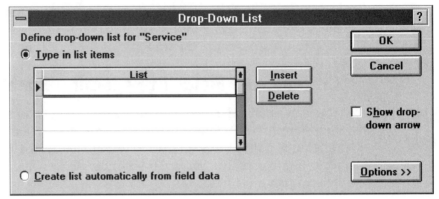

on the list. In the example, choose Drop-down list. The Drop-
Down List dialog box appears (see Fig. 7.13).

5. In the **T**ype in list items list box, type the first item you want to
appear when the user places the insertion point in the field.

6. Repeat step 5 for each value you want to appear in the list. For the
example, use the list below. If you make a mistake, highlight the
mistake in the List box and choose the **D**elete command button.

- Keypunch/Bookkeeping
- Compilation
- Financial Statement Preparation
- Financial Statement Review
- Quarterly Payroll Taxes
- W-2s/1099s
- Tax Return Preparation
- Consulting
- None

7. When you finish adding values to the list, choose the OK command button.

In the example database, also create a drop-down list for the
Required Return field on the Returns Data Entry form. Use the
steps above and the choices in the list that follows:

- 1120
- 1120S

- 1065
- 1041
- 5500
- None

Moving a Repeating Panel

You can move a repeating panel to any location you want. When you pass the mouse pointer over the bottom of the repeating panel, the shape changes to a hand. Drag the repeating panel to its new location.

Deleting a Repeating Panel

You can delete a repeating panel by selecting it (pass the mouse pointer over it; when the pointer shape appears like a hand, click) and then pressing the **Del** key. The repeating panel and all fields on it disappear from your form.

Using Database Information to Perform Math

You can use the information you store in your databases to perform mathematical calculations. You can tell Lotus Approach to calculate numbers based on information in your database. You calculate by defining a special field type—a calculated field. You define calculated fields the same way you define other fields—using the Field Definition dialog box. You use the Options command button to supply the formula for the calculation. You can define calculated fields anywhere on a form, including in a repeating panel.

You can perform basic math—addition, subtraction, multiplication, or division—or you can use more advanced mathematical functions, such as calculating averages or present values or using If statements to perform function-based comparisons.

A calculated field is part of a view file, but it is not part of a database because Lotus Approach doesn't store the results of a calculated field in the database. You can't edit the results of a calculated field.

Performing Basic Math

Using a calculated field, you can perform basic math—addition, subtraction, multiplication, or division. The Review Date field in the BUSRETS view file, which stores a date by which a return must be reviewed before it can be filed, should be calculated based on the due date of the return.

To set up the formula that tells Lotus Approach to set the value that will appear in the Review Date field as the date occurring 15 days before the Due Date:

1. If necessary, switch to the Returns Data Entry form in the BUS-BACK database and switch to Design mode.

2. Open the **C**reate menu and choose the Field Definition command. The Field Definition dialog box appears.

3. If necessary, open the Data**b**ase list box and choose the BUS-RETS database.

4. Highlight the Review Date field and change its **T**ype to Calculated. You see the dialog box shown in Figure 7.14.

5. Open the Fields list box and choose the BUSRETS database.

6. From the list of fields, choose Due Date. BUSRETS."Due Date" appears in the Formula box.

7. Choose the minus sign (–) from the Op**e**rators list box.

8. In the Formula box, immediately after the minus sign, type **15**.

9. Choose the OK command button. You may see a warning about data in the field being truncated because you changed the field type. Choose the OK command button (because we haven't entered any data yet).

In the example, you did not need to use the Functions list box. You use the functions in the Functions list box as needed to create a formula. Later in this chapter, you use the Functions list box when you learn how to calculate summary values using summary functions such as SSum or SAverage.

Figure 7.14

The Field
Definition
dialog box for
a Calculated
field.

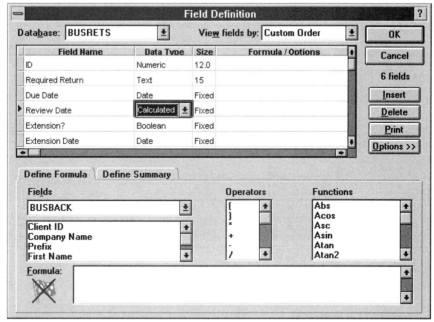

Using Mathematical Functions to Summarize Data in a Repeating Panel

Using certain functions—summary functions—that are available when you define calculated fields, you can summarize data in a repeating panel. For example, you can add up or average values that you display. You also can count the number of records that you display in the repeating panel. In the example database, we can show the total number of services performed for a given client.

To show the number of records that appear in the repeating panel:

1. Switch to Design mode in the Background Data Entry form.

2. Open the Create menu and choose the Field Definition command. The Field Definition dialog box appears. Make sure the database to which you want to add the calculated field appears in the Database list box. In the example, switch to BUSSERV.

3. Scroll to the bottom of the Field Name column and type **Number of Records** in the empty space. In the Data Type column, choose Calculated. The Formula dialog box appears (see Fig. 7.15).

Figure 7.15

The Field
Definition
dialog box
showing
options for a
calculated
field.

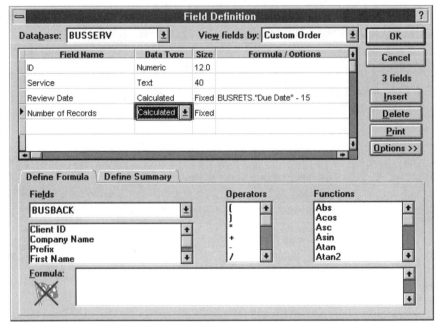

4. Open the Fields list box and choose the BUSSERV database.

5. Place the insertion point in the Formula box and choose the SCount function from the Functions list.

6. Choose the Service field from the Fields list. The dialog box should look like the one in Figure 7.16 when you finish setting up the formula.

7. Choose the Define Summary tab.

8. Open the Summarize on: list box and choose "Summary of all records in BUSSERV."

9. Choose the OK command button. The Add Field window appears, showing the new field you just defined.

10. Drag the new field, Number of Records, onto the form at the bottom right side of the repeating panel for services.

11. Close the Add Field window.

You may want to save your work at this point.

Figure 7.16

The Formula box after setting up a summary formula.

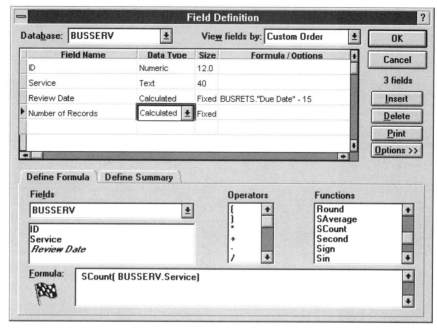

Chapter Summary

In this chapter, you learned how create repeating panels on forms so that you can view many records from a detail database on the same form as its related record in the main database. You learned how to move, size, and delete repeating panels, how to add fields to repeating panels, and how to change the options for repeating panels. You also learned how to use the information in your database to perform basic math and to use mathematical functions to summarize data in a repeating panel.

In the next chapter, you will learn how to enter data into the databases we have created and then to find that information.

Entering, Finding, and Editing Information in the Database

Once you create databases, join them (if applicable), and set up data entry forms, you are ready to enter information into the database system. In this chapter, you will learn how work in Browse mode to enter information into the database. You will also learn how to work in Find mode to find records that meet criteria you specify and modify them or delete them. Last, you will learn how to sort records.

Entering Information into the Database

In Lotus Approach, you typically use forms, which show one record at a time, to enter data. You can use reports (such as List) to enter data, but typically data entry is cumbersome when you are viewing more than one record at a time.

Open the BUSBACK database and switch to the Background Data Entry form.

Understanding Browse Mode

When you first open a database, Lotus Approach automatically places you in Browse mode. Until now, we have worked in Design mode to set up databases. To enter information into a database, work in Browse mode.

The appearance of the screen changes somewhat when you work in Browse mode (see Fig. 8.1). First, you will note that the SmartIcon bar contains some new and different SmartIcons. Remember, you can determine the function of any SmartIcon by pointing at it.

Tip
If you are working on either a worksheet or a crosstab, the SmartIcon bar changes to display icons appropriate for those types of views.

The status bar has also changed. You can still identify the form and mode in which you are working from the first and second boxes at the left edge of the status bar. The third box, however, identifies the number of the record you are currently viewing. As you enter records, you can move forward or backward one record by clicking on the arrows on either side of the third box. The fourth box tells you, if you are searching for records, the number of records that meet the search criteria.

Like in Design mode, the menu bar can change while you work in Browse mode, depending on the view in which you are working and the type of field in which you place the insertion point. If you place the insertion point in a PicturePlus field, you will see the PicturePlus menu next to the Create menu. For most views, you will see the Browse menu next to the Create menu. If, however, you are viewing a worksheet, you will see the Worksheet menu next to the Create menu; if you are viewing a crosstab, you will see the Crosstab menu next to the Create menu.

Figure 8.1

The Lotus Approach screen on a form in Browse mode.

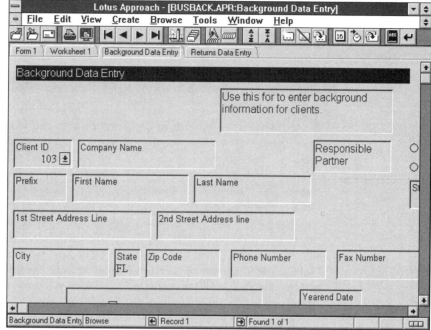

Entering Data into the Database

To enter data into a database, you select a view from which to enter the data and switch to Browse mode. In the example, choose the Background Data Entry view in the BUSBACK database. To start a new record, choose the New Record SmartIcon or open the **B**rowse menu and choose the **N**ew Record command. You also can press **Ctrl+N** to start a new record.

Tip
If, during the previous chapters, you played around in Browse mode in the example database, you probably saw an error message when you tried to switch out, asking you to enter a value into the Company Name field. If you pressed Esc or chose the Cancel command button, Lotus Approach then let you switch, but the Client ID number field was incremented. Since we want to start with record number 101, reset the Client ID number. Switch to Design mode and select the Client ID field. Open the Create menu and choose the Field Definition command to display the Field Definition dialog box. Place the insertion point in the Client ID field and choose the Options command button. Change the number that appears in the Serial number starting at text box to 101 and choose the OK command button. Then, switch back to Browse mode.

When you start a new record, Lotus Approach presents you with a blank version of the form you are viewing. Use either the **Tab** key or the mouse to select a field.

Tip
Pressing the Tab key moves the pointer forward from field to field; pressing Shift+Tab moves the pointer backward from field to field. The order in which the insertion point moves (called the *tab order*) is based upon the order in which you defined the fields when you set up the database. Later in this chapter, you will learn to change the tab order; finish entering the first record before you try. Note that you cannot press the Tab key to move from row to row in the repeating panel, since the repeating panel on the Background Data Entry form represents one field. You can click in a new row to add a repeating panel choice. Once the choice list appears, you can highlight your choice by using the arrow keys or by typing the first letter of the choice. If two choices begin with the same letter, Lotus Approach will highlight only the first one.

Once you select a field, enter information as required. In most types of fields, you enter information exactly as you would expect. In the next section, you will learn more about entering data into various types of fields. In the example, when you start a new record, Lotus Approach automatically places the next record number in the ID field because of the field options we specified for the ID number field. During data entry, simply press the **Tab** key to accept the number and move to the next field. After you learn about entering data in various types of fields, you will enter a complete record.

Typing on a Form During Data Entry

You add information to fields in forms to complete a record. To move from field to field, you can use the mouse or press the **Tab** key. In the next section, you will learn how to change the order Lotus Approach uses when you press the **Tab** key to move from field to field.

In list fields, you can choose an item by clicking on it, or you can highlight your choice by using the arrow keys or by typing the first letter of the choice. If two choices begin with the same letter, Lotus Approach will highlight only the first one. To choose the item, press the **Enter** key.

You can select either an option button or a check box by using the mouse or by pressing the **Spacebar**. You can deselect a check box by pressing the **Spacebar** again. You can deselect an option button by choosing a different option button.

In most types of fields, you enter information exactly as you would expect. In text and memo fields, you can enter numbers, letters, and symbols. If you format a text field, you can, for example, enter information in lowercase and let Lotus Approach redisplay the information in uppercase.

In numeric fields, you can type only numbers. You can format a numeric field just like you can format a text field.

In date fields, you type numbers that represent dates. If you don't type a year, Lotus Approach assumes the current year. You can type just the number that represents the day of the month and Lotus Approach will assume both the current month and the current year from the system date of your computer. If you want to tab into a date field and to type a single digit number for a month or day (e.g., 9 for September), you can type the single-digit number and separate it from the next part of the date field (e.g., the day number) by pressing the **Spacebar**. You can format date fields just like you can format text and numeric fields.

In time fields, you can type numbers that represent times. Lotus Approach uses the same basic rules for time fields as for date fields.

When you type in Boolean fields, you type either **Y** or **1** for a Yes answer or **N** or **0** for a No answer. When the insertion point leaves the field, either "Yes" or "No" appears in the field.

In option button and check box fields, you select the option button or the check box to select the choice. In a drop-down list, you select from the values that appear in the list. If you defined the field as a field box & list, you can either type a value that doesn't appear in the drop-down list or choose from the list.

In PicturePlus fields, you paste OLE objects from other applications or draw in the field to create an image. Any image you enter into a PicturePlus field appears only on the current record. See Chapter 14 for more information about entering OLE objects into PicturePlus fields.

For the first record in the BUSBACK database, enter the information shown in Table 8.1 using the Background Data Entry form:

In the Mailing Lists box, choose Monthly Newsletter, Tax Law Changes, and Holiday List.

When you place the pointer into the Services Performed for the Client repeating panel, a list box appears—the custom values list we created for the Services field. Click on a value, and Lotus Approach places the value into the repeating panel. Click on the next blank line

Table 8.1 Record 1 for the BUSBACK database	
Field	**Information to enter**
ID #	101 (Just press **Tab** to insert this number)
Company Name	Orange Juice Special
Prefix	Mr.
First Name	O.J.
Last Name	Drinker
1st Street Address Line	1 Healthy Way
2nd Street Address Line	Suite 100
City	Tampa
State	(Leave this at FL)
Zip Code	33344
Phone Number	8131111111
Fax Number	8132222222
Year End Date	0430
Prepare Additional Returns?	Y
Staff Person Assigned	Jeff
Responsible Partner	Jim

to accept the value (and insert a record into the BUS-SERV database). To add another service, simply click on the same blank line again, and the list will reappear. Add, to the first record, the following services:

- Keypunch/Bookkeeping
- Compilation
- Tax Return Preparation

Click on the Enter Record SmartIcon to save the new record.

Tip

If you find that a field doesn't repeat in a repeating panel, it may not be placed properly. It must appear in the top row of the repeating panel and fit within the boundaries of the repeating panel. To make sure that a field is part of a repeating panel, switch to Design mode and try moving the panel. Any field that doesn't move with the panel is not part of the panel. Resize or move the field so that it fits within the boundaries of the repeating panel.

You can finish entering a record and save it in one of four ways:

- Choose the Enter Record SmartIcon—this method leaves the record you just entered displayed.
- Choose the Create New Record SmartIcon—this method saves the record and displays a blank form on which you can enter another record.
- Press **Ctrl+N**—this method saves the record and displays a blank form on which you can enter another record.
- Open the **R**ecord menu and choose the **N**ew Record command—this method saves the record and displays a blank form on which you can enter another record.

If you decide, in the middle of entering a record, that you don't want to enter that record, you can press the **Esc** key. Lotus Approach will not enter the record you started. In the example database, however, you will find that the ID number will still increment by one even though no record is inserted in your database. Because you didn't complete the record, no record in your database contains that number; however, Lotus Approach will not redisplay the number for you to use again. Essentially, Lotus Approach will skip a number as it assigns numbers to your customers. In Chapter 13, you will learn a technique to renumber your records.

Changing the Data Entry Order

When you enter data in Browse mode and press the **Tab** key to move from field to field, Lotus Approach moves the mouse pointer in the order in which you originally defined fields in the database. As you enter records, you may discover that the tab order of the mouse pointer does not match the way you want to enter data.

You can change the tab order of the fields so that the pointer moves into fields in the order you want to enter data.

To change the tab order:

1. Switch to Design mode.

2. Open the **View** menu and choose the Show Data Entry Order command. Numbers appear in gray boxes at the edge of each field.

3. Click on any of the boxes. An insertion point appears in the box. Change the number in the box. Lotus Approach renumbers subsequent fields as appropriate.

4. To use the tab order you establish, open the **View** menu and choose the Show Data Entry Order command again. The gray boxes disappear from the screen and, when you enter data and press the **Tab** key, the pointer moves in the order you specified.

Tip

If you plan to use the Tab key while entering data on the Returns Data Entry form, you may want to change the tab order so that the Required Return field in the repeating panel is the first field to which Lotus Approach moves the insertion point when you press the Tab key. Number the rest of the fields in the repeating panel consecutively and make the Company Name field and the Yearend Date field the last fields on the form. That way, you will use the Next Record button (on the status bar or the SmartIcon) to display the appropriate record, and then use the keyboard to type and move in the repeating panel.

Finding Records

Once you have entered records into the database, you may need to find them to view their contents, to modify them, or to delete them. To be able to test the functions you are about to learn about, you need to enter a few more records using the Background Data Entry form. Enter the additional records shown in Table 8.2.

In the Mailing Lists box, choose Monthly Newsletter and Holiday List.

Add the following services in the repeating panel:

* Compilation
* Tax Return Preparation
* Financial Statement Preparation

Table 8.2 Record 2	
Field	**Information to enter**
ID #	(Leave this at the suggested number)
Company Name	Papaya Juice Special
Prefix	(Leave this blank)
First Name	Papa
Last Name	Papaya
1st Street Address Line	2 Healthy Way
2nd Street Address Line	Suite 200
City	Tampa
State	(Leave this at FL)
Zip Code	33333
Phone Number	8133333333
Fax Number	8134444444
Year End Date	1231
Prepare Additional Returns?	Y
Staff Person Assigned	Tim
Responsible Partner	Harvey

Table 8.3 Record 3	
Field	**Information to enter**
ID #	(Press **Tab** to insert this number)
Company Name	Tomato Juice Special
Prefix	Ms.
First Name	Red Hot
Last Name	Drinker
1st Street Address Line	400 Juicey Street
2nd Street Address Line	(Leave this blank)
City	Tampa
State	(Leave this at FL)
Zip Code	33333
Phone Number	8135555555
Fax Number	8136666666
Year End Date	0930
Prepare Additional Returns?	N
Staff Person Assigned	Kelly
Responsible Partner	Jim

Click on the New Record SmartIcon to save the new record and display a new data entry form for you to complete (see Table 8.3).

In the Mailing Lists box, choose Monthly Newsletter, Holiday List, and 11-Month Planning.

Add the following services in the repeating panel:

- Keypunch/Bookkeeping
- Financial Statement Review
- Tax Return Preparation
- Consulting

Click on the New Record SmartIcon to save the new record and display a new data entry form for you to complete (see Table 8.4).

Table 8.4 Record 4	
Field	Information to enter
ID #	(Leave this at the suggested number)
Company Name	Apple Juice Special
Prefix	Mr.
First Name	Johnny
Last Name	Appleseed
1st Street Address Line	1 Delicious Drive
2nd Street Address Line	Suite 2001
City	Tampa
State	(Leave this at FL)
Zip Code	33343
Phone Number	8137777777
Fax Number	8138888888
Year End Date	1231
Prepare Additional Returns?	Y
Staff Person Assigned	Tim
Responsible Partner	Harvey

In the Mailing Lists box, choose Annual Payroll Summaries, Tax Law Changes, and 11-Month Planning.

Add the following services in the repeating panel:

- Keypunch/Bookkeeping
- Compilation
- Tax Return Preparation
- W-2s/1099s

Click on the New Record SmartIcon to save the new record and display a new data entry form for you to complete (see Table 8.5).

In the Mailing Lists box, choose Monthly Newsletter, Annual Payroll Summaries, and Holiday List.

Table 8.5 Record 5	
Field	**Information to enter**
ID #	(Leave this at the suggested number)
Company Name	Pineapple Juice Special
Prefix	Ms.
First Name	Carmen
Last Name	Coconut
1st Street Address Line	46 Yellow Circle
2nd Street Address Line	Room 5080
City	Tampa
State	(Leave this at FL)
Zip Code	33355
Phone Number	8139999999
Fax Number	8130000000
Year End Date	0930
Prepare Additional Returns?	Y
Staff Person Assigned	Jeff
Responsible Partner	Jim

Add the following services in the repeating panel:

- Compilation
- Quarterly Payroll Taxes
- W-2s/1099s
- Tax Return Preparation

Click on the Enter Record SmartIcon to save the new record.

Moving to a Record

As you add records to the database, Lotus Approach places the record at the end of the database, or at the end of the last set you found, by setting up criteria that Lotus Approach uses to select only certain records. Records remain in that order until you refresh your database. To refresh your database, open the **B**rowse menu and choose the **R**efresh command. Lotus Approach reorders the records so that they appear in the order in which they were entered.

You can move directly to a specific record. As you enter information into the database, Lotus Approach assigns a record number to each record. You can use that record number to go directly to a record. Click in the status bar on the section that tells you the current record number. You see a dialog box into which you can type a number for the record you want to see.

In Browse mode, you can use SmartIcons to move to the next, previous, first, or last records in the database or in a set of records that you found.

Finding a Record or Group of Records

Once you have entered records into the database, you often want to find a particular record or a set of records that share a common characteristic—for example, you may want to browse through all the records in the database to see which clients are supposed to receive 11-month planning information.

To find records, you work in Find mode on the form that can display the information you want to find. You can change to Find mode using either the Mode list on the status bar or the Find SmartIcon. Lotus Approach presents a *find request form*, which is blank form on which you specify criteria that describe the records you want to find. You fill information into a field (or several fields), and Lotus Approach finds the records that match the criteria you set. While you are viewing a blank form on which you want to specify a find request, you refer to the fields in which you type the search criteria as *search fields*.

When you specify search criteria, you type in fields the same way you type while entering data—the same rules and restrictions apply. In search fields, you can type characters alone or you can include operators. When you type characters alone, Lotus Approach searches for information in the field that begins with the characters you type. In the example database, if you type **1** in the 1st Street Address Line of a find request form, Lotus Approach will find two records: Orange Juice Special at 1 Healthy Way, and Apple Juice Special at 1 Delicious Drive.

When you include operators, you provide Lotus Approach with a way to compare the records in the database with the information you want to see. For example, you may want to see the records of clients whose numbers are less than 103. Or, you may want to see the records of all clients whose names begin with O through P. Or, you may want to see all the records where the contact's last name is Smith.

Tip

If the search criterion contains an apostrophe ('), type the apostrophe twice. For example, to search for O'Malley, type **O''Malley** in the search field.

Add one of the operators in Table 8.6 to the characters in a search field to help specify criteria for the search.

You can make a search case-sensitive by preceding the characters in the search field with an exclamation point. Case-sensitive searches are not typically necessary in either a dBASE or a FoxPro database.

You can use option button fields and check box fields in searches. Just select the option button or check box for which you want Lotus Approach to search. If you select an option button, Lotus Approach will display all records where that option button is selected. If you select a check box, Lotus Approach will display all records where the check box is selected.

Tip

If you want to see all records where a particular check box is *not* selected, place an "X" in the check box and then remove the "X" from the check box. Then, perform the find request. Lotus Approach will display the records on which that particular check box is not selected. You can test this particular feature using the Monthly Newsletter check box. If you find only those records where the Monthly Newsletter check box is *not* selected, Lotus Approach will find only the Apple Juice Special record.

Table 8.6 Operators Used When Searching	
Include this operator	**To find records where the information stored in the database**
=	exactly matches the information in the search field. If used alone (with no search characters), this character tells Lotus Approach to find records where the search field is blank.
<>	does not match the information in the search field. If used alone (with no search characters), this character tells Lotus Approach to find records where the search field is not blank.
<	is less than the information in the search field.
>	is greater than the information in the search field.
<=	is less than or equal to the information in the search field.
>=	is greater than or equal to the information in the search field.
*	matches any characters in the search field.
?	matches any character at specific positions in the search criteria.
...	falls between the values in the search field (for example, O...Pz). Note that you must use three periods to specify this operator.
~	sounds like the information specified in the search field (this kind of search is effective when you're not sure how to spell the data stored in the field).

You can make comparisons within one search field by using the And and Or operators. To specify that records should contain two values in the search field, type the search characters and connect them with an ampersand (&). For example, to find all records that include *both* "apple" and "special" in the Business Name field in the example database, type ***apple*&*special*** in the Business Name field of a find request form. A search of this type will yield two records: Apple Juice Special and Pineapple Juice Special. Note that if you exclude the wildcard asterisk (*), Lotus Approach won't find any records because no records begin with "apple" and "special."

To find all records where the search field contains one of two values (an Or relationship), type the search characters and connect them with a comma. For example, to find all the records that include *either* "apple" or "special" in the Business Name field in the example database, type ***apple*,*special*** in the Business Name field of a find request form. A search of this type will find all five records in the database, since all the clients' names contain the word "special."

As you might guess, And searches yield fewer records than Or searches. In addition, you can type criteria into more than one field on the find request form. Lotus Approach treats information in more than one field on a form as an And request—Lotus Approach will retrieve only records that meet the specifications of *both* search fields. Viewed another way, as you complete more search fields, fewer records will match your criteria; therefore, specifying more information yields fewer records found.

You can build If statements to formulate find requests. You type If statements into an unused field on a find request form. If statements can include constant values, other fields, and operators. Enclose non-numeric constants in single quotation marks. Under the following conditions, enclose the field name in double quotation marks:

- If the field name begins with a number or contains a space, a period, or a comma.

- If the field name contains any of the following characters:

  /

  #

  +

  -

  <

  >

  (

)

In the sample database, you could use an If statement to find all records where the responsible partner is Harvey or the staff person assigned is Kelly by typing, in any blank field of a find request form, the following statement:

If((″Responsible Partner″='Harvey') or (″Staff Person Assigned″='Kelly'))

Lotus Approach would find three records: Papaya Juice Special, Tomato Juice Special, and Apple Juice Special.

Let's try a few sample find requests using the example database:

To find one client's record in the example database:

1. Switch to Find mode by choosing the Find SmartIcon. Lotus Approach displays a find request form (see Fig. 8.2)

2. Place the insertion point in the ID field and open the list box. A list appears that contains client names for the records we entered into the database. This list is the list we created for the ID number field in Chapter 5.

3. To view a specific record, click on the client's name. Lotus Approach will fill in the client's ID number.

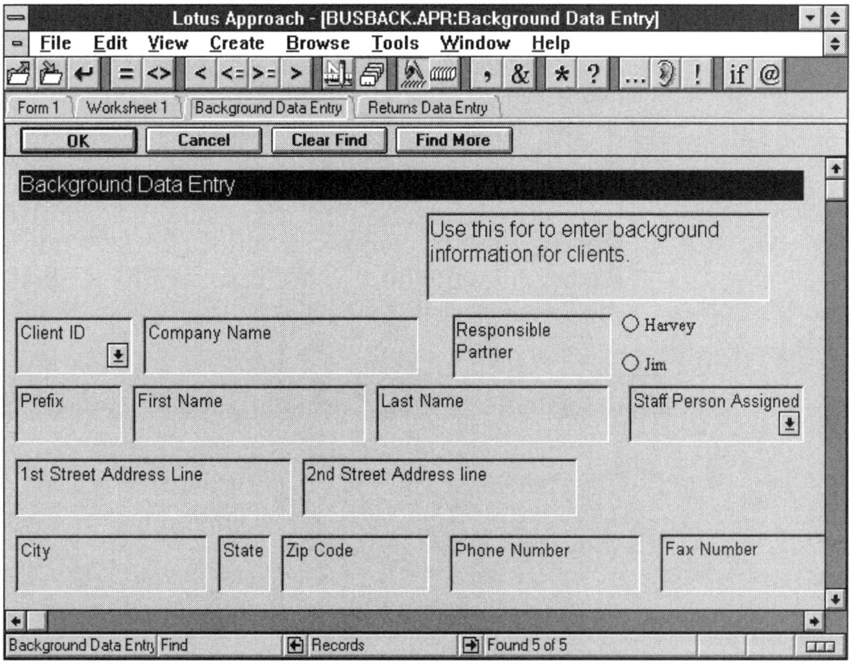

Figure 8.2

A find request form.

4. Choose the OK command button to find the record. Lotus Approach fills in the rest of the client's record.

To find all the records where the zip code is 33333:

1. Switch to Find mode by choosing the Find SmartIcon.

2. Place the insertion point in the Zip Code field and type **=33333**.

3. Choose the OK command button. Lotus Approach finds two records: Papaya Juice Special and Tomato Juice Special.

To find all the records where the business name starts with O and P:

1. Switch to Find mode by choosing the Find SmartIcon.

2. Place the insertion point in the Company Name field and type **O...Pz**. Be sure to use three periods to separate O and Pz.

Tip

The logic behind using Pz (as opposed to just P) may not be obvious. If you used just P, Lotus Approach would find all records beginning with O and ending with Oz—unless one record contained a company name of just P. To include all businesses whose names begin with O *and* all businesses whose names begin with P, you must extend the search beyond the letter P. If you search for O...Pa, you will see all the Os and those businesses whose names begin with Pa. If you search for O...Pz, you will see all the businesses whose names begin with O and all the businesses whose names begin with P.

---

3. Choose the OK command button. Lotus Approach finds three records: Orange Juice Special, Papaya Juice Special, and Pineapple Juice Special.

Tip

If you find a set of records and then start adding records, you may want to update your view of the found set to include any of the new records that meet the criteria. Open the Browse menu and choose the Refresh command.

Tip

After finding a set of records and working with them, you will eventually want to display all the records in your database again. To show all records in the database, choose the Find All SmartIcon.

Speeding Up Searches and Sorts

You can index fields when you define them (or go back and change the field definition in Design mode) to speed up searches and sorts in a database. However, indexing fields slows down data entry. In addition, Lotus Approach will build an index for a field the first time you find or sort using that field; therefore, you should be able to let Lotus Approach index fields as needed. You will learn about sorting records at the end of this chapter.

Editing and Deleting Records

After finding records, Lotus Approach returns you to Browse mode. You can edit one or more of the records you found by typing in them the same way as when you are adding records. Choose the Enter SmartIcon when you finish modifying a record to save the changes.

You also can delete one or more of the records you find, or you can delete an entire set of records you find.

Filling a Field with a Specific Value

You can quickly update records by filling one field in each record with the same data. You can update a set of records in the same way by finding the set first and then filling the field in question. Suppose, in the example database, that you needed to update zip codes because the post office changed zip code 33333 to 33332.

To fill the zip code field of all records containing 33333 with 33332:

1. Find the set of records you want to modify. In the example, find all records where the zip code equals 33333. Lotus Approach finds two records: Papaya Juice Special and Tomato Juice Special.

2. Place the insertion point in the field that you want to fill. In the example, click in the Zip Code field.

3. Open the **Browse** menu and choose the Fill Field command. The Fill Field dialog box appears (see Fig. 8.3).

4. Type the new value for the field in the text box. In the example, type **33332**.

5. Choose the OK command. Lotus Approach changes all the zip codes in the found set to 33332.

Duplicating a Record

Once you have added a record, you may find that most of the information on that record is the same as the information for another record you want to add.

To duplicate a record:

1. Make sure that you are viewing the record you want to duplicate.

2. Open the **Browse** menu and choose the **Duplicate Record** command.

Finding Duplicate Records

You can ask Lotus Approach to compare values in specified fields and find all records that have the same value in the specified fields. Using this technique, you can find duplicate records in your database.

Suppose you enter another record into the database for Papaya Juice Special, but you accidentally type the name **Papaya Juice**

Figure 8.3

The Fill Field dialog box.

For each record in the found set, set field "BUSBACK.Postal Code" to:

33332

Specials (where Special is plural). In reality, you have two records in the database, under two different ID numbers, for the same client. You can find the duplicates and then delete the extra.

To search for duplicates in your database:

1. To search through all records in the database, choose the Find All Records SmartIcon.

2. Open the **B**rowse menu and choose the Find Special command. The Find Special dialog box appears (see Fig. 8.4).

3. Identify whether you want to find duplicate records or unique records. In the example, choose the Find **d**uplicate records in the current found set option button.

4. If you want Lotus Approach to display only the second record entered, choose the Exclude first record found in each set of duplicates option button. If you want Lotus Approach to display all records for the matching set, choose the Find All option button.

5. From the Database fields list box, choose the fields you want Lotus Approach to compare while searching for duplicates and choose the **A**dd command button. In the example, you would

Figure 8.4

The Find Special dialog box.

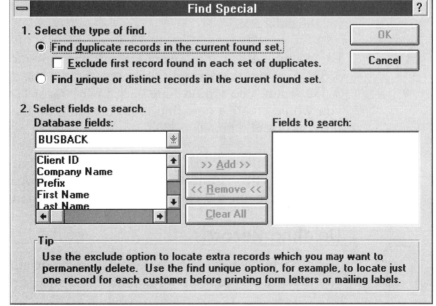

add the First Name field, the Last Name field, and, possibly, the 1st Street Address Line field to help identify the duplicate records.

6. Choose the OK command button. Lotus Approach displays a set of records for which the values are identical in the fields you selected.

Hiding or Displaying Records

You can hide records so that they are unavailable for editing, sorting, calculating, printing, or exporting. Hiding records does not delete them from the database; they simply aren't used when performing any of the activities just listed. You can use the hide and display features in Lotus Approach to work with a particular set of records—you find and hide the records with which you *don't* want to work.

To hide a record:

1. Find the record or records you want to hide.

2. Open the **Browse** menu and choose the **Hide Record** command.

3. Repeat step 2 for each record in the found set to hide all the records with which you don't want to work.

4. Start a new find request that finds all the rest of the records in the database.

For example, if you don't want to work with any record in zip code 33332, you would find all the records where the zip code equals 33332. Then, you would hide each of the records you find. Last, you would create a new find request to find all the records where the zip code *is not equal to* 33332.

To redisplay the records you hid, choose the Find All SmartIcon (eighth SmartIcon from the left edge of the SmartIcon bar), or open the **Browse** menu and choose the Show **All** command.

Deleting Records

You can remove records from the database by deleting them. When you delete a record, you are not affect the structure of your database, just the contents. When you remove records using a form created for joined databases, the join options control whether records in the joined database are also deleted. For the sample databases, we set up the join options so that deleting a record in the main database would also delete any records in the detail database. See Chapter 4 for more information on join options.

> **Tip**
>
> Deleting records is permanent—you must reenter a record if you accidentally delete it; you cannot undo the action. Before you delete large numbers of records, you might want to back up your database.

To delete a record, you select it, either by viewing it or finding it. Then, you choose the Delete Record SmartIcon or open the **B**rowse menu and choose the Delete Record command. If you found a set of records, you can open the **R**ecords menu and choose the Delete Found Set command.

If you are deleting records from a form created using joined databases (like the Background Data Entry form), you may want to refresh the database after deleting to ensure that all detail databases are properly updated. Open the **B**rowse menu and choose the **R**efresh command.

Sorting Records

Sometimes, you need to see the records in your database in a different order than the natural order—that is, the order in which you create the records. When you need to change the order, you can sort the records in the database. You can sort records in alphabetical order by sorting on a text field, you can sort records in numerical order by sorting on a numeric field, and you can sort records in chronological order by sorting on a date or time field. You can sort a set of records or all records in the database.

For example, suppose you want to see the records in the example database in alphabetical order by client name.

Tip

You can perform a simple alphabetical or numerical sort, in either ascending or descending order, using SmartIcons. Place the insertion point in the field by which you want to sort and choose the Ascending Sort SmartIcon or the Descending Sort SmartIcon.

To sort the records in your database:

1. In Browse mode, choose the Show All SmartIcon to find all the records in the database or create a find request to find the records you want to sort. In the example, we want to sort all records in the database.

2. Open the **B**rowse menu and choose the Sort command. The Sort submenu appears.

3. Choose the Define command. The Sort dialog box appears (see Fig. 8.5).

4. If necessary, open the list box showing the database and switch to the database containing the field by which you want to sort. In the example, leave the database at the BUSBACK database.

5. In the Database fields list, highlight the field by which you want to sort. In the example, choose the Zip Code field.

6. Choose the **A**dd command button. The field you chose appears in the Fields to sort on list box.

7. Repeat steps 4 and 5 until all the fields by which you want to sort appear in the **S**ort list box. You can select only one field unless you expect more than one record in the database to contain the same value in the sort field; Lotus Approach uses the additional fields you choose to break ties. In the example, since

Figure 8.5

The Sort dialog box.

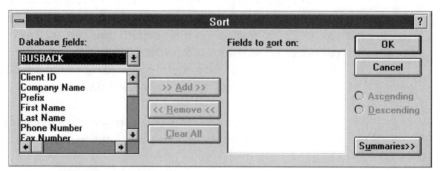

we are sorting by zip code, we want to also choose the Company Name field to sort records with the same zip code into some additional order (either alphabetical or numerical order). If you make a mistake while adding sort fields, highlight the field in the Fields to sort on list box and choose the **Remove** command button.

8. Choose whether to sort in Ascending or **D**escending order by selecting an option button.

9. Choose the OK command button. When you look through the records in the database, you will find them appearing in the following order:

Record 1	Papaya Juice Special	ID # 102
Record 2	Tomato Juice Special	ID # 103
Record 3	Apple Juice Special	ID # 104
Record 4	Orange Juice Special	ID # 101
Record 5	Pineapple Juice Special	ID # 105

You can resort the records into any order by repeating the steps above. To return the records to their original, natural order, choose the Show All SmartIcon or open the **B**rowse menu and choose the Show **A**ll command.

Tip

During any one session, if you sort records and then add new records to the database, you may want to update your view of the sorted set to include any of the new records. Open the Browse menu and choose the Refresh command.

The sort order remains effective only for the current session until you sort the records in a different order, find a set of records, or choose the Show All SmartIcon. You can specify a permanent sort order either by using a macro that resorts your database into the desired order when you open the database or by periodically exporting your data, sorted in the desired order, to a new file. In Chapter 13, you will learn about macros; in Chapter 14, you will learn about exporting and importing.

Chapter Summary

In this chapter, you learned how work in Browse mode so that you could enter records into a database. Then, you learned how work in Find mode so that you could find records that you entered. You learned how to modify records; to save updating time, you learned how to fill one field on a selected set of records with the same value, and you learned how to duplicate records. You learned how to search the database for duplicate records and you learned how to delete records. Last, you learned how to sort the database into an order other than the natural order (the one in which you enter information).

In the next chapter, you will learn how to create and run reports in Lotus Approach.

CHAPTER 9

Designing Reports for the Database

So far, you have learned how to set up a database, join two databases, enter information into a database, and find information in the database. In this chapter, you will learn how to produce reports from the information in the database using three basic types of reports:

- Standard
- Columnar
- Summary

The good news here is that much of what you learned about forms in Chapters 5 and 6 also holds true for reports. For example, when you create a report, you work in Design mode. You move, size, and format fields on a report the same way you formatted them on a form. You add text objects, fields, graphics, or drawn objects to a report the same way you added them to a form.

Before you begin creating reports, let's add some data to the database using the Returns Data Entry form to give you more information about which to report.

To add data to the database using the Returns Data Entry form:

1. If necessary, open the BUSBACK database.

2. Switch to the Returns Data Entry form by clicking on the Returns Data Entry tab. In the Company Name field, you see the name you typed in one of the records in the Background Data Entry form, along with the year end date you typed on that record.

3. Place the insertion point in the first field of the repeating panel and use the information in the following lists to complete the repeating panel for each record you entered on the Background Data Entry form. Remember, you can press the space bar to specify the separators between each portion of a date; the system will calculate the Review By date for each return.

4. As you finish entering each record for the company, choose the Enter Record SmartIcon to save the current record. Remember, each row is *part* of the record for the company, so wait until you have entered all the information on all the rows.

5. To bring up the next record, click on the Next Record SmartIcon or the Next Record arrow in the status bar. Do *not* use the Company Name list box.

For Orange Juice Special, enter the following information:

Return	1120
Due By	7 1594
Extension?	N
Return	5500
Due By	113094
Extension?	N

For Papaya Juice Special, enter the following information:

Return	1120S
Due By	3 1594
Extension?	N

For Tomato Juice Special, enter the following information:

Return	1120

Due By	121594
Extension?	N
Return	5500
Due By	4 3095
Extension?	N

For Apple Juice Special, enter the following information:

Return	1065
Due By	5 1594
Extension?	N

For Pineapple Juice Special, enter the following information:

Return	1120
Due By	121594
Extension?	Y
Extension Date	6 15 95

Creating Reports

Much of what you learned about forms in Chapters 5 and 6 also holds true for reports. To create reports, you will work in Design mode. You will format fields on a report the same way you formatted them on a form. You can add text objects, fields, graphics, or drawn objects to a report the same way you added them to a form.

> ### Tip
>
> Note that while you work on a report, the menu choices are slightly different than those you saw while working on forms. Next to the Create menu, you see the Report menu. In addition, the SmartIcon bar in Design mode contains SmartIcons useful for creating reports.

In Lotus Approach, you can create three basic types of reports:

- **Standard:** Use a standard report when you want each piece of information to appear on a separate row on the report (see Fig.

9.1). You can make a standard report print so that records run down the left side of the page and then start again at the top of the page on the right side (similar to the way newspaper columns read).

- **Columnar:** Use a columnar report to display each piece of information in a separate column on the report. When you set up a columnar report, all information for one record appears in one row across the report (see Fig. 9.2).

- **Summary:** Use a summary report when you don't want to display information for individual records in the database, but want instead you want the information in specified fields. You typically use summary reports to add up all the values in a given field on each record and display the total on the report (see Fig. 9.3).

To view the results of a report, you must switch to Browse or Preview mode ,using either the status bar or the Browse or Preview SmartIcon. You can see the results of Summary reports only in Preview mode.

Figure 9.1

A sample standard report.

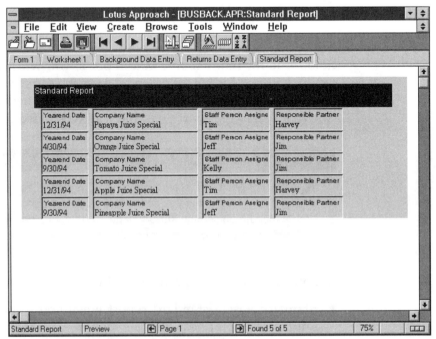

Figure 9.2

A sample columnar report.

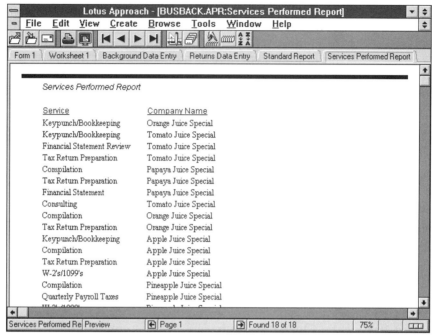

Figure 9.3

A sample summary report.

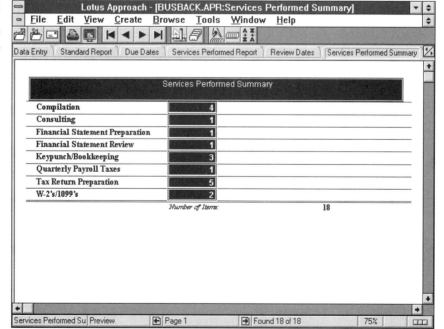

The type of report you choose to create depends entirely on what you want to see and the way you want to see it. From the examples in Figures 9.1 and 9.2, you can see that you can use the same information and display it as either a standard report or a columnar report.

Regardless of the type of report you want to create, you follow the same basic steps. In this chapter, you will learn how to create standard and columnar reports and then to summarize information in reports in a variety of ways, including by creating a summary report. You will then learn how to format a report.

Creating a Standard Report

Let's create a simple report in standard format for the BUSBACK database that will show each company name, the staff person assigned, the responsible partner, and the year end date for the company.

1. Open the database on which you want to base the report. In the example, open the BUSBACK database.

2. Switch to Design mode using either the SmartIcon bar or the Mode list in the status bar.

3. Open the **C**reate menu and choose the **R**eport command. You see the Report Assistant dialog box (see Fig. 9.4).

4. You can type the name of the report in the View name & title text box, or you can change it later. In the example, type Standard Report.

5. From the SmartMaster style list box, choose a report style. Watch the Sample Form box to see what your form will look like. For the example, choose Chisel2. (Like form styles, you may want to experiment with these styles some—several of them are quite nice-looking.)

6. From the SmartMaster layout list box, choose a report style. In the example, choose Standard.

7. Click on the Next command button or the Step 2:Fields tab.

8. If necessary, change the database that appears in the Database fields list box. In the example, don't change the database that appears in the Database fields list box.

Figure 9.4

The Report Assistant dialog box.

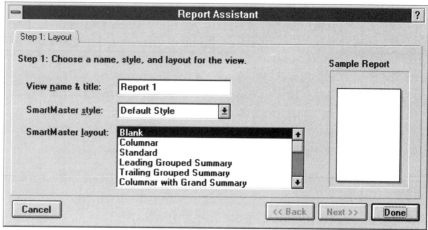

9. Select the fields you want on your report from the Database fields list box and choose the Add command button. Those fields then appear in the Fields to place on view list box. Select the fields in the order you want them to appear on the report. In the example, choose the following fields:

   • Year End Date

   • Company Name

   • Staff Person Assigned

   • Responsible Partner

10. When you finish, choose the Done command button. You see the report you created on-screen.

11. Switch to Preview mode to see your report.

This same report might be more useful in a columnar layout, because you can group information for easier readability in a columnar report. You may want to try recreating it after you learn, in the next section, how to create a columnar report.

Creating a Columnar Report

In the sample CPA system, we have several reports to create based on joined databases, including a columnar report. You create reports of the information contained in joined databases in much the same way you create reports based on a single database, and in much the same way you created forms for joined databases. When you finish creating the report, Lotus Approach asks you to designate the main database. For a report to produce accurate information, you must make sure that you have established correctly the main-to-detail relationship of the databases. As with forms based on joined databases, Lotus Approach assumes that the main database for the report is the database from which you first add a field to your report. In reports, you typically display a many-to-one relationship, so the main database on a report is the database in which the the join field is *not* unique.

The Services Performed report, for which we will use a basic columnar layout, shows the clients for whom various services are performed. Later in this chapter, you will learn to use Lotus Approach's PowerClick reporting feature to group information on the report.

The Services Performed report uses two databases: the BUSSERV database and the BUSBACK database. The relationship between the two databases for this report is a many-to-one relationship, and the BUSSERV database is the main database for the report.

To create a Services Performed Report:

1. Open the BUSBACK database and switch to Design mode.

2. Open the **C**reate menu and choose the **R**eport command. The Report Assistant dialog box (see Fig. 9.5) appears.

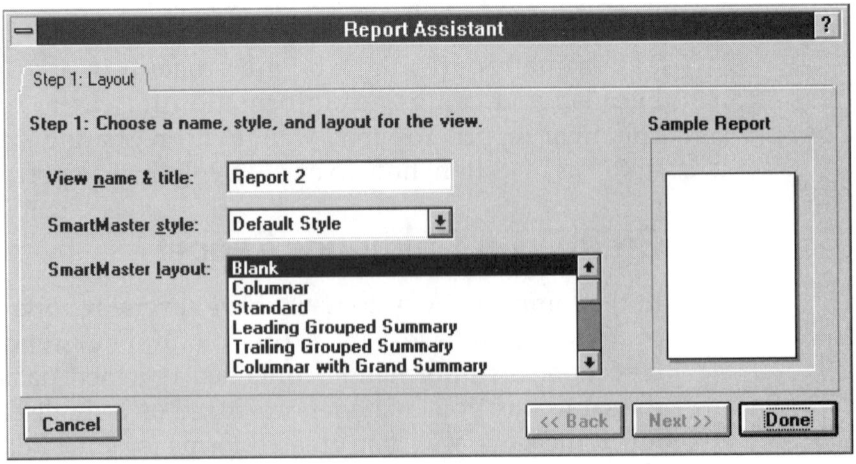

Figure 9.5

The Report Assistant dialog box.

3. In the View name & title text box, type the title for the report. In the example, type **Services Performed report**.

4. From the SmartMaster style list box, choose a style for your report. In the example, choose B&W2.

5. From the SmartMaster layout list box, choose a layout for your report. In the example, choose Columnar.

6. Click on the Next command button or the Step 2:Fields tab.

7. From the Database fields list box, choose the main database for the report. In the example, choose the BUSSERV database.

8. From the Database fields list, choose the fields you want to appear on the report. In the example, choose Service and choose the **Add** command button.

9. (Optional) If you want to include fields from a joined database, reopen the Database fields list box and choose the that database. In the example, switch to the BUSBACK database.

10. From the Database Fields list, choose the fields you want to add to the report. In the example, choose Company Name and choose the **Add** command button.

11. Choose the Done command button. You will see the Define Main Database dialog box (see Fig. 9.6), from which you can specify the main database for the report.

12. Select the correct main database and choose the OK command button. In the example, make sure the main database is BUSSERV. The Services Performed report appears on-screen in

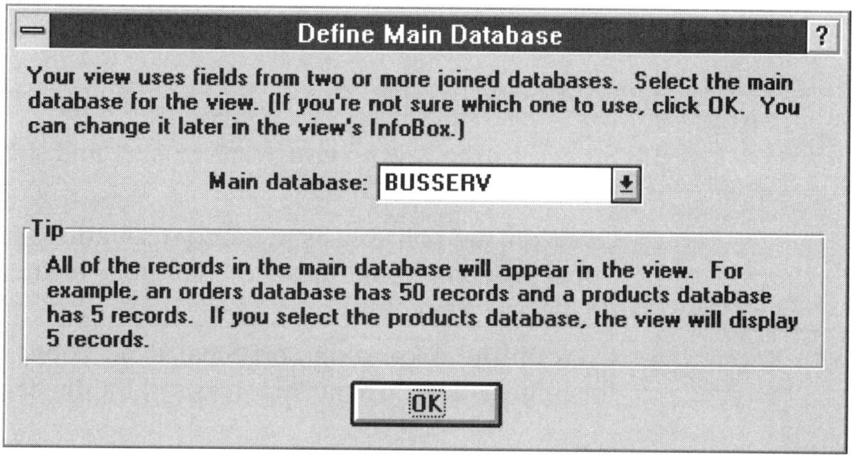

Figure 9.6

The Define
Main
Database
dialog box.

Define Main Database

Your view uses fields from two or more joined databases. Select the main database for the view. (If you're not sure which one to use, click OK. You can change it later in the view's InfoBox.)

Main database: BUSSERV

Tip

All of the records in the main database will appear in the view. For example, an orders database has 50 records and a products database has 5 records. If you select the products database, the view will display 5 records.

OK

Figure 9.7

The Services
Performed
report in
Browse mode.

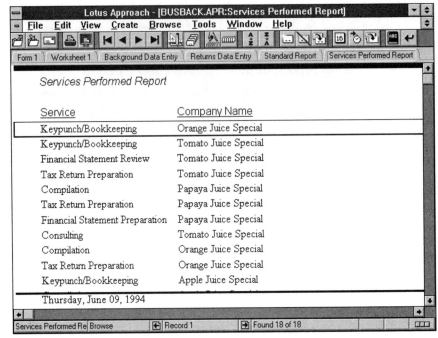

Design mode. You can switch to Browse mode to see all the records presented in the database, each showing the service and the corresponding client for whom that service is performed (see Fig. 9.7).

Sorting Information on a Report

The information on the Services Performed report would be more useful if we could see it organized by service, so that we could see the clients for whom we perform a particular service.

To use the SmartIcon bar to quickly sort the report:

1. Switch to the report you want to sort and switch to Design mode.

2. Click on the column by which you want to sort the report. Lotus Approach highlights the column. In the example, click on the Services column.

3. Click on the Ascending Sort SmartIcon. Lotus Approach sorts the information on your report based on the field you selected.

In the example, the Services Performed report now appears in Service order.

Tip
If you want more control over sorting, you also can sort from the Sort dialog box. Open the Report menu and choose the Sort command. The Sort submenu appears. Choose the Define command. The Sort dialog box appears (see Fig. 9.8).

In the next section, you will learn how to display information in summarized format, showing the service only once and listing, next to it, the clients for whom the service is performed.

Summarizing Information

You can summarize information on reports in several ways.

- You can group information.

- You can subtotal and total information on a report.

- You can create a summary report, which contains only summary information and no detail information.

In each case, Lotus Approach utilizes a *summary panel* to create the summarized information (see Fig. 9.9).

You can add a summary panel containing a field to a report either when you are creating the report or after you have created it. The

Figure 9.8

The Sort dialog box.

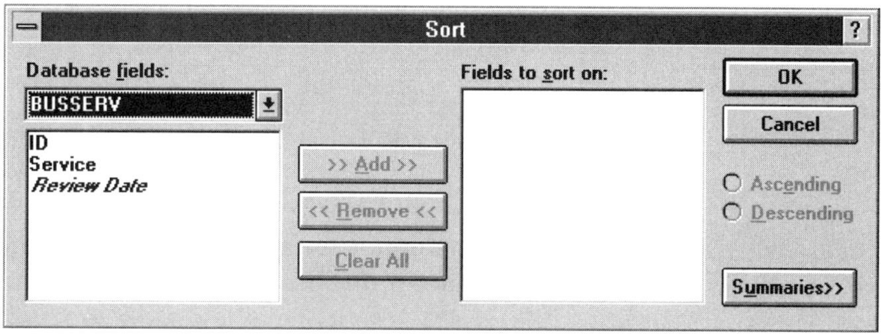

Sort

Database fields:

BUSSERV

ID
Service
Review Date

>> Add >>

<< Remove <<

Clear All

Fields to sort on:

OK

Cancel

◯ Ascending
◯ Descending

Summaries>>

Figure 9.9

Sample report with a summary panel.

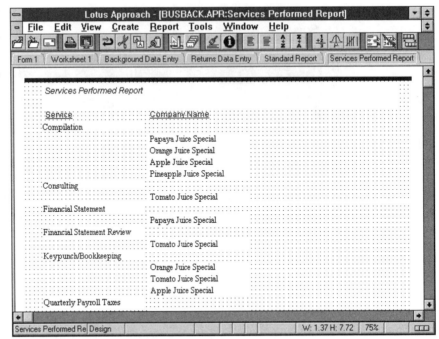

summary panel tells Lotus Approach the field by which you want to summarize information and where to place the summarized information—before or after the detail information. Typically, you want the field to appear before the detail information, when you want to group information; you then use a leading summary panel. Similarly, you want the field to appear after the detail information if you are subtotaling or totaling number; you then use a trailing summary panel.

> ### Tip
>
> The physical placement of the field inside the summary panel affects whether the summary panel actually works. If the field is not completely contained inside the summary panel, Lotus Approach will not summarize the information properly. As you work through the examples in this section, you will learn how to check to make sure the field appears inside the summary panel.

A summary report is not really an exception to any of the above information, because it does contain a summary panel. However, a summary report contains no detail information. You learn more about summary reports at the end of this section.

Grouping Items in a Report

You can group the information on standard or columnar reports so that certain items appear together. For example, we can create groups on the Services Performed report by listing the Service only once when listing the clients for whom that service is performed.

Adding a Summary Panel to an Existing Report

You can add a summary panel to an existing report in two ways in Lotus Approach. You can use the Summary dialog box or you can use the SmartIcon bar. If you use the Summary dialog box, you have more control over the placement of the summary panel (see Fig. 9.10).

You access the Summary dialog box by opening the Create menu and choosing the Summary command.

If you use the SmartIcon bar, Lotus Approach automatically adds centered leading or trailing summary panels based on a field you specify.

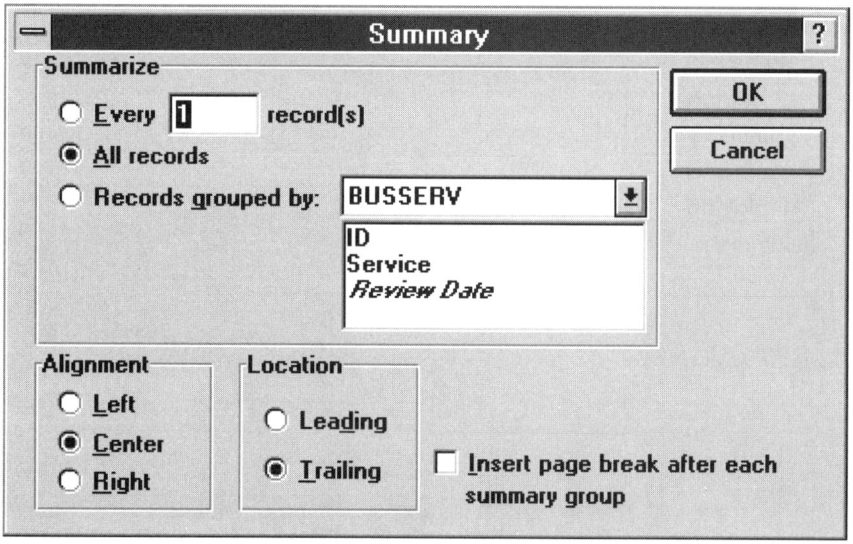

Figure 9.10

The Summary dialog box.

Summary	?

Summarize

○ Every [1] record(s)
● All records
○ Records grouped by: | BUSSERV | ± |

ID
Service
Review Date

OK

Cancel

Alignment
○ Left
● Center
○ Right

Location
○ Leading
● Trailing

☐ Insert page break after each summary group

To add a summary panel to the Services Performed report to group the services using SmartIcons:

1. Open the BUSBACK database and switch to the Services Performed report.

2. If necessary, switch to Design mode.

3. Click on the column you want to summarize. In the example, click on the Service column.

4. Click on the Leading Summary SmartIcon. Lotus Approach adds a summary panel to the report and separates the items in the selected column into groups. You may not notice the new summary panel until after the next step.

5. We need to display fields names instead of data on the report. Either click on the Show Field Names SmartIcon or open the **V**iew menu and choose the S**h**ow Data command to remove the check mark. The example report should look similar to the one in Figure 9.11.

6. Drag the Service field up into the blank summary panel. Make sure the entire field appears inside the summary panel (see Fig. 9.12).

Figure 9.11

The Services Performed report after inserting a leading summary panel and displaying field names.

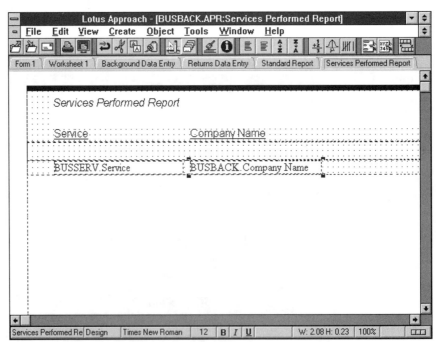

Figure 9.12

The Services
Performed
report after
you move the
Service field.

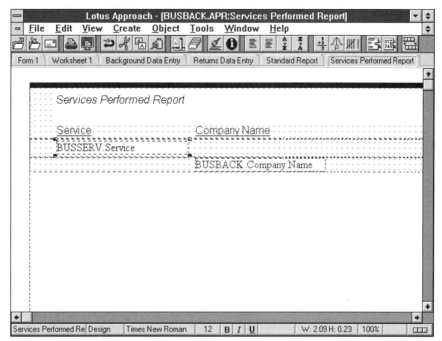

7. Redisplay data instead of field names, either by clicking on the Show Field Names SmartIcon again or by opening the **V**iew menu and choosing the S**h**ow Data command again. Your report should look similar to the one in Figure 9.13.

Creating a New Report Containing a Summary Panel

If you know, when you create the report, that you want to group items, you can set up the report to group the items when you create the report. For the example system, we need to create a Due Dates for Returns report. To show this information, we will create a report that shows, in a columnar fashion, the due date, the required return, and the client. The information will be sorted in due date order and grouped by due date.

The Due Dates for Returns report uses information from two joined databases: the BUSBACK database and the BUSRETS database. The relationship between the two databases for this report is a many-to-one relationship, and the BUSRETS database is the main database.

Figure 9.13

The Services
Performed
report after
redisplaying
data.

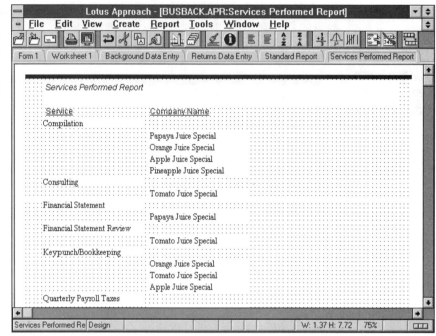

To create the Due Dates for Returns report:

1. Open the BUSBACK database and switch to Design mode.

2. Open the Create menu and choose the Report command. The Report Assistant dialog box (see Fig. 9.14) appears.

3. In the View name & title text box, type the name for the report. In the example, type **Due Dates**.

4. From the SmartMaster style list box, choose a style. In the example, choose B&W3.

5. From the SmartMaster layout list box, choose the type of summary report you want to create. In the example, choose Leading Grouped Summary.

Tip

Leading Grouped Summary and Trailing Grouped Summary require the same information—the only difference between them is the placement of the summarized field on the report. The summarized field appears above the group on a Leading Grouped Summary. The summarized field appears below the group on a Trailing Grouped Summary.

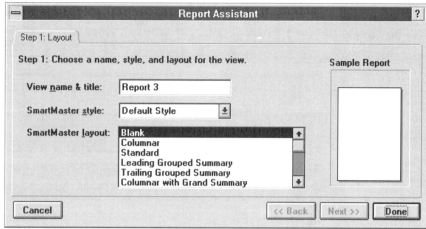

6. Choose the Next command button or the Step 2: Fields tab.

7. Open the database you want to use as the main database for the report. In the example, open the Database fields list box and choose the BUSRETS database.

8. From the Database fields list box, choose the fields you want to appear on the report. In the example, choose the Due Date field and choose the **A**dd command button. Also, choose the Required Return field and choose the **A**dd command button.

9. (Optional) If you want to include fields from any joined databases, reopen the Database fields list box and choose the next database. In the example, switch back to the BUSBACK database. Then, add fields from the new database that you want on the report. In the example, add the Company Name field.

10. Choose the Next command button or click on the Step 3: Leading Summary tab.

11. Choose the **S**elect a field that groups the records check box and then select a field on which to group the records. In the example, open the list box and switch to the BUSRETS database. Then, choose the Due Date field.

12. Choose the Done command button. The Define Main Database dialog box appears.

13. Choose the main database for the report In the example, the main database should be the BUSRETS database.

Figure 9.15

The Due Dates report in Preview mode.

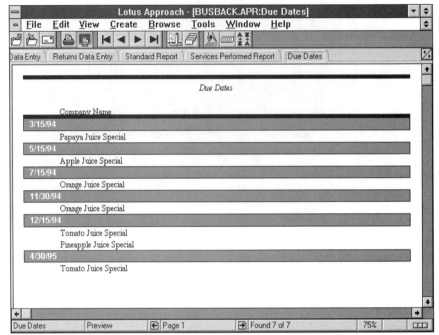

14. Choose the OK command button. You may see a dialog box asking if you want to regroup the information on your report. Choose the **Yes** command button. The report appears on-screen in Design mode. Switch to Preview mode to see the report. The Due Dates report should look similar to the one in Figure 9.15.

Using Subtotals and Totals on Reports

You can place calculated fields in summary panels to create subtotals and grand totals on reports. In the last section, you learned how to group items. Building on that concept, if your report contains numbers, you can subtotal the groups and then create a grand total at the end of the report that adds up the subtotals. If your report does not contain numbers, you can count the items and the total the counts.

When you place a calculated field in a summary panel to generate a subtotal or grand total, the summarize options of the calculated field must match the summary panel's options. You can handle this requirement in two ways:

• You can create a calculated field for each summary panel when you need calculated fields and make sure that the options match.

- You can create a calculated field that is defined as "where placed," meaning that you can use it in any summary panel. This type of calculated field is smart enough to be able to determine the options for the summary panel and perform the correct calculation. You can, therefore, use a "where placed" calculated field many different times.

To create a "where placed" calculated field that we can add to the Services Performed report:

1. Open the Create menu and choose the Field **D**efinition command.

2. Open the database into which you want to add the field and move to the bottom of the list. In the example, switch to the BUSSERV database.

3. In the Field Name column, supply a name for the field. In the example, type **Subtotal**.

4. In the Data Type column, choose Calculated. The Options portion of the Field Definition dialog box appears (see Fig. 9.16).

5. On the Define Formula panel, set up the formula you want to calculate. In the example, choose the SCount function from the

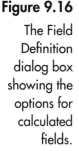

Figure 9.16

The Field Definition dialog box showing the options for calculated fields.

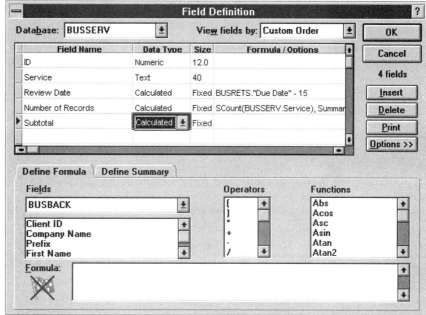

Functions list box and, from the Fields list box, choose the Services field from the BUSSERV database.

6. Switch to the Define Summary panel and make sure the Summarize on: list box shows Summary panels where this field is placed.

7. Choose the OK command button. The Add Field window appears, showing the new field.

Adding Subtotals and Totals to Existing Reports

Suppose, for example, you had created a report that included charges, by client, for each service. On the report, you might want to subtotal the charges by service, and then create a grand total of charges for all services.

Or suppose, for example, that on the Services Performed report, you want to add a field that counts, for each service you perform, the number of clients for whom you are performing the service. Then, you want to add up the total number of services you are performing. I'm stretching this example a bit to demonstrate conditions under which you would create a subtotal and a grand total; in reality, the grand total on this report may not be particularly meaningful. The subtotal, however, does give you some information—from the subtotals, you can get a fairly good idea of the types of work you perform predominantly. You can use this information, in conjunction with other earnings-related information, to help make decisions on the direction you want to take your business.

Now we are ready to add a calculated field in a summary panel to the Services Performed report to count the number of clients for whom a service is performed.

To add a calculated field in a summary panel to a report:

1. Switch to the report to which you want to add a calculated field and switch to Design mode. In the example, switch to the Services Performed report.

2. Click on the column you want to calculate. In the example, click on the Company Name column, since we want to count the number of companies.

Tip

You will see a dialog box telling you that the values in the column you clicked on are not grouped together and asking if you want to sort them. Choose the Yes command button.

---

3. Display field name information on the report either by clicking on the Show Field Name SmartIcon or by opening the View menu and choosing the Show Data command to remove the check mark. The example report should look similar to the one in Figure 9.17.

4. Click on the Add Trailing Summary SmartIcon. Lotus Approach adds a summary panel to the report (see Fig. 9.18).

5. Drag the calculated field from the Add Field window into the blank summary panel. Make sure the entire field appears inside the summary panel (see Fig. 9.19).

6. Hide field name information either, by clicking on the Show Field Name SmartIcon again or by opening the View menu and choosing the Show Data command again. Your report should look similar to the one in Figure 9.20.

Figure 9.17

The Services Performed report displaying fields instead of data.

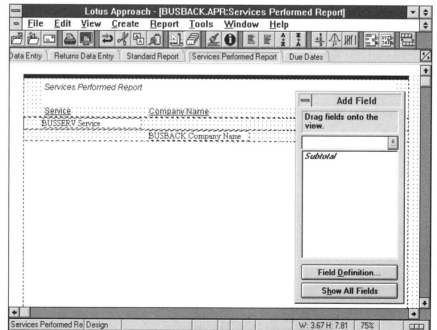

Figure 9.18

The Services Performed report after inserting a trailing summary panel and displaying field names.

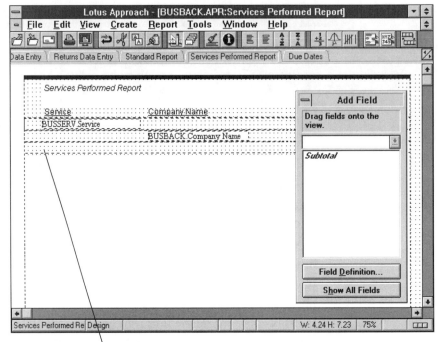

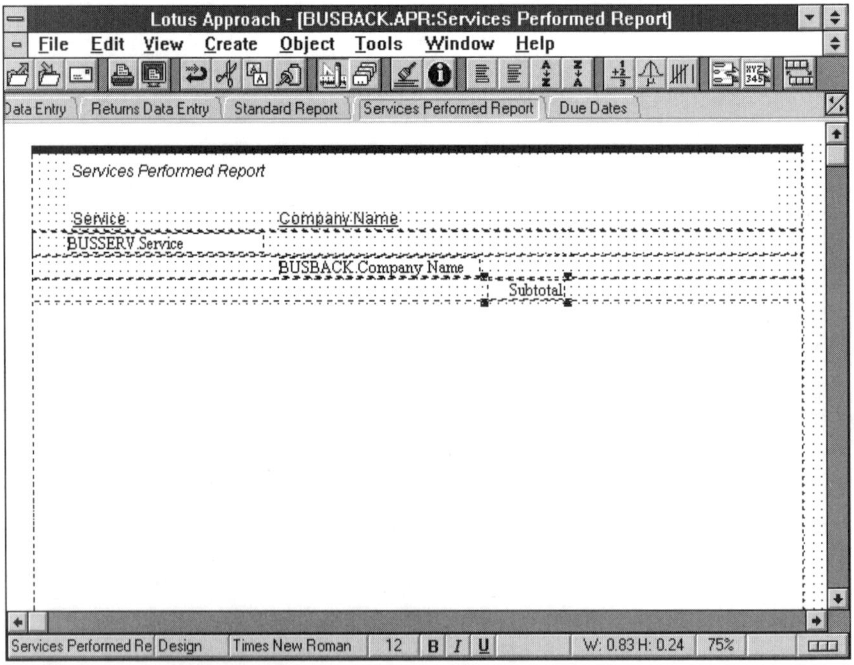

Trailing Summary Panel

Figure 9.19

The Services Performed report after adding the Subtotal field.

Figure 9.20

The Services Performed report.

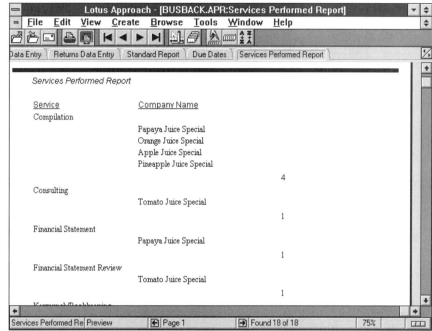

```
Lotus Approach - [BUSBACK.APR:Services Performed Report]
 File   Edit   View   Create   Browse   Tools   Window   Help

Data Entry │ Returns Data Entry │ Standard Report │ Due Dates │ Services Performed Report

    Services Performed Report

    Service              Company Name
    Compilation
                         Papaya Juice Special
                         Orange Juice Special
                         Apple Juice Special
                         Pineapple Juice Special
                                                          4
    Consulting
                         Tomato Juice Special
                                                          1
    Financial Statement
                         Papaya Juice Special
                                                          1
    Financial Statement Review
                         Tomato Juice Special
                                                          1

Services Performed Re│ Preview      │ Page 1        │ Found 18 of 18      │ 75% │
```

Tip

You can print the report (after previewing) by choosing the Print SmartIcon. You will learn more about printing in Chapter 12.

Including Subtotals and Grand Totals on New Reports

Suppose, for example, that you want to create a Review Date report that shows, by Review Date and Staff Person Assigned, each client and return due. To help plan your workload, you want to count the total number of returns to be reviewed on each review date. In this case, you would create a Leading Grouped Summary report that groups the information by review date and also counts the number of returns due.

Tip

Because Lotus Approach adds fields to the report in the order you select the field, you will notice, while working in the Report Assistant to set up this report, some switching back and forth between databases to choose fields.

To create a new report containing subtotals and totals:

1. Open the Create menu and choose the Report command. The Report Assistant dialog box appears (see Fig. 9.21).

2. In the View name & title text box, type the name for the report. In the example, type **Review Dates**.

3. From the SmartMaster style list box, choose a style. In the example, choose Executive.

4. From the SmartMaster layout list box, choose the type of summary report you want to create. In the example, choose Leading Grouped Summary.

Tip

Leading Grouped Summary and Trailing Grouped Summary require the same information—the only difference between them is the placement of the summarized field on the report. The summarized field appears above the group on a Leading Grouped Summary. The summarized field appears below the group on a Trailing Grouped Summary.

---

5. Choose the Next command button or the Step 2: Fields tab.

6. Open the database you want to serve as the main database for the report. In the example, open the Database fields list box and choose the BUSRETS database.

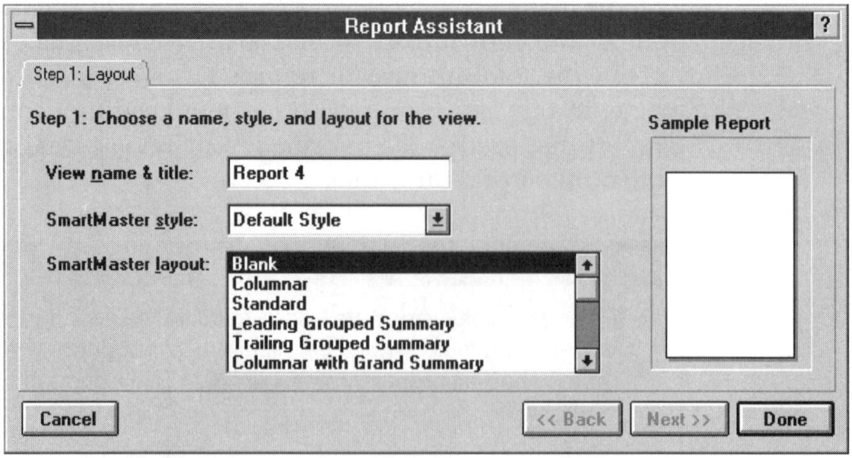

Figure 9.21

The Report Assistant dialog box.

Report Assistant

Step 1: Layout

Step 1: Choose a name, style, and layout for the view.

Sample Report

View name & title: Report 4

SmartMaster style: Default Style

SmartMaster layout:
Blank
Columnar
Standard
Leading Grouped Summary
Trailing Grouped Summary
Columnar with Grand Summary

Cancel   << Back   Next >>   Done

7. From the Database fields list box, choose the fields you want to appear on the report. In the example, choose the Review Date field and choose the Add command button.

8. (Optional) If you want to include fields from any joined data-bases, reopen the Database fields list box and choose the next database. In the example, switch back to the BUSBACK data-base. Then, add fields from the new database that you want on the report. In the example, add the Staff Person Assigned field and the Company Name field.

9. If necessary, switch to other joined databases to add additional fields. In the example, switch back to the BUSRETS database, choose the Required Return field, and choose the Add com-mand button.

10. When you finish adding fields to the report, choose the Next command button or click on the Step 3: Leading Summary tab.

11. Choose the Select a field that groups the records check box and then select a field on which to group the records. In the exam-ple, open the list box and switch to the BUSRETS database. Then, choose the Review Date field.

12. Place an "X" in the Calculate the: check box and open the list box and choose number of items.

13. In the of field list box, highlight the field you want to calculate. In the example, switch to the BUSRETS database and choose the Review Date field.

14. Choose the Done command button. The Define Main Database dialog box appears.

15. Choose the main database for the report. In the example, the main database should be the BUSRETS database.

16. Choose the OK command button. The report appears on-screen in Design mode. Switch to Preview mode to see the report. After you print the Review Dates report, it should look similar to the one in Figure 9.22.

Tip

You may see a dialog box telling you that the values in the column you clicked on are not grouped together and asking if you want to sort them. Choose the Yes command button.

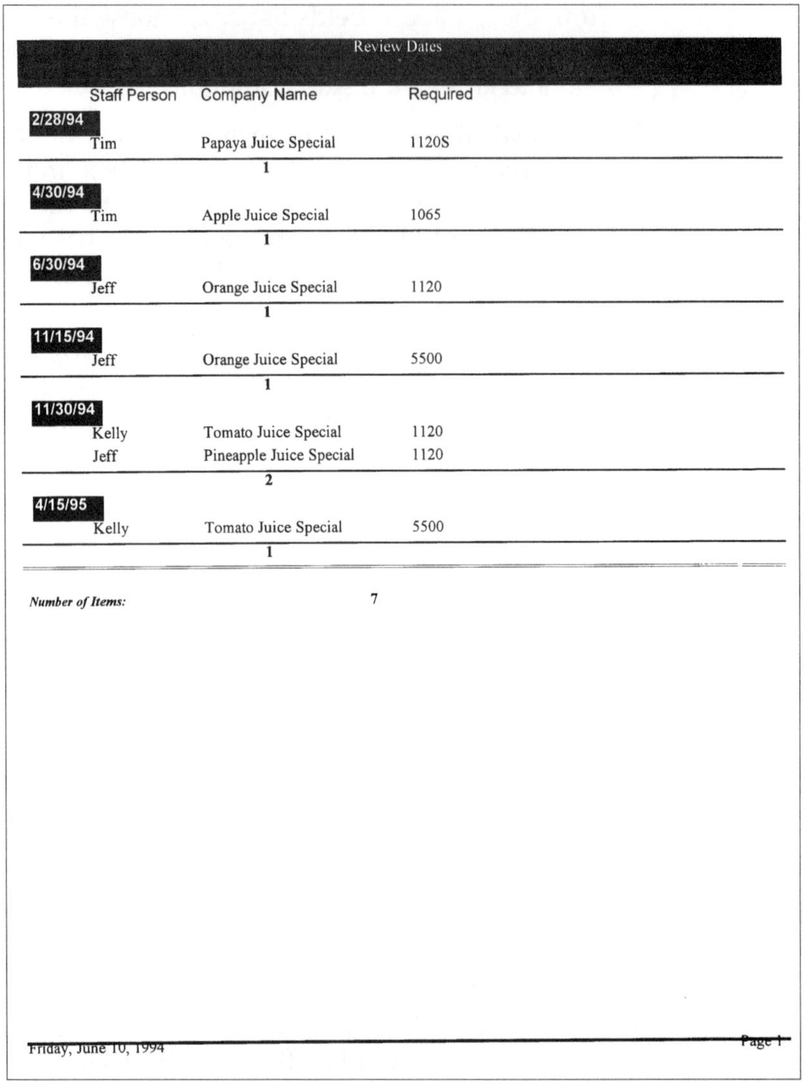

Figure 9.22

The Review
Dates report.

	Review Dates		
	Staff Person	Company Name	Required
2/28/94			
	Tim	Papaya Juice Special	1120S
		1	
4/30/94			
	Tim	Apple Juice Special	1065
		1	
6/30/94			
	Jeff	Orange Juice Special	1120
		1	
11/15/94			
	Jeff	Orange Juice Special	5500
		1	
11/30/94			
	Kelly	Tomato Juice Special	1120
	Jeff	Pineapple Juice Special	1120
		2	
4/15/95			
	Kelly	Tomato Juice Special	5500
		1	

Number of Items: 7

Friday, June 10, 1994   Page 1

Tip

If you don't see the grand total at the end of your summary report, make sure that the grand total field lies entirely inside the summary panel. To check the placement of the field, display field names on your report, either by clicking on the Show Field Names SmartIcon or by opening the View menu, and choose the Show Data command to remove the check. If the Auto_Count field at the end of the report appears to extend outside the report, move the field inside the boundaries.

Creating a Summary Report

In standard and columnar reports, you can show both detailed information and summarized information. In a summary report, you
show only the summarized information; you don't show any detail.
In previous examples of the Services Performed report, we created
subtotals and a grand total. In a summary report for the same information, none of the clients' names would appear on the report.
Instead, you would see just the service, the subtotal representing the
number of clients for whom you perform the service, and a grand
total representing the total number of services performed. Your
report would look something like the one in Figure 9.23.

When you create a summary report, Lotus Approach creates a
report with a trailing summary panel that contains a summary calculated field. Part of the calculated field's name will include
"Auto." This field stores the calculation for the summary report.

To create a summary report:

1. If necessary, switch to Design mode.

Figure 9.23

A sample
summary
report of
Services
Performed.

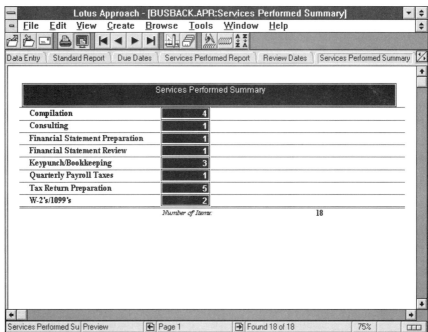

Figure 9.24

The Report
Assistant
dialog box.

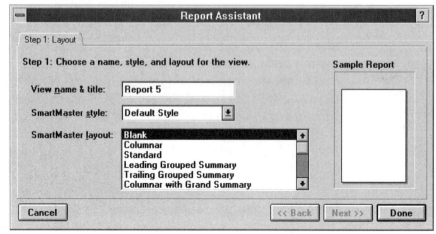

2. Open the Create menu and choose the Report command. The Report Assistant dialog box appears (see Fig. 9.24).

3. In the View name & title text box, type the name for the report. In the example, type **Services Performed Summary**.

4. From the SmartMaster style list box, choose a style. In the example, choose Simple2.

5. From the SmartMaster layout list box, choose the type of summary report you want to create. In the example, choose Summary Only.

6. Choose the Next command button or the Step 2: Trailing Summary tab.

7. Choose the Select a field that groups the records check box and then select a field on which to group the records. In the example, open the list box and switch to the BUSSERV database. Then, choose the Service field.

8. Choose the Calculate the: check box, open the list box and choose number of items.

9. Open the of field list box and choose the database containing the field you want to summarize. In the example, choose the BUSSERV database. Then, choose the Service field.

10. Choose the Done command button. The report appears on-screen in Design mode. Switch to Preview mode to see the report. The Services Performed Summary report should look similar to the one in Figure 9.25.

Figure 9.25

The Services
Performed
Summary
report in
Preview mode.

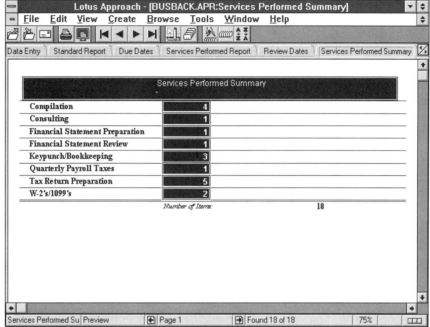

Formatting a Report

You can format reports the same way you formatted forms: you can use field labels, move and resize fields, add field, text, graphic, and drawing objects to a report, color objects, change fonts, and format fields. You can make all these changes the same way you made them for forms, using the Info box. In addition to these formatting options, you can insert, remove, and modify header and footer information, create a title page for a report, keep information together on a report, and remove blank spaces from reports.

Understanding the Report Environment

While you work in one report, you may notice that the menu choices are slightly different than those you saw while working on forms. Next to the Create menu, you see the Report menu. In addition, the SmartIcon bar in Design mode contains SmartIcons useful for creating reports.

In previous sections, you learned how to create reports and you added summary panels to reports to group and total information, so you know that a report can consist of many different panels. In addition to summary panels, reports contain body panels and can contain header panels and footer panels. You can see the panels in any report by clicking on the SmartIcon that shows report panel labels, or by opening the View menu and choosing the Show Panel Labels command. In Figure 9.26, you see the Review Dates report with the report panel labels displayed.

The labels help you identify the various summary panels on a report in case you need to make modifications to the report and the way it summarizes.

Changing Report Specifications

You can change the field labels that appear on standard reports using the Label panel of the Info box. The report title in the header and the column labels Lotus Approach automatically supplies on columnar reports are text objects; you can edit them the same way you edit any text object to make the column titles more meaning-ful. Choose the Text Object SmartIcon (the ABC SmartIcon) and then click on the title you want to change. The insertion point

Figure 9.26

The report panel labels for the Review Dates report.

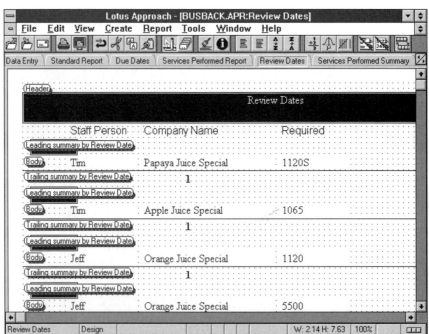

appears in the text box containing the title. Make your changes and then click outside the column title anywhere on the report.

You can change the number of columns for a standard or columnar report using the Basics panel Info box. By default, Lotus Approach defines the report with only one column. If you increase the number of columns to two, Lotus Approach will print the information newspaper-style—down the left side of the page and then at the top of the right side of the page. If your information will fit across in less than 6½ inches (8½ inches minus a one-inch margin at the left and right sides of the page), you may want to increase the number of columns for your report. To change the number of columns, open the Info box. Then, open the list box at the top to display the settings for the report and switch to the Basics panel (see Fig. 9.27).

From this panel, you can change the number of columns for the report, the main database for the report, the report name, and the attached menu bar. You also use this panel to tell Lotus Approach to keep records together instead of printing some on one page and the rest on another page.

You also can change the line and color settings for any of the panels on the report from the Lines and Colors tab of the Info box. Click on the appropriate panel and then display the Info box.

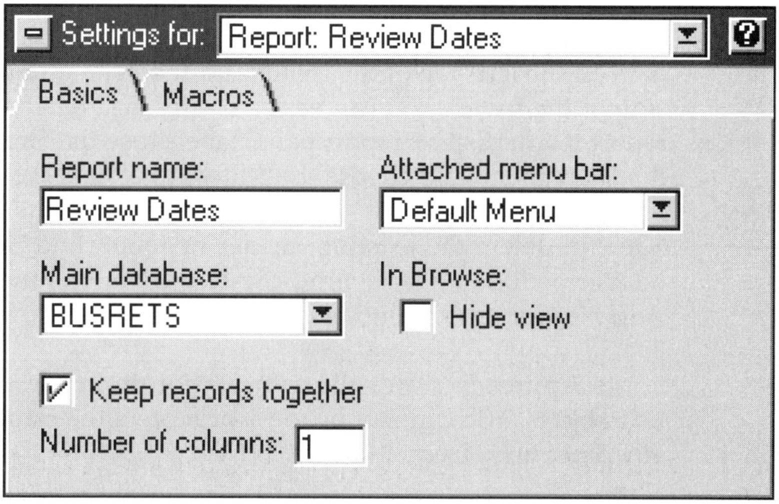

Figure 9.27

The Basics panel of the Info box for the Report.

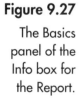

Settings for: Report: Review Dates

Basics \ Macros \

Report name: Attached menu bar:
Review Dates   Default Menu

Main database: In Browse:
BUSRETS   ☐ Hide view

☑ Keep records together
Number of columns: 1

Depending on the area of the report you select, you may be able to change fonts (text objects), formatting, location, and labels.

Moving or Deleting a Summary Panel

You can move or delete a summary panel that you added to a report. First, display the report and switch to Design mode. You will also find these tasks easier if you display field names instead of data (click on the Show Field Names SmartIcon or open the View menu and remove the check from the Show Data command). Then, select the summary panel by holding down the **Ctrl** key and clicking the left mouse button anywhere in the summary panel. Lotus Approach highlights the panel with a wide gray border.

- To delete the panel, press the **Del** key.
- To move the panel, pass the mouse pointer over it—the mouse pointer shape changes to a hand. Drag the panel to its new location.

Adding a Footer or Header to a Report

You can use headers and footers on reports. Headers contain information that appears at the top of every page of the report; footers contain information that appears at the bottom of every page of the report. On standard and summary-only reports, Lotus Approach automatically adds a header that contains the report title to every report. On columnar reports, Lotus Approach automatically adds a header that contains the column headings as well the report title. Lotus Approach also adds a footer to every report that contains the date on the left side of the footer and the page number on the right side of the footer. You can easily see the headers and footers for a report if you display report panel labels (use the SmartIcon or open the View menu and choose the Show Panel Labels command).

You can delete the existing header or footer and then add a new header or footer by opening the **R**eport menu and choosing the Add **H**eader or Add **F**ooter command.

Lotus Approach stores the information in headers and footer as text objects. You can edit headers or footers the same way you edit any other text object.

To tell Lotus Approach to print the current date, time, or page number in your header or footer:

1. Draw a text object completely inside the header or footer area.

2. While the insertion point appears in the text object, open the **R**eport menu and choose the **In**sert command.

3. From the Insert submenu, choose either the **P**age# command, the **D**ate command, or the **T**ime command. Be sure that the text object containing the page number command or the date command rests entirely inside the boundaries of the header or footer.

Tip

You can add text, such as "Page," to the field that Lotus Approach inserts.

Creating Report Title Information

You can add report title information to the first page of each report you create. Although Lotus Approach refers to this information as a *title page*, don't misunderstand—you are not creating a separate page on which only title information will print. You are adding information to the first page of your report.

Title information will not appear on the report in Browse mode. You can view the title page (and add information to it) in Design mode if you choose to show data on-screen while in Design mode. If you don't show data, you can control whether you see the title page by opening the **R**eport menu and placing or removing a check mark from the Show Title Page command. To see title information the way it will appear on the report, you must either print the report or switch to Preview mode.

To add title information to the first page of the Standard Report we created earlier in this chapter, create a special header for the first page of the report:

1. Open the BUSBACK database and switch to the Standard Report.

2. Switch to Design mode if necessary.

3. Open the **View** menu and make sure you are *not* showing data (for purposes of these steps only—you can add a title page with data showing, but you won't have access to the Show Title Page command mentioned in the next step).

4. Open the **Report** menu and choose the Add Title **Page** command. The title of your report (in the header area) seems to disappear. You can bring it back by opening the **Report** menu and choosing the Show Title Page command (to remove the check mark).

5. Switch to Preview mode. "Title Page" appears in the status bar at the bottom of the screen, to indicate that you are looking at the page on which title information will appear.

6. Switch back to Design mode.

7. Draw a text object completely inside the "empty" header or footer area.

You can hide the title information by switching to Design mode, opening the **Report** menu, and choosing the Add Title Page command again, removing the "X."

Duplicating Reports

On the Background Data Entry form, you specified mailing lists on which to place the client. We need to build a report that shows, by mailing list, the clients on that list. Therefore, we need to build one report for each type of mailing list. Fortunately, all the reports look the same, so we can create one report and then duplicate that report for the other mailing lists.

Each Mailing List report uses two joined databases: the BUSBACK database and the BUSMAIL database. The relationship between the two databases for this report is a many-to-one relationship, and the BUSMAIL database will be the main database.

To create a mailing list report:

1. Open the BUSBACK database and switch to Design mode.

2. Open the **Create** menu and choose the **Report** command. The Report Assistant dialog box (see Fig. 9.28) appears.

Figure 9.28

The Report
Assistant
dialog box.

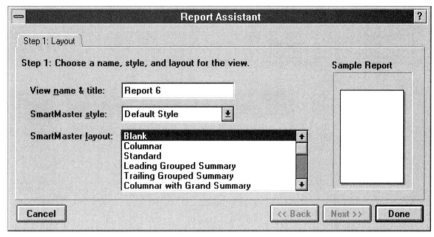

3. In the View **n**ame & title text box, type **Monthly Newsletter**.

4. From the SmartMaster **s**tyle list box, choose B&W4.

5. From the SmartMaster **l**ayout list box, choose Columnar.

6. Choose the Next command button or the Step 2: Fields tab.

7. Make sure the BUSBACK database appears in the Database fields list box.

8. From list of fields, choose Company Name and choose the **A**dd command button.

9. Open the Database fields list box and choose the BUSMAIL database.

10. From the list of fields, choose Monthly Newsletter and choose the **A**dd command button.

11. Choose the Done command button. The Define Main Database dialog box appears.

12. Choose BUSMAIL for the main database and choose the OK command button. The Monthly Newsletter report appears on-screen in Design mode (see Fig. 9.29).

Tip

You may not be able to see the full title for the Monthly Newsletter column. Since it is a text object, you can resize it to make it larger so that you can read the entire label.

Figure 9.29

The Monthly Newsletter report in Design mode.

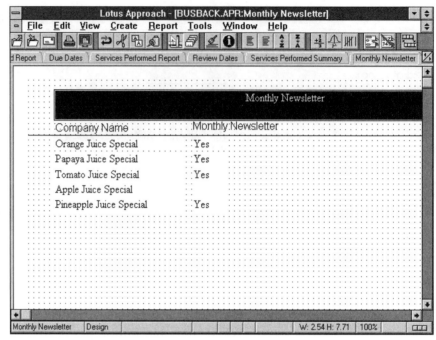

In the body of the report, you see either "Yes" or a blank space, depending on whether an "X" appeared in the Monthly Newsletter checkbox on the Background Data Entry form.

To see just the clients for whom an "X" appeared:

1. If necessary, switch to Browse mode.

2. Choose the Find SmartIcon.

3. Click in the Monthly Newsletter field and type **Y**.

4. Choose the OK command button. You see only those records for which you checked the Monthly Newsletter box on the Background Data Entry form. The "X" you placed the box was stored as a Boolean "Yes" in the BUSMAIL database.

Often, you may find that the information you need on one report resembles quite closely the information you need on another report; the layouts for the two reports could be identical. You can copy a report in Lotus Approach.

To copy the Monthly Newsletter report so that you can create a report that shows the clients who receive notification of tax law changes:

1. Open the BUSBACK database and switch to the Monthly Newsletter report.

2. Switch to Design mode if necessary.

3. Open the **Edit** menu and choose the **Duplicate Report** command. Lotus Approach creates a copy of the report, adding "Copy of" to the name of the original report. On-screen, you are viewing Copy of Monthly Newsletter.

To change this report so that it shows clients who should receive holiday greeting cards:

1. Show field names instead of data either using the SmartIcon or the View menu.

2. Click on the Monthly Newsletter field (*not* the column heading) and press the **Del** key to remove it from the report.

3. Open the **Report** menu and choose the **Add Field** command. The Add Field window appears (see Fig. 9.30).

Figure 9.30

The Add Field window.

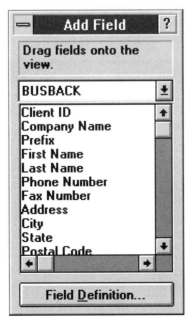

4. Open the database list box and choose the BUSMAIL database.

5. From the list of fields that appears below the database name, drag the Holiday List field into the summary panel where the Monthly Newsletter field had been.

6. Display the Info box.

7. If necessary, use the Font panel to change the font and point size for the field to match the Company Name field.

8. If necessary, resize the Holiday List field so that it appears on the same line as the Company Name field and fits entirely with the panel on-screen (see Fig. 9.31).

9. Change the column label text object so that it reads **Holiday List**.

10. Change the Report Title, both on the report and in the Info box, to Holiday List.

You can repeat the above process to create a report for each of the other mailing lists.

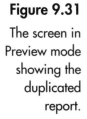

Figure 9.31

The screen in Preview mode showing the duplicated report.

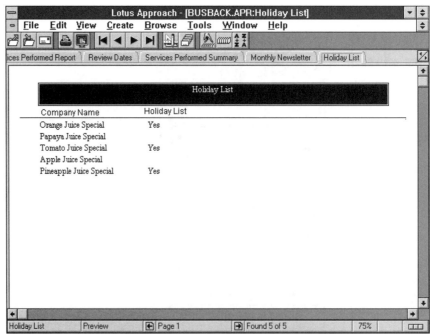

Chapter Summary

In this chapter, you learned how to create standard reports, columnar reports, and summary reports. You also learned how to summarize information. Using summary panels, you learned how to group information and subtotal information. Last, you learned that you can format reports in many of the same ways you formatted forms. You learned how to display report panel labels to see the parts of a report, and you learned how to use the Info box to change basic specifications for a report, including the number of columns included in the report. You learned how to move and delete a summary panel and how to modify the header and footer Lotus Approach automatically supplies with every report. You learned how to duplicate reports to create reports with formats similar to existing reports.

In the next chapter, you will learn how to work with form letters in Lotus Approach.

CHAPTER

10

Creating Form Letters and Mailing Labels

In this chapter, you will learn how to use your Lotus Approach data to prepare form letters and mailing labels.

Sending Form Letters to Customers

You can use Lotus Approach and the information you store in your databases to send form letters. The information in your database to appears on the form letter as the changing information.

You can create a form letter using joined databases; all of the rules associated with joined databases apply to this type of view. For example, you must decide which database is the main database and which is the detail database. To help you decide which database is the main database, be aware that Lotus Approach will create one form letter for each record in the main database.

The basic process for creating a form letter is similar to creating a form or a report. You use the Form Letter Assistant dialog box to select fields that you want to include on the form letter. You will find it easiest to add fields to the form letter in the order you intend to use them. After you add the fields to the form letter, you can type the body of the form letter—the unchanging information. If necessary, you can use a field more than once in a form letter, and you can add fields to the form letter after you close the Form Assistant dialog box.

While you work in Design mode on a form letter, the menus, the SmartIcon bar, and the status bar all change to reflect the form letter environment.

Setting Up a Form Letter

To create a form letter, you create a new view of your data and add fields to it. You must set up each page of a form letter as a separate view. When you work with a form letter, Lotus Approach treats the information on-screen as one large text object. You create the form letter in Design mode, and then you can use other Lotus Approach features, such as the Find feature, to decide which clients should receive the form letter. Suppose, for example, you want to send a form letter to all clients you notify of tax changes, telling them about changes in the payroll tax laws. The letter you are sending might look something like the one in Figure 10.1, with field names from the database appearing where you would want them on the form letter.

To create a form letter:

1. Open the database that will serve as the main database and switch to Design mode. In the example, open the BUSBACK database.

2. Open the **Create** menu and choose the Form Letter command. The Form Letter Assistant dialog box appears (see Fig. 10.2).

3. In the View **n**ame & title text box, type a name for the Form Letter view. In the example, type **Payroll Form Letter**.

4. From the SmartMaster **s**tyle list box, choose a letter style. In the example, choose Business.

5. From the SmartMaster **l**ayout list box, choose a letter layout. In the example, choose Block.

6. Click on the Next command button to display the Step 2: Return Address panel.

Figure 10.1

A sample form letter.

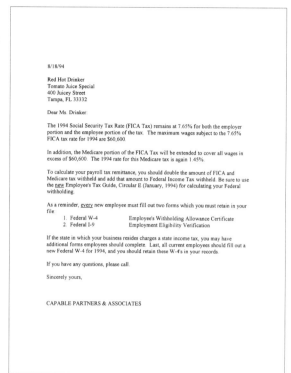

8/18/94

Red Hot Drinker
Tomato Juice Special
400 Juicey Street
Tampa, FL 33332

Dear Ms. Drinker:

The 1994 Social Security Tax Rate (FICA Tax) remains at 7.65% for both the employer portion and the employee portion of the tax. The maximum wages subject to the 7.65% FICA tax rate for 1994 are $60,600.

In addition, the Medicare portion of the FICA Tax will be extended to cover all wages in excess of $60,600. The 1994 rate for this Medicare tax is again 1.45%.

To calculate your payroll tax remittance, you should double the amount of FICA and Medicare tax withheld and add that amount to Federal Income Tax withheld. Be sure to use the new Employee's Tax Guide, Circular E (January, 1994) for calculating your Federal withholding.

As a reminder, every new employee must fill out two forms which you must retain in your file.
  1. Federal W-4   Employee's Withholding Allowance Certificate
  2. Federal I-9   Employment Eligibility Verification

If the state in which your business resides charges a state income tax, you may have additional forms employees should complete. Last, all current employees should fill out a new Federal W-4 for 1994, and you should retain these W-4's in your records.

If you have any questions, please call.

Sincerely yours,

CAPABLE PARTNERS & ASSOCIATES

7. If you want a return address to appear on the inside of the letter, type it into the text box. Otherwise, choose the **N**one option button. You might want to use a return address if you don't intend to print your form letters on letterhead paper. In the example, choose **N**one.

Figure 10.2

The Form Letter Assistant dialog box.

Form Letter Assistant

Step 1: Layout   Step 2: Return Address   Step 3: Inside Address   Step 4: Salutation   Step 5: Close

Step 1: Choose a name, style, and layout for the view.   **Sample Letter**

View _n_ame & title: Form Letter 1

SmartMaster _s_tyle: Default Style

SmartMaster _l_ayout: **Block**
                        Modified Block
                        Personal

Cancel   << Back   Next >>   Done

8. Click on the Next command button to display the Step 3: Inside Address panel.

9. Choose a layout for the inside address from the Address layout list box. In the example, choose 5 lines.

10. From the appropriate database, choose the fields you want to appear in the inside address in the order you intend to use them. In the example, select the following fields from the BUSBACK database, choosing the **A**dd command button after selecting each field:

    • First Name

    • Last Name

    • Company Name

    • Address

    • Address2

    • City

    • State

    • Zip Code

11. Choose the Next command button to display the Step 4: Salutation panel.

12. From the appropriate database, choose the fields you want to appear in the salutation, in the order you want them to appear. In the example, choose the Prefix field from the list box on the left and the Last Name field from the list box on the right.

13. Choose the Next command button to display the Step 5: Close panel.

14. Change the closing that appears in the text box so that it suits your needs. In the example, do not change anything on this panel.

15. Choose the Done command button. On-screen, you see the form letter you created in Design mode (see Fig. 10.3). The fields you selected appear in enclosed in pairs of angle brackets (<<>>).

Adding Text to the Body of a Form Letter

To add text to the body of the letter, place the insertion point on the left margin two lines below the salutation and start typing. You may need to click twice to see an insertion point—when you click

Figure 10.3

A form letter immediately after it is created.

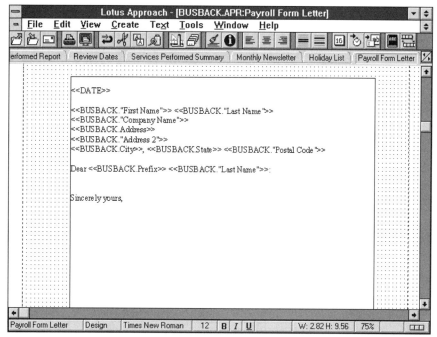

the first time, you will select the form letter text object (you will see handles surrounding the form letter); when you click the second time, you will see an insertion point.

Type the unchanging information in the letter just as you would type in a word processor. Lotus Approach uses word wrap, so you won't need to press **Enter** to start a new line. To underline text (such as "new" and "every" in the example), type the text, select it by dragging, and click on the Underline icon in the status bar—or open the Text menu and choose the Underline command. To try typing in a form letter, place the following text in the body of the form letter we just created:

The 1994 Social Security Tax Rate (FICA Tax) remains at 7.65% for both the employer portion and the employee portion of the tax. The maximum wages subject to the 7.65% FICA tax rate for 1994 are $60,600.

In addition, the medicare portion of the FICA Tax will be extended to cover all wages in excess of $60,600. The 1994 rate for this medicare tax is again 1.45%.

To calculate your payroll tax remittance, you should double the amount of FICA and Medicare tax withheld and add that amount to Federal Income Tax withheld. Be sure to use the *new* Employee's Tax Guide, Circular E (January, 1994) for calculating your Federal withholding.

As a reminder, *every* new employee must fill out two forms, which you must retain in your file:

1. Federal W-4   Employee's Withholding Allowance Certificate

2. Federal I-9   Employment Eligibility Verification

If the state in which your business resides charges a state income tax, you may have additional forms that employees should complete. Last, all current employees should fill out a new Federal W-4 for 1994, and you should retain these W-4s in your records.

If you have any questions, please call.

Sincerely,

CAPABLE PARTNERS & ASSOCIATES

Tip
You can check the spelling in your form letter using the SmartIcon bar.

You can change the font by selecting the text and fields you want to change (as a shortcut, open the Edit menu and choose the Select All command) and then using the Info box or the status bar.

You can see your form letter on-screen by switching to Browse mode. Lotus Approach replaces the field names with data from the database. You can check the general layout of the form letter by switching to Preview mode.

Tip
You can set selected text for single- or double-spacing using the SmartIcon bar.

Adjusting the Size and Placement of the Fields

You can move the fields on-screen the same way you would move text in a text object. For example, if you want to place the form letter on letterhead, you should move all the fields down on the page. Display the ruler (open the **View** menu and choose the Show **Ruler** command). Then, select the form letter by clicking on any border of the form letter until you see black handles in the corners of the form letter (see Fig. 10.4).

Pass the mouse pointer over the form letter until you see a hand. Then, drag the form letter down so that the top border appears just below the 2-inch mark, leaving two inches for your logo or letterhead.

Because a form letter is one large text block and the fields you see on-screen are actually inside a text block, you cannot move a field in a form letter by dragging. Instead, you must cut and paste the field. Make sure the Text Object SmartIcon (the ABC icon) is selected. Highlight the field, open the **Edit** menu, and choose the **Cut** command. Then, click at the location where you want the field to appear, open the **Edit** menu, and choose the **Paste** command.

Figure 10.4

A selected form letter.

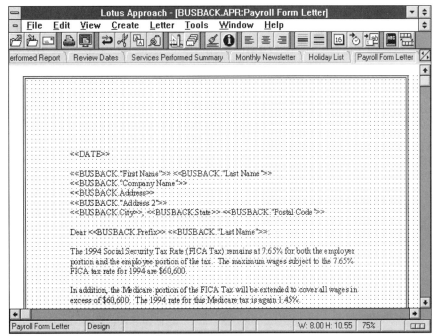

You can add a field to a form letter. Suppose, for example, you want to personalize a form letter by adding a reference, in the body of the letter, to the person to whom the letter is addressed.

To personalize a form letter:

1. Click where at the location where the field should appear. Black handles appear around the form letter and the **O**bject menu appears in the menu bar.

2. Open the **O**bject menu and choose the **A**dd Field command. The Add Field window appears.

3. From the Add Field window, drag the field you want to appear onto the letter.

Producing Form Letters for Selected Clients

By following the steps described previously, you produce a form letter for all your clients. In the example, however, we only wanted to send this form letter to those clients we notify about tax law changes. You can combine searching with producing form letters so that you can send a form letter to only some clients.

To send a form letter to selected clients, add a nonprinting field to the letter—a field we use for the search criteria:

1. Switch to the form letter you want to send to only some clients. In the example, switch to the Payroll Form Letter.

2. Switch to Design mode and click on the body of the form letter.

3. Open the **L**etter menu and choose the **A**dd Field command. The Add Field window appears (see Fig. 10.5).

4. Open the database list box and choose the database that contains the field by which you want to search. In the example, choose the BUSMAIL database.

5. Drag the field by which you want to search onto the form letter outside the box that contains the form letter information. In the example, choose the Tax Law Changes field.

6. (Optional) Close the Add Field window.

7. With the Tax Law Changes field selected, open the Info box.

8. From the Basics panel, choose Nonprinting.

Figure 10.5

The Add Field
window.

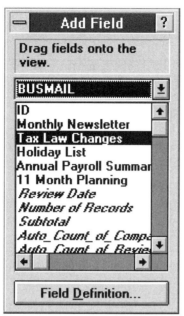

9. To select only specific records, switch to Browse mode, choose the Find SmartIcon, set up the find criteria in the nonprinting field, and choose the OK command button to find the records. In the example, type **Y** in the Tax Law Changes field. Lotus Approach displays form letters only for the clients who meet the criteria.

Creating Mailing Labels for Customers

You can use the information in your database to create mailing labels. You can use one of many predefined Avery style labels, or you can create your own custom label. You create mailing labels similar to the way you created a form letter.

Setting Up Mailing Labels

Mailing labels will be another view in the database, and if you need to include information from a joined database, the main-to-detail relationship is still important. You determine the main database for labels the same way you determined the main database for form letters. Lotus Approach creates one mailing label for each record in the main database.

If you are not using a standard Avery mailing label, skip the follow steps and refer to the next set of steps.

To create a mailing label view using a standard Avery label:

1. Open the database that will serve as the main database and switch to Design mode. In the example, open the BUSBACK database.

2. Open the **C**reate menu and choose the **M**ailing Labels command. The Mailing Label Assistant dialog box appears (see Fig. 10.6).

3. In the **M**ailing label name text box, type a name for the Mailing Label view. In the example, type **Tax Change Labels**.

4. On the Basics panel of the Mailing Label Assistant dialog box to select a mailing label layout. In the example, choose 5 Lines from the **S**elect a SmartMaster address layout list box.

Figure 10.6

The Mailing Label Assistant dialog box.

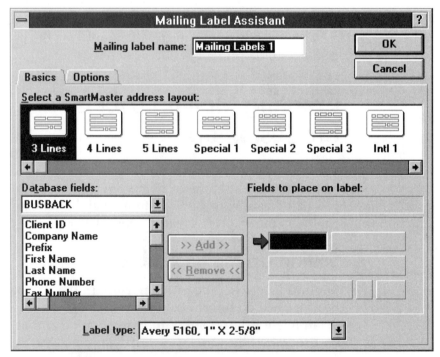

5. From the main database, choose the fields you want to appear on the labels in the order you intend to use them. In the example, select the following fields, choosing the **Add** command button after selecting each field:

   - First Name
   - Last Name
   - Company Name
   - Address
   - Address2
   - City
   - State
   - Zip Code

6. Add any fields from joined databases by opening the Database list box, selecting the joined database, and adding the appropriate field from that database.

7. To use a standard Avery label, open the Label type list box and select the type of labels you want to use. If you don't want to use a standard Avery label, skip this step. In the example, choose Avery 5162, 1-1/3" × 4".

8. (Optional) If you want to create your own custom labels, click on the Options tab to display the Options panel of the Mailing Label Assistant dialog box and specify label margins, the number of labels per page, and the arrangement of labels on the page (see Fig. 10.7).

9. Choose the OK command button. On-screen, you see a mailing label view in Design mode (see Fig. 10.8).

Adjusting the Size and Placement of the Fields

For mailing labels, Lotus Approach automatically closes up the extra space that might appear when data in fields does not extend to the full length of the field. If you want, however, you can move and size the fields on mailing labels the same way you would move text in a form. You can drag fields and use sizing handles to change their size.

Figure 10.7

The Options panel of the Mailing Label Assistant dialog box.

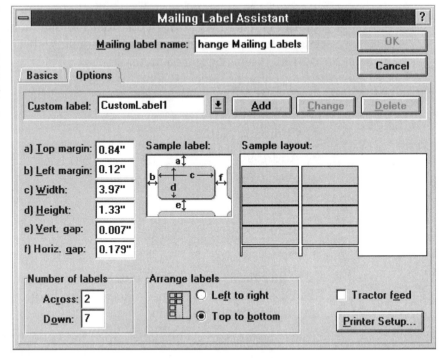

Figure 10.8

A mailing label view in Design mode.

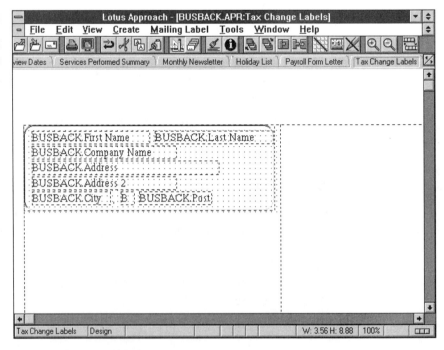

You can align the fields on the mailing label the same way you aligned fields on forms and reports—select the fields to align, open the Object menu, and choose the Align command.

You can see your mailing labels on-screen by switching to Browse mode and then to Preview mode. Lotus Approach replaces the field names with data from the database.

Tip

You can create mailing labels for selected clients the same way you created a form letter for selected clients. Add a nonprinting field to your mailing label and use it to select the clients for whom you want to produce mailing labels.

Adjusting the Appearance of Mailing Labels

You can change the appearance of mailing labels by adding text blocks containing specialized text (perhaps with bold or italics) that will appear on each label, or you can add graphics to mailing labels. Perform these functions the same way you added text blocks and graphics to forms. If you need to change the layout of the mailing labels, use the Info box for mailing labels. Click anywhere on the mailing label view *except* inside or on the rounded rectangle that represents the mailing label. Open the Info box and display the Basics panel (see Fig. 10.9).

Figure 10.9

The Basics panel of the Info box for mailing labels.

Settings for: | Mailing Labels: Tax Change Labels |

Basics \ Macros \

Mailing labels name:
Tax Change Labels

Attached menu bar:
Default Menu

Main database:
BUSBACK

In Browse:
☐ Hide view

Named styles:

Edit label options...

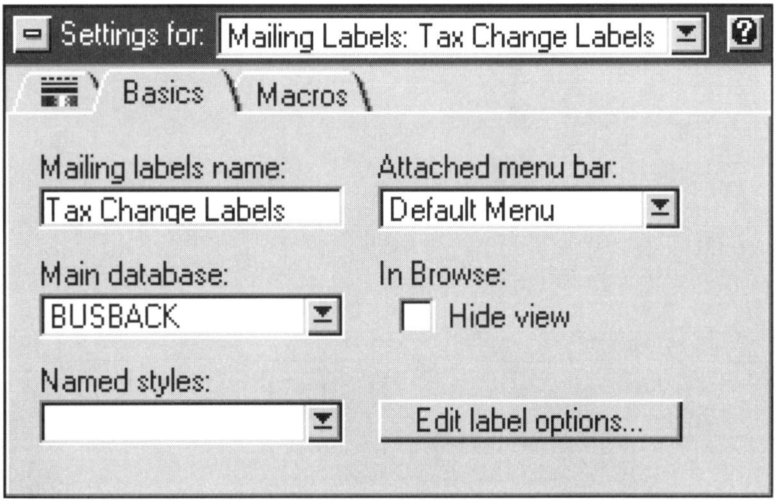

Figure 10.10

The Mailing Label Options dialog box.

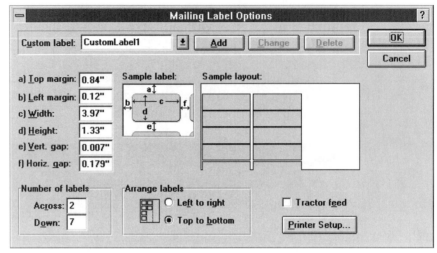

Use the Edit label options command button in the Info box to open the Mailing Label Options dialog box, from which you can change the margins of the labels, the number of labels that appear down and across, and the arrangement of the labels (see Fig. 10.10).

Chapter Summary

In this chapter, you learned how to create a form letter in Lotus Approach and send that form letter to only selected clients. You also learned how to create mailing labels in Lotus Approach.

In the next chapter, you will learn how to create cross-tabulation views in Lotus Approach.

Analyzing Data in Lotus Approach

In addition to being able to produce forms, reports, form letters, and mailing labels from your data in Lotus Approach, you can also analyze your data using worksheets, cross-tabulation, and charts. In this chapter, you will learn how to create and work with worksheets, cross-tabs, and charts.

Working with Worksheet Views

Worksheets present a row-and-column view of your data, where a *row* represents one record in your data and a *column* represents one field from your data. When you first create a database, Lotus Approach creates one form and one worksheet view for your data. You can modify the original worksheet view, or you can create new worksheets.

Understanding the Worksheet View

Unlike other views, you can change in a worksheet view in either Browse mode or Design mode. To be able to work effectively in worksheet view, you should understand the parts of the screen.

Figure 11.1

The default
worksheet.

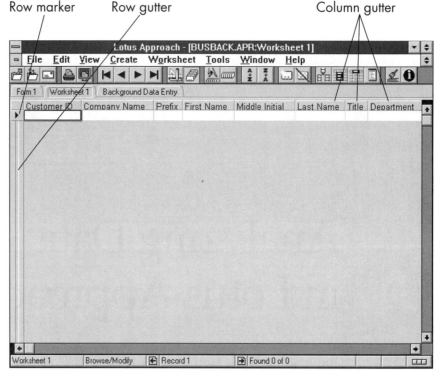

In the BUSBACK database, switch to Worksheet 1, the default
worksheet that Lotus Approach created when you created the
database. Also, switch to Browse mode. In Figure 11.1, you see the
parts of the screen when you view a worksheet.

On any worksheet view, you see rows that represent records of
your data and columns that represent fields in your database. The
intersection of any row and column is called a *cell*. Along the left
edge of the screen, you see an area called the row gutter, which you
use to convert a worksheet to a crosstab. You also see, across the top
edge of the worksheet, the column gutter, which you also can use to
convert a worksheet to a crosstab. Later in this chapter, you will
learn how to convert a worksheet to a crosstab. The row marker
indicates the row containing the currently selected cell or row.

Creating a Worksheet View

You can easily create additional worksheet views of your data. You
also can create worksheet views based on joined databases. As you

might expect, you follow the same rules for establishing a main database and a detail database when creating worksheets based on joined databases. The main database for the worksheet will be the database from which you want to see the most records.

To create a worksheet view using data from joined databases:

1. Open the **C**reate menu and choose the **W**orksheet command. The Worksheet Assistant dialog box appears (see Fig. 11.2)

2. From the Database **f**ields list box, select the fields you want to appear on your worksheet. Each field will appear as a column heading. In the example, choose the Company Name field from the BUSBACK database and the Service field from the BUSSERV database.

3. Choose the Done command button. You will see the Define Main Database dialog box, from which you should identify the main database for the worksheet. In the example, choose the BUSSERV database as the main database, since we want to see all the services being performed in this worksheet.

4. Lotus Approach creates a worksheet containing, as column headers, the fields you selected (see Fig. 11.3).

Tip

You can change both the worksheet name and the main database for the worksheet from the Basics panel of the Info box.

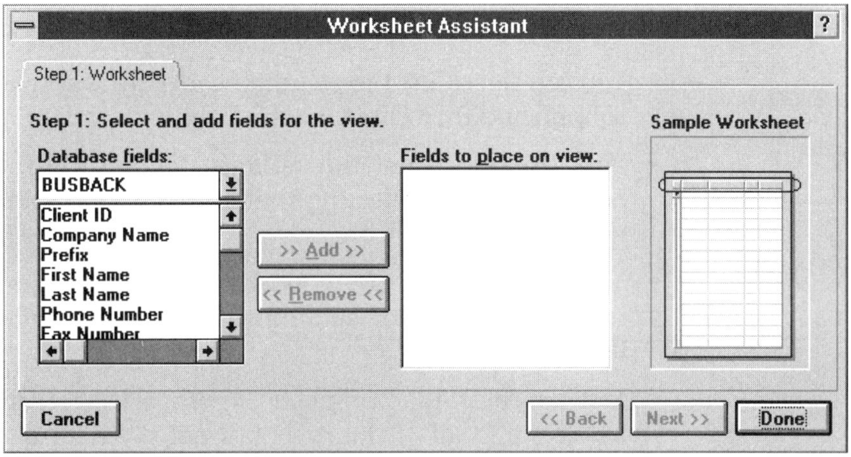

Figure 11.2

The Worksheet Assistant dialog box.

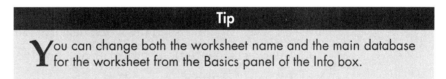

Figure 11.3

A sample worksheet based on joined databases.

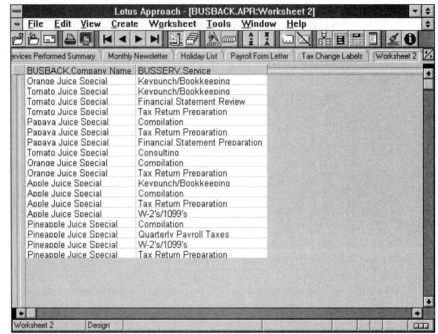

Selecting and Navigating in a Worksheet

You can select within a worksheet in the following ways:

- You can select single cells in the worksheet by clicking on the cell.

- You can select a contiguous group of cells by dragging.

- You can select entire rows by clicking immediately to the left of the first cell in the row.

- You can select entire columns by clicking on the column header.

- You can select just the column header by first selecting the entire column and then choosing the Column Header SmartIcon.

- You can select just the cells in the column (not the column header) by first selecting the entire column and then choosing the Column SmartIcon.

- You can select the entire worksheet by clicking in the upper left corner of the worksheet, immediately to the left of the first column header.

- You can select the perimeter of the worksheet (all of the column headers and all of the rows but not the data in the worksheet) by clicking twice in the upper left corner of the worksheet. (You might want to select this way to resize all of the columns or all of the rows in the worksheet at one time.)

You can move around a worksheet with the keyboard by pressing the **Tab** key.

Resizing Rows and Columns

You can resize individual rows or columns or you can resize, simultaneously, all rows or all columns.

To resize:

1. Select the row or column you want to resize. In the example, in Worksheet 2, select the entire worksheet.

2. Place the mouse pointer in either the row gutter or the column gutter, depending on whether you want to resize rows or columns. In the example, place the mouse pointer in the column gutter.

3. Place the mouse pointer between the rows or columns you want to resize. In the example, place the mouse pointer between the Company Name column and the Service column.

4. When the mouse pointer changes to a heavy black line with arrows pointing outward in either direction, drag the row or column boundary in the direction you want to change size. To make a row larger, drag down. To make a column larger, drag to the right.

Adding and Removing Fields in a Worksheet View

To add fields to a worksheet view using the Add Field window:

1. Click the Add Field SmartIcon. The Add Field window appears (see Fig. 11.4).

2. Drag the field you want to add to the worksheet into the column gutter. In the example, drag the Client ID field into the column gutter. Lotus Approach adds a new column to the worksheet and displays the information for that field (see Fig. 11.5).

Figure 11.4

The Add Field window.

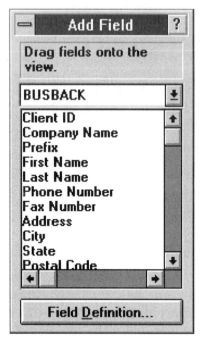

Figure 11.5

Worksheet 2 after adding a field.

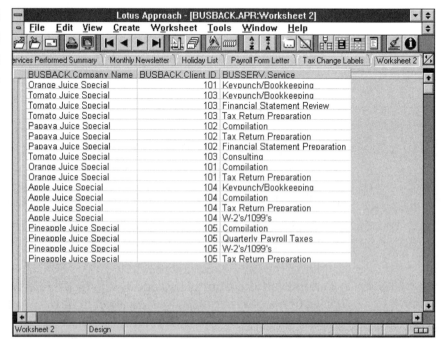

To remove a column (delete a field) from a worksheet view, drag the column header up off the worksheet view. In the example, remove the Client ID from Worksheet 2.

Moving Columns

You can move columns in a worksheet view. For example, we can switch the Service column with the Company Name column.

To move columns:

1. Select the column you want to move. You can move more than one column by selecting more than one column header. In the example, select the Service column.

2. Slide the mouse pointer over the column header of the selected column. The mouse pointer changes to the shape of a hand.

3. Drag the column in the direction you want to move it. A vertical black line appears as you move the column to let you know where the column will appear if you release the mouse button. In the example, drag the Service column to the left until you see the black vertical line on the left side of the Company Name column. When you release the mouse button, the Company Name column and the Service column should be reversed (see Fig. 11.6).

Inserting Columns

To insert a blank column in a worksheet view:

1. Place the mouse pointer above the column and at the edge where you want to insert a column. The mouse pointer changes to a wedge shape (see Fig. 11.7).

2. Click the mouse pointer. Lotus Approach inserts a blank column in the worksheet.

Working with Crosstabs

You can perform cross-tabulations of the data in your databases in Lotus Approach. You use a crosstab view to perform cross-tabulations.

Figure 11.6

Worksheet 2 after switching the Service column and the Company Name column.

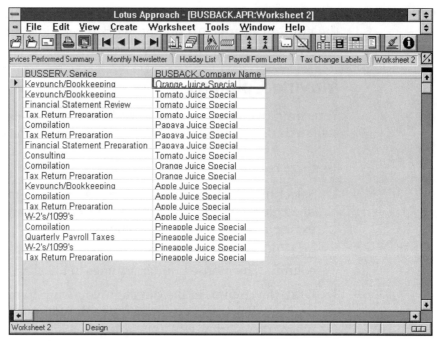

Mouse pointer

Figure 11.7

The mouse pointer positioned to insert a blank column.

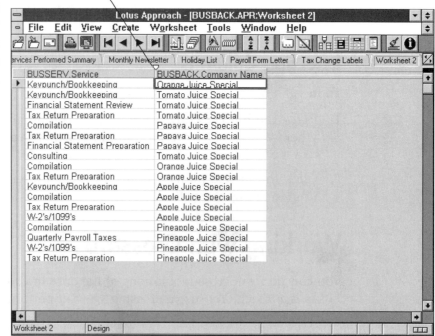

A crosstab view lets you categorize and summarize information in a worksheet format. Using a crosstab, you can count or add up groups of records. In the following sections, we will create a crosstab that counts the number of clients for whom various services are performed, the number of returns (by return type) that must be reviewed by a specifed date, the number of returns that must be reviewed by specified staff persons and review dates, and the number of returns (by return type) that each staff person must review by specified review dates. Later in this chapter, after we create the crosstabs, we will chart some of them to present a graphic representation of the information.

Creating a Crosstab from a Worksheet

You can use information already stored in a worksheet to create a crosstab. Basically, when you create a crosstab from a worksheet, you are trying to summarize the information in the worksheet by one column in the worksheet. For example, we can create a crosstab from Worksheet 2 that shows each service and the number of that service performed—Lotus Approach will be adding up the number of client records on which a particular service appears and supply that number in the crosstab.

To create a crosstab from a worksheet:

1. Select the field by which you want to summarize the information in the worksheet. In the example, select the Service field column header.

2. Drag the field over to the left edge of the worksheet and down into the row gutter area. You will know you have found the row gutter area when the left side of the worksheet (the row gutter area) changes colors to appear highlighted.

3. Release the mouse button. Lotus Approach reorganizes your worksheet, summarizing by the field you dragged. In the example, Worksheet 2 would look like Figure 11.8.

Adding a Summary to a Crosstab

You can add a row or column to a crosstab to summarize information in the crosstab. For example, we can add a summary row to Worksheet 2 to identify the total number of services performed.

Figure 11.8

Worksheet 2
after
converting it
into a
crosstab.

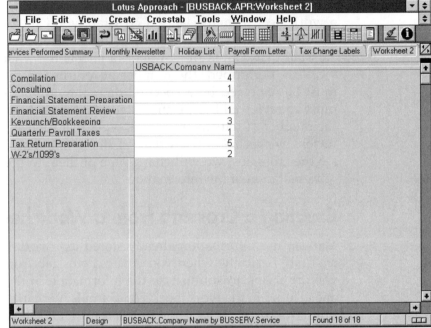

To add a summary row:

1. Position the mouse pointer next to the column or below the row you want to summarize. In the example, place the mouse pointer below the last row in Worksheet 2, at the left edge of the screen. The mouse pointer shape turns into a small, white wedge.

2. Click the mouse pointer. The wedge momentarily increases in size, and then Lotus Approach inserts a "Total" row, with the total number appearing at the bottom of each column in the worksheet. In the example, Worksheet 2 should appear similar to Figure 11.9.

Creating a New Crosstab

You can create crosstabs without first creating a worksheet. You use the Crosstab Assistant. You can create crosstabs that display data from joined databases; as you would expect, you will need to identify the main database. We will create three new crosstabs to help give you a feeling for creating crosstabs.

In the first crosstab we create, we will show, for each return and review date, the number of returns that must be reviewed. In this

Figure 11.9

Worksheet 2 after adding a summary row.

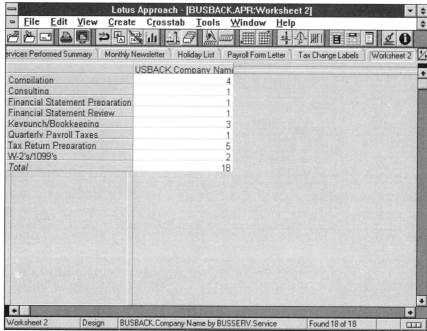

crosstab, tax returns appear as columns, review dates appear as rows, and the number of returns appears in the grid.

To show the number of returns to be reviewed:

1. Open the **C**reate menu and choose the Crosstab command. The Crosstab Assistant dialog box appears (see Fig. 11.10).

2. Select the field you want to appear as rows in the crosstab and choose the **A**dd command button. In the example, choose the Review Date field from the BUSRETS database.

3. Choose the Next command button to switch to the Step 2: Columns tab.

4. Select the field you want to appear as columns in the crosstab and choose the **A**dd command button. In the example, choose the Required Return field from the BUSRETS database.

5. Choose the Next command button to switch to the Step 3: Values tab.

6. Open the **C**alculate list box and choose the formula you want Lotus Approach to calculate. In the example, choose number of items.

Figure 11.10

The Crosstab
Assistant
dialog box.

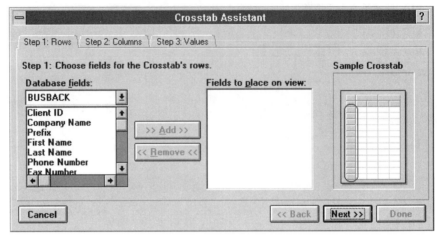

7. Select the field you want to calculate from the of field list box. In the example, choose the Required Return field from the BUS-RETS database.

8. Choose the Done command button. Lotus Approach displays the crosstab (see Fig. 11.11).

Figure 11.11

A new
crosstab from
the example
database.

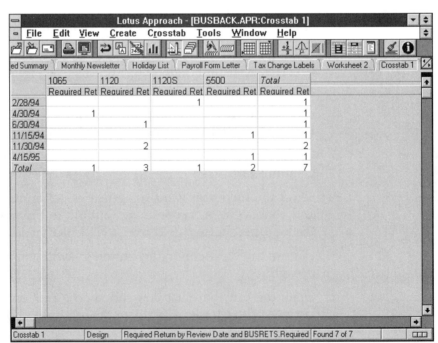

In the second crosstab we create, we will use information in two joined databases to show the number of returns that must be reviewed on each review date by each staff person. In this crosstab, the staff person assigned appears as columns, review dates appear as rows, and the number of returns appears in the grid.

To do this:

1. Open the Create menu and choose the Crosstab command. The Crosstab Assistant dialog box appears.

2. Select the field you want to appear as rows in the crosstab and choose the Add command button. In the example, choose the Review Date field from the BUSRETS database.

3. Choose the Next command button to switch to the Step 2: Columns tab.

4. Select the field you want to appear as columns in the crosstab and choose the Add command button. In the example, choose the Staff Person Assigned field from the BUSBACK database.

5. Choose the Next command button to switch to the Step 3: Values tab.

6. Open the Calculate list box and choose the formula you want Lotus Approach to calculate. In the example, choose number of items.

7. Select the field you want to calculate from the of field list box. In the example, choose the Required Return field from the BUSRETS database.

8. Choose the Done command button. Lotus Approach displays the crosstab (see Fig. 11.12).

In the last crosstab we create, we will summarize information within the summary. We will show, for each person and review date, the number of each type of required return that must be reviewed. In this example, the required return appears in the rows, and we will define two column sets: the review date and the staff person assigned. The number of returns appears in the grid. When you use two column fields, Lotus Approach nests the information so that you will see, for each review date, all the staff people.

Figure 11.12

The second crosstab example.

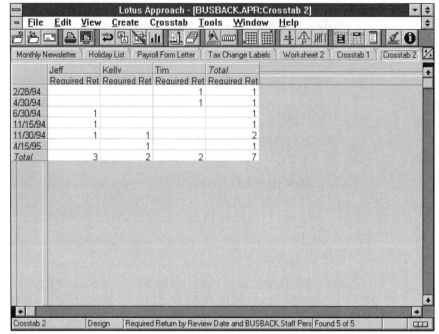

To do this:

1. Open the **Create** menu and choose the Crosstab command. The Crosstab Assistant dialog box appears.

2. Select the field you want to appear as rows in the crosstab and choose the **Add** command button. In the example, choose the Required Return field from the BUSRETS database.

3. Choose the Next command button to switch to the Step 2: Columns tab.

4. Select the field you want to appear as columns in the crosstab and choose the **Add** command button. In the example, choose the Staff Person Assigned field from the BUSBACK database and then choose the Review Date from the BUSRETS database.

5. Choose the Next command button to switch to the Step 3: Values tab.

6. Open the **Calculate** list box and choose the formula you want Lotus Approach to calculate. In the example, choose number of items.

Figure 11.13

The third crosstab example.

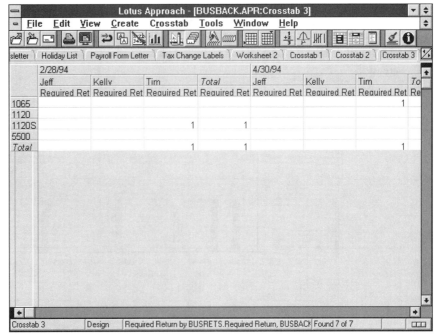

7. Select the field you want to calculate from the of field list box. In the example, choose the Required Return field from the BUS-RETS database.

8. Lotus Approach displays the Define Main Database dialog box; choose the BUSRETS database.

9. Choose the Done command button. Lotus Approach displays the crosstab (see Fig. 11.13).

Working with Charts

Often, a picture conveys the meaning of numbers more effectively than the numbers themselves. You can chart the information in a crosstab view to create a picture of the numbers. You also can create a new chart based on the information in a worksheet or crosstab.

Creating an Instant Chart from a Crosstab

You can easily create a chart from the information displayed in a crosstab. Switch to the crosstab containing the information you

Figure 11.14

A chart
created from a
crosstab.

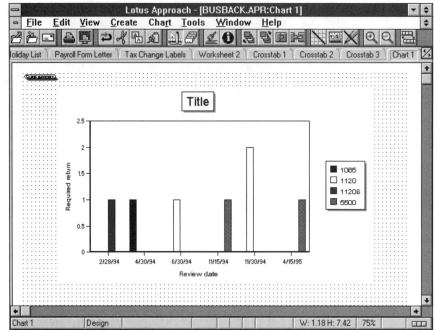

want to chart. Then, either choose the Chart SmartIcon or open the Crosstab menu and choose the Chart Crosstab command. Lotus Approach creates a chart view. In Figure 11.14, you see a chart created from the data in the first crosstab example we created in the last section.

Creating a New Chart

You can create a new chart using information in your database. You use the Chart Assistant to create a new chart.

Let's create basically the same chart we just created (see Fig. 11.14), but let's use the Chart Assistant:

1. Open the database that contains the information you want to chart. You don't need to be looking at a particular view and you don't need to be in Design mode.

2. Open the Create menu and choose the Chart command. The Chart Assistant dialog box appears (see Fig. 11.15).

3. In the View name & title text box, type a name for the chart. In the example, type **Return Review Chart**.

Figure 11.15

The Chart
Assistant
dialog box.

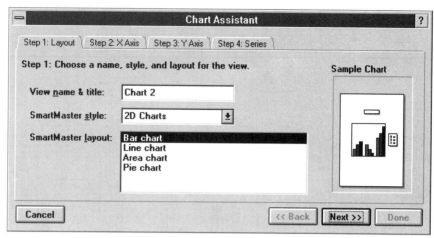

4. In the SmartMaster style list box, choose a style for your chart. For the example, choose 2D Charts.

5. In the SmartMaster layout list box, choose a type of chart. In the example, choose Bar chart.

6. Choose the Next command button to display the Step 2: X Axis tab.

7. Use the X-axis field list boxes to select the database and field you want to appear on the horizontal axis of your chart. In the example, choose, from the BUSRETS database, the Review Date field.

8. Choose the Next command button to display the Step 3: Y Axis tab.

9. From the Chart list box, choose the value you want charted. In the example, choose number of items.

10. Use the of field list boxes to select the database and field you want Lotus Approach to calculate. This value will appear on the vertical axis of your chart. In the example, choose, from the BUSRETS database, the Required Return field to plot the number of required returns.

11. (Optional) Switch to the Step 4: Series tab and identify a field on which you want Lotus Approach to group the data that you intend to plot on the X axis. In the example, group on the Required Return field in the BUSRETS database.

12. Choose the Done command button. Lotus Approach displays the chart (see Fig. 11.16).

Figure 11.16

A 2D bar chart created with the Chart Assistant.

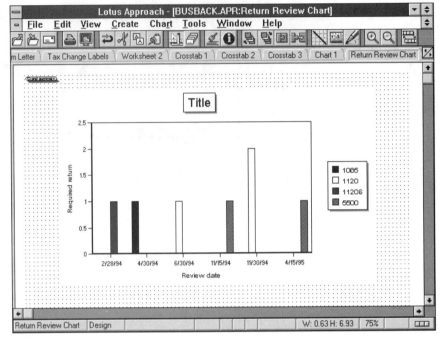

When you create pie charts, the Chart Assistant dialog box changes to ask questions related only to pie charts (see Fig. 11.17).

The layout tab looks the same as the one you saw in Figure 11.15, but you see only one tab for steps. If we wanted to create a pie chart that showed the number of returns needing review by each

Figure 11.17

The Chart Assistant for pie charts.

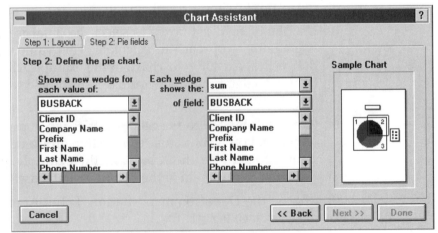

Figure 11.18

A pie chart.

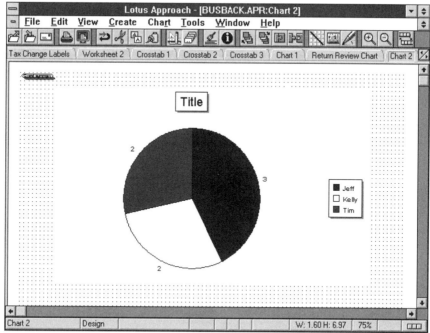

staff person, we would select the Staff Person Assigned field from the list box on the left in the Chart Assistant, and in the list box on the right, we would choose the number of items for the Required Return field in the BUSRETS database. The pie chart would look similar to the one in Figure 11.18.

Modifying a Chart

Once you create a chart, you can make changes to it. You can change the data that appears in the chart, the type of chart, and the appearance of the chart.

Changing the Chart Data

Even though you specify one set of data to appear in a chart when you create it, you can change the data in the chart. For example, suppose we want to change the pie chart to see the total number of each type of return needing preparation, instead of the number of returns to be reviewed by each staff person.

To change the data in a chart:

1. Open the Chart menu and choose the Chart Data Source command. You see the Chart Data Source Assistant dialog box (see Fig. 11.19).

2. Select different fields to chart. In the example, change the list box on the left to display the Required Return field from the BUSRETS database. The list box on the right would show the same information: the number of items for the Required Return field.

3. Choose the Done command. Lotus Approach displays the new chart (see Fig. 11.20).

In the example, you could make chart more meaningful with labels on the pie slices; later in this chapter, you learn how to add these labels.

Changing the Appearance of a Chart

After you initially create a chart, you can change its appearance, including the chart type and layout. Suppose, for example, that you want to change the bar chart we created earlier from a two-dimensional bar chart to a three-dimensional bar chart.

To do this:

1. Switch to the chart you want to change and switch to Design mode.

Figure 11.19

The Chart Data Source Assistant dialog box.

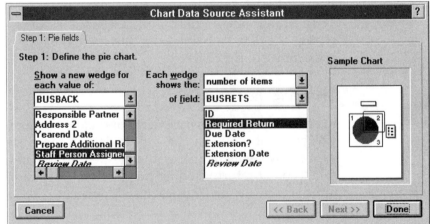

Figure 11.20

The pie chart after changing the data.

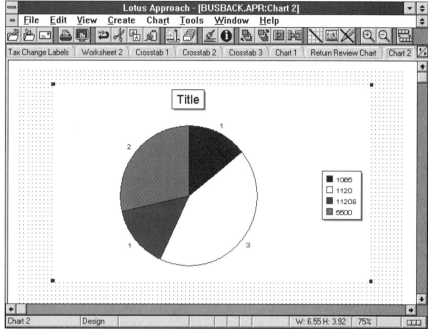

2. Double-click on the chart. Lotus Approach displays the chart's Info box (see Fig. 11.21). Note that the tabs for the panels appear at the bottom of the Info box.

3. Click on the Type button to open the pictorial view of the various chart types.

4. Choose a new chart type. In the example, choose the picture that appears in the middle of the second row.

Earlier in the chapter, we created a pie chart and then changed the data that we used to create the pie chart. After changing the pie chart's data, the chart looked confusing because the labels were unclear. You can use the chart Info box to change the labels.

To change the chart labels:

1. If necessary, switch to the pie chart and switch to Design mode.

2. Double-click on the pie chart to display the Info box.

3. Open the Chart list box and choose Slice labels.

4. Choose the Use legend text as labels check box to display the type of return each pie slice represents. Optionally, you can add

Figure 11.21

The Basics panel of the Info box for a chart.

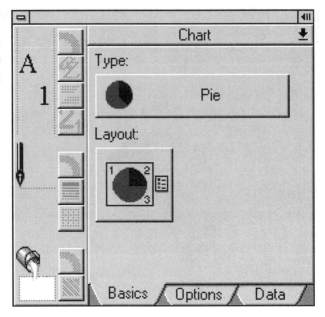

Figure 11.22

The pie chart with labels and titles.

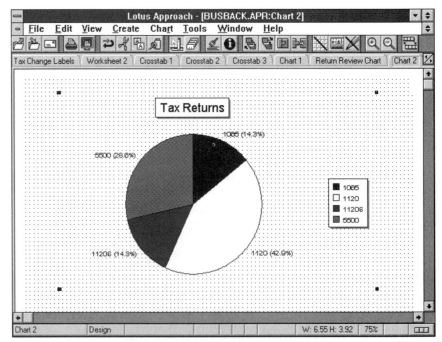

or remove checks from the other check boxes to display the chart the way you want.

The title on the chart is a text object that you can edit by double-clicking on it and changing it. You also can place a subtitle, legend, or note on the chart, all from the same list box in the Chart Info box. In Figure 11.22, you see the pie chart with labels, a title, and a subtitle.

Chapter Summary

In this chapter, you learned how you can use tools in Lotus Approach to analyze the data you store in databases. You learned how to create worksheet views, cross-tabulation views that summarize information, and charts.

In the next chapter, you will learn about printing in Lotus Approach.

Printing Information in the Database

Once your database contains information, you may want to print some or all of that information. When printing information from your database, you can print from forms, reports, form letters, mailing labels, worksheets, crosstabs, or charts.

When you print information from forms, Lotus Approach prints one record on a page; when you print information from reports, Lotus Approach prints multiple records per page. If you use the Preview mode feature in Lotus Approach, you can think of what you see on-screen as what you get when you print.

In this chapter, you will learn about printing in Lotus Approach. You can print the data in your database, or you can print the various views you create without any data in them. You will learn how to preview the view before you print it, and you learn how to change the printer's settings. In certain cases, you may need to close up the space between fields on a view; in this chapter, you will learn how to slide fields and reduce field boundaries.

Previewing before Printing

To see what your printout will look like before you print, you can use Preview mode. While you are not forced to switch to Preview mode, you will often find that viewing a particular report or form in Preview mode helps you find mistakes in appearance before printing. Also, for summary reports and views that contain summary calculations over a range of records Lotus Approach makes the calculation when you preview or print. You also see, while in Preview mode, the effects of sliding fields, about which you will learn later in this chapter.

Tip

Usually, Lotus Approach calculates summarized values when you print or preview; however, Lotus Approach will calculate values for summaries of line items in a repeating panel in Browse mode.

To preview a report or form before printing, click on the Preview SmartIcon. By default, Lotus Approach displays the current view in Preview mode at 75 percent of normal size (see Fig. 12.1).

Figure 12.1

Preview mode.

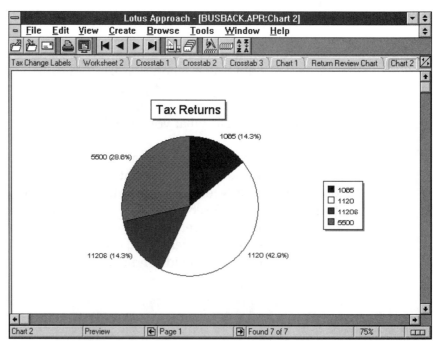

The status bar shows that you are in Browse/Preview or Design/Preview and the mouse pointer changes shape to indicate that you can click the mouse button to change the size of the view. If you click the left mouse button, you enlarge the view (zoom in); if you click the right mouse button, you reduce the view (zoom out). You also can change the size of the view using the Zoom list on the status bar, or by opening the **View** menu and choosing the **Zoom In** command, the Zoom **Out** command, or the **Actual Size** command.

The SmartIcon bar in Preview mode contains icons to create and open files, print, move to other records, and find and sort records.

When you use Preview mode, you get a sense of whether you need to reset the margins for a form or report or whether you want to change the paper orientation.

Reducing Gaps between Data when Printing

When you create a report, extra blank space can appear between records on the report, within a specified field, or between fields. You can remove the extra blank space that might appear on a report. You can use the same technique to reduce space between fields on a form or form letter. When you create mailing labels, Lotus Approach automatically reduces the space between the fields for you, but if you add a field after creating the mailing labels, you may want to reduce the space between the new field and existing fields.

You can tell Lotus Approach to slide fields up and to the left on a report, form, form letter, or mailing label. You use the Dimensions panel of the Info box. Select the field you want to adjust to eliminate blank space and open the Info box. Then, switch to the Dimensions panel and place checks in the two check boxes associated with sliding fields. For Lotus Approach to close up the gap between two fields on the same line, you must slide both fields to the left. For Lotus Approach to close up the gap between fields on two rows, you must slide both fields up. In addition, to slide fields (either to the left or up), the two fields must be aligned along their bottom edges.

To reduce space within a specific field, you want to reduce the boundaries of the field. Then, when you print or preview, Lotus Approach will automatically scale the field based on the amount of text appearing in it. By reducing the boundaries of a field, you reduce the amount of space required by the selected field, based on the data that appears in the field on the current record.

Last, by default, Lotus Approach keeps all the fields of one record together on a page. You can change this option from the Info box by viewing the report you want to change in Design mode, opening the Info box, and clicking on the report header to display the Info box settings for the report. Then, from the Basics panel, remove the check in the Keep records together check box.

Changing Printer Setup

If your printer supports such changes, you can change the paper size or orientation before you print. Changes you make to printer setup remain in effect until you change them again.

To change printer setup:

1. Open the File menu and choose the Print Setup command. Lotus Approach displays the Print Setup dialog box (see Fig. 12.2).

2. If your printer supports landscape printing, you can change the orientation from Portrait to Landscape.

3. If your printer supports form sizes other than 8½ × 11 inches, you can change the paper size.

4. When you finish changing the setup for your printer, choose the OK command button.

The settings you select remain in effect until you reopen this dialog box and select new settings.

Tip

You also can open this dialog box from inside the Print dialog box by choosing the Setup command button.

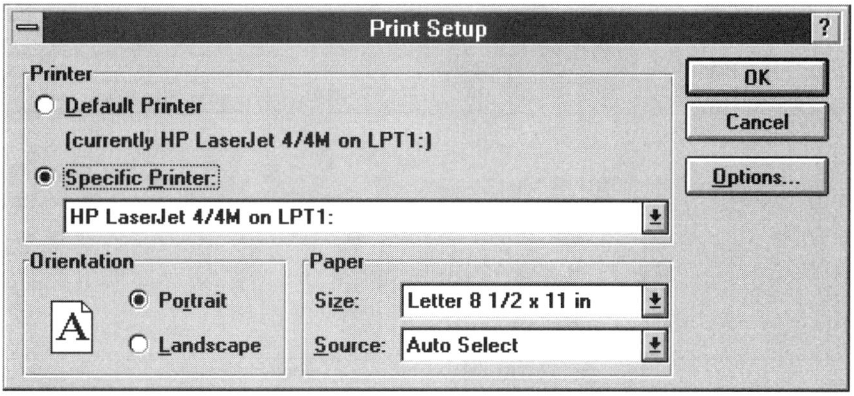

Figure 12.2

The Print Setup
dialog box.

Printing Forms and Form Letters

You can print the data that appears on a form. Because forms usually show only one record, when you print a form, Lotus Approach usually prints only one record on the page.

Tip

Lotus Approach prints the selected set of records. If you don't want to print all the records in the database, search for the records you want to print before you print. If you want to print the records in a specified order, sort the records before you print.

To print a form:

1. Open the database containing the form you want to print.

2. Display the form you want to print.

3. Switch to Browse mode.

4. (Optional) Switch to Preview mode.

5. Choose the Print SmartIcon, or open the File menu and choose the **Print** command. The Print dialog box appears (see Fig. 12.3)

6. In the Print Range box, choose a print range.

7. Make any other necessary changes to the Print dialog box.

8. If you want to make changes to the form size or orientation, choose the **Setup** command button to display the Print Setup

Figure 12.3

The Print
dialog box.

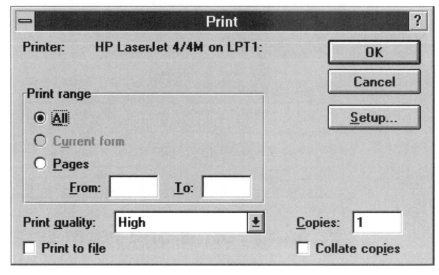

dialog box. Make any changes and choose the OK command
button to return to the Print dialog box.

9. Choose the OK command button. Lotus Approach prints the
selected information.

Because form letters are a variation on a form, Lotus Approach
prints only one form letter per page. The steps are the same as out-
lined above; make sure you select the form letter you want to print
in step 2.

Printing Reports and Mailing Labels

To print a report, follow all the same steps described in the previous
section. You will note only one major difference between printing
forms and printing reports: when Lotus Approach prints reports,
multiple records appear on a page.

You can, on reports that include summary panels, insert a page
break if needed. In Design mode, display the report view on which
you want to insert a page break. Select the summary panel after
which you want a page break and then open the Info box. Switch
to the Basics panel, where you will see a check box that lets you
insert a page break.

If a columnar report contains too many columns to fit on the page with the orientation you have selected, Lotus Approach wraps the extra columns to the next line, essentially printing two rows for each record instead of one row. To correct the problem, try changing the paper orientation from portrait to landscape in step 8.

Mailing labels behave like a report when you print them—Lotus Approach typically produces one mailing label for each record in the database and prints multiple records on a page. Occasionally, you may need to print more than one mailing label for the same addressee. To print multiple mailing labels for the same addressee, duplicate the addressee's record. Create an additional duplicate record for each mailing label you want to print. After printing the mailing labels, delete the duplicate records.

Printing Worksheets and Crosstabs

You can print worksheets and crosstabs the same way you print forms, reports, form letters, and mailing labels. You can, if you want, use the Info box to set print parameters (see Fig. 12.4).

You can choose to print the title, the grid, the date, and the page number. The options are the same for crosstabs.

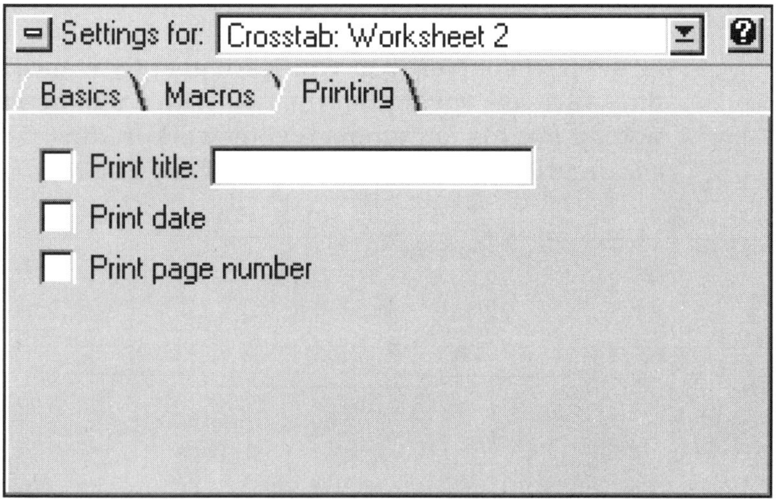

Figure 12.4

The Print panel of the Info box for a worksheet.

Settings for: Crosstab: Worksheet 2

Basics \ Macros \ Printing \

☐ Print title: [   ]

☐ Print date

☐ Print page number

Printing the Design vs. Printing Data

In addition to printing data from your databases, you can print your report and form designs.

To print a form or report design:

1. Open the database containing the form or report design you want to print.

2. Display the form or report you want to print.

3. Switch to Design mode.

4. Open the **File** menu and choose the **Print** command. The Print dialog box appears.

5. Choose the OK command button. Lotus Approach prints the image you see on-screen in Design mode.

Chapter Summary

In this chapter, you learned that you print data in your databases by printing a view containing the information you want to print. Lotus Approach prints one record on a page for forms and form letters, and multiple records on a page for reports and mailing labels. If your printer supports alternate paper sizes and orientations, you can selectively print views with different printer settings.

In the next chapter, you will learn about advanced database features such as copying information within and between view files, writing macros to automate your work, setting database options and security, and creating and modifying SmartIcon bars.

Advanced Database Features

In this chapter, you will learn about some of the more advanced features in Lotus Approach. You will learn how to create, edit, and delete *macros*, tools that making working in your database easier. Using macros, you will learn how to create a menu system within Lotus Approach and to switch automatically from one form to another. You will learn how to set database options and database security, and you will learn how to customize the SmartIcon bar.

Creating Macros

You can create macros in Lotus Approach to simplify your work. In this section, you will learn how to create one of the most common (and the most simple) macros—a macro that switches automatically from one view to another view. In the example database, this macro would be particularly useful for connecting the two data entry forms, Background Data Entry and Returns Data Entry. By creating a macro that lets you switch automatically from Background Data Entry to Returns Data Entry, you help the user to remember to enter all the necessary information for a new client.

Later in this chapter, you will also learn how to place a find request and a sort request in a macro. You will learn how to assign a macro to a button or to a field and to use buttons and macros to create a menu system for your database. You will also learn how to renumber records in your database to maintain a sequential numbering system.

To create a macro that lets you switch from one view to another:

1. Open the database in which you want to store the macro. In the example, open BUSBACK.

2. Open the **T**ools menu and choose the **Macros** command. The Macros dialog box appears (see Fig. 13.1).

3. Choose the **New** command button. The Define Macro dialog box appears (see Fig. 13.2).

4. In the Macro **N**ame text box, type a name for the macro. In the example, type **Switch**.

Tip

To create a macro that runs each time you open or close a Lotus Approach file, name the macro OPEN or CLOSE.

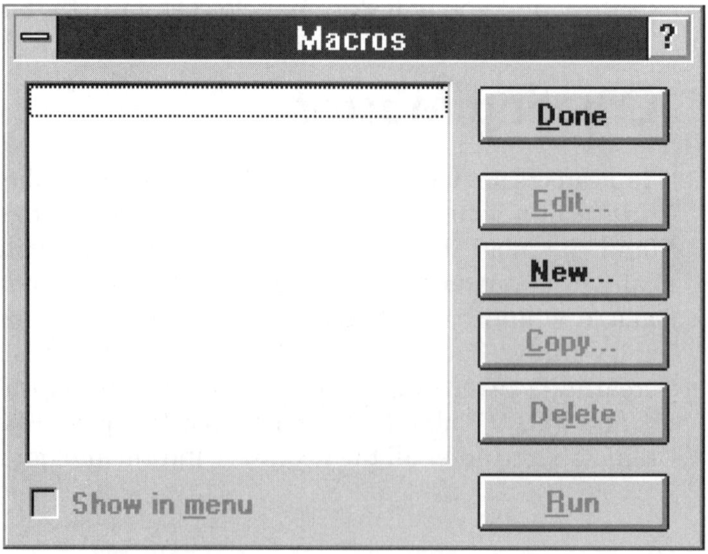

Figure 13.1

The Macros dialog box.

Figure 13.2

The Define Macro dialog box.

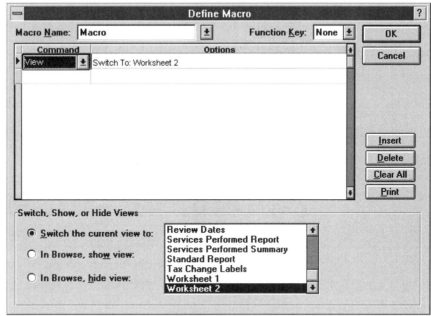

5. (Optional) If you want to be able to run the macro by pressing a function key, open the Function **K**ey list box and choose a function key. In the example, don't assign the macro to a function key.

6. Use the Commands list box to select the first command you want Lotus Approach to perform in the macro. Use the options that appear below the Commands list to specify options for the command you selected. The options that appear below the command list show only the options available for the command you select, so as you change commands, the options change. By default, Lotus Approach always choose the View command. In the example, you want to use the View command, and you want to choose the first option button, **S**witch the current view to, and choose Returns Data Entry from the list of available views.

Tip

You cannot use a macro to switch from one .APR file to another.

7. (Optional) Repeat Step 6, selecting commands in the order in which you want Lotus Approach to execute them. In Table 13.1, you will find a list of the various macro commands and their purposes. For the example macro, you don't need to select any additional commands.

8. Choose the OK command button. The Macros dialog box reappears, with an "X" appearing in the Show in **m**enu check box.

9. Choose the **D**one command button. Lotus Approach saves the macro you just created.

Tip

You run macros from Browse mode. You can run the macro you just created by switching to Browse mode, then opening the Tools menu and choosing the Run Macro command. Your macro appears in a submenu. Select it to run it.

Table 13.1 Macro Commands and Their Functions	
Use this Macro command	**When you want a macro to**
Browse	Change to Browse mode.
Close	Close the current file.
Delete	Delete the current record, the found set of records, or the Lotus Approach file. By default, warnings appear before anything is deleted.
Dial	Use a modem and have Lotus Approach dial a telephone number in the selected field.
Edit	Use the Cut, Copy, Paste, or Select All commands on the Edit menu, primarily to place information on the Clipboard.
Enter	Accept the current record.
Exit	Close Lotus Approach software program.
Export	Set export options, either now or when the macro is run. If you set them now, the export occurs automatically when the macro is run.
Find	Find all records in the database, find records based on a stored find request, or refresh the found set.

Continued

Table 13.1 Macro Commands and Their Functions *(continued)*

Use this Macro command	When you want a macro to
Find Special	Set Find Special options, either now or when the macro is run.
Import	Set import options, either now or when the macro is run. If you set them now, the import occurs automatically when the macro is run.
Mail	Set mailing options, either now or when the macro is run. If you set them now, mail is sent automatically when the macro is run.
Menu Switch	Switch to the specified menu set.
Message	Display a dialog box containing a message.
Open	Set file open options, either now or when the macro is run. If you set them now, the file opens automatically when the macro is run.
Preview	Change to Preview mode.
Print	Set printing options, either now or when the macro is run. If you set them now, printing occurs automatically when the macro is run.
Records	Move to a record, create a new record, hide a record, or duplicate a record.
Replicate	Set replicate options, either now or when the macro is run. If you set them now, replication occurs automatically when the macro is run. (This command is for users of Lotus Notes.)
Run	Run another macro or continue running the same macro under conditions you specify.
Save	Set file saving options, either now or when the macro is run. If you set them now, saving occurs automatically when the macro is run.
Set	Set a particular field to the value you specify or formula you define.
Sort	Set sort criteria, either now or when the macro is run. If you set them now, the sort occurs automatically when the macro is run.
Spell Check	Check spelling.
Tab	Tab forward or backward a specified number of times.
View	Change to a specified view.
Zoom	Enlarge or reduce the current window.

Editing or Deleting a Macro

To edit macros using the Define Macro dialog box:

1. Open the database containing the macro. In the example, open BUSBACK.

2. Open the **T**ools menu and choose the **M**acros command. The Macros dialog box appears.

3. Choose a macro from the list box and choose the Edit command button. In the example, choose Switch. The Define Macro dialog box appears (see Fig. 13.3).

4. To modify the macro, make whatever changes you want and choose the OK command button. In the following sections, you find some examples of changes you might want to make to the macro. In the example, open the Function **K**ey list box and choose F3.

5. Choose the OK command button.

Figure 13.3

The Define Macro dialog box.

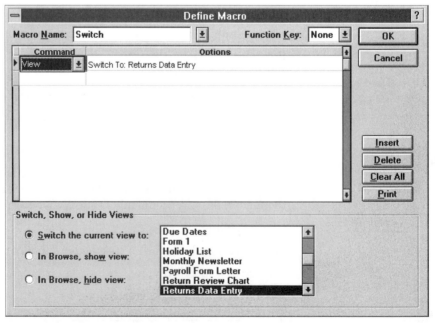

Adding and Removing Commands in a Macro

You can add or remove lines in a macro. Remember, the lines in a macro should appear in the order you want Lotus Approach to execute them. To remove a line from a macro, click in the row marker area to the left of the command list to select the entire line. Then, choose the **D**elete command button.

Tip

Use the Clear All command button to erase *all* macros commands from the dialog box.

To add a command to a macro:

1. Select the row you want to appear *below* the new command by clicking in the row marker area to the left of the command list of that row.

2. Choose the Insert command button. Lotus Approach inserts a blank row above the selected row.

3. Open the Commands list box and select the command you want to add to the macro and set options for the command as appropriate.

Moving a Macro Command

You can move commands in a macro if you discover you need them to appear in an order different from the one you originally set up. Follow these steps:

1. Select the row you want to move by clicking in the row marker area to the left of the command list of that row.

2. Move the mouse pointer over the selection marker until the mouse pointer shape changes to a hand.

3. Drag the line to its new position.

Using Macros to Perform Repetitive Tasks

Macros are ideally suited for performing repetitive tasks in Browse mode. You can create a loop in your macro to tell Lotus Approach to select a record, perform a series of tasks, and then select the next record and repeat the set of tasks. With a looping macro, you can tell Lotus Approach to quit after it reaches the last record. If you have additional actions you want the macro to take after finishing the repetitive actions, you can tell Lotus Approach to continue running the macro after it reaches the last record in the loop. You can also tell Lotus Approach to start another macro and, when it finishes that macro, continue running the original macro.

To create a loop in a macro that ends when Lotus Approach encounters the last record:

1. In the Define Macro dialog box, start the loop by selecting the Records command. Note that you can include other commands before the Records command, but they will not be performed as part of the loop.

2. Set the Options for the Records command to Next.

3. Enter the commands you want performed as part of the loop.

4. To complete the loop, select, as the last command in the loop, the Run command.

5. Set the Options for the Run command by opening the **Run** macro list box and choosing the current macro (in which you are defining a loop). Lotus Approach runs the loop macro through all the records in the database or found set and then stops executing the macro when it encounters the last record. Your macro should look like the one in Figure 13.4.

To create a loop that continues executing the current macro, follow the steps above, but add a command after Step 2 to check to see if Lotus Approach has reached the last record in the database. The command to add is a Run command. For its options, choose the **If** option button and click on the **Formula** command button to open the Formula dialog box. In the Formula dialog box, choose IsLastRecord() from the **Functions** list box. Then, open the is true list box and choose continue this macro. The macro will look similar to the one in Figure 13.5, where the command in the loop is a View command.

To create a loop that branches to another macro and then returns to the original macro to continue executing, follow the instructions in

Figure 13.4

A macro that loops and stops after reaching the last record in the database.

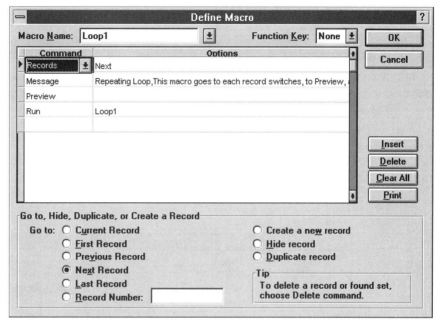

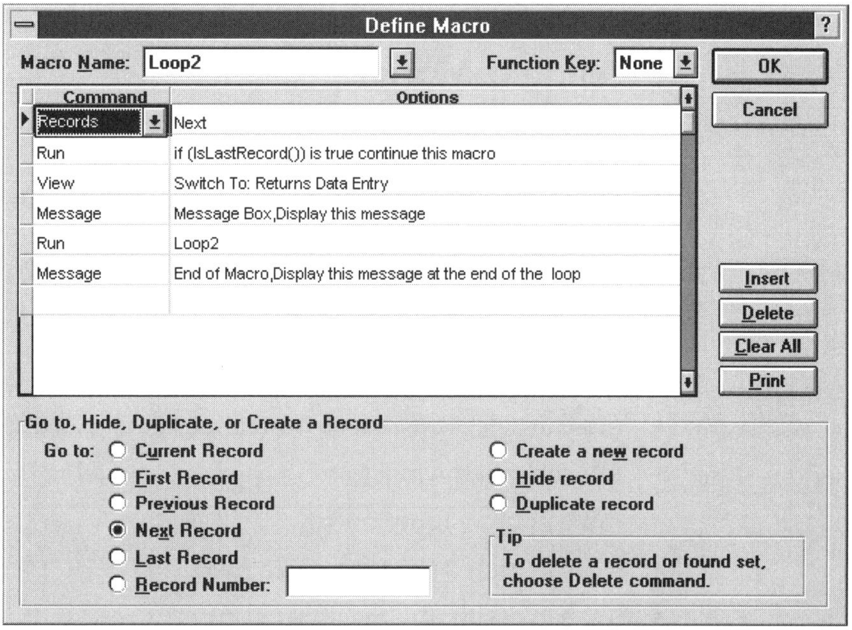

Figure 13.5

A macro that loops and continues to execute after reaching the last record in the database.

Figure 13.6 Looped section

A macro that
loops and
branches to
another macro
before
returning to
complete.

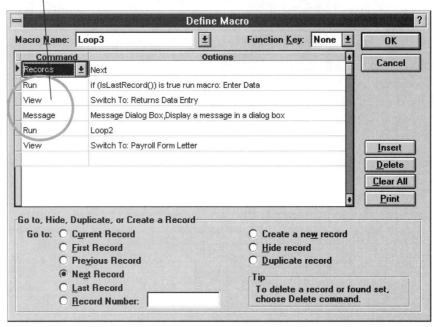

the previous paragraph, but in the is true list box, choose run macro: and specify the macro to which you want to branch. Your macro will look similar to the one in Figure 13.6.

Deleting a Macro

To delete the macro, open the Macros dialog box (from the Tools menu, choose the Macros command). Highlight the macro you want to delete and choose the Delete command button.

Running a Macro

You can run a macro using five possible methods:

- You can select the macro from a menu.
- You can run the macro from the Macros dialog box.
- You can use a function key.
- You can assign the macro to a field.
- You can assign the macro to a button.

You can run the macro from the **T**ools menu. Open the **T**ools menu and choose the **R**un Macro command. Choose the macro from the submenu.

If you reopen the Macros dialog box by choosing **M**acros from the **T**ools menu, you can highlight the macro and choose the **R**un command button.

If, when you defined the macro, you established a function key for the macro, you can simply press the function key to run the macro.

You can assign a macro to a field so that when you tab into or out of the field, Lotus Approach runs the macro. Similarly, you can also create a button and assign a macro to the button so that you can run the macro by clicking on the button. See the next section for more information on creating buttons and assigning macros to them.

Assigning a Macro to a Field

You can assign up to three macros to any field on any form. To assign a macro to a field, switch to Design mode and select the field. Double-click on the field to display its Info box and switch to the Macros panel (see Fig. 13.7).

Open the appropriate list box and assign a macro. You can tell Lotus Approach to execute a macro in Browse mode when you tab

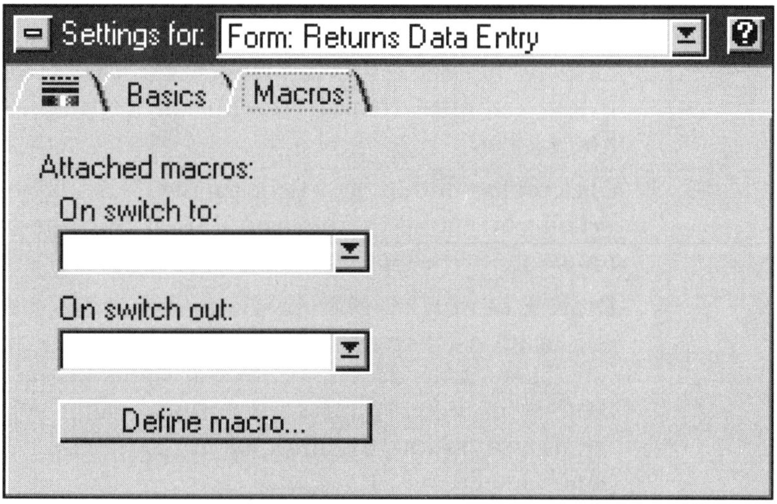

Figure 13.7

A sample Macros panel in the Info box.

into a field, when you tab out of a field, or when you change data in a field.

Assigning a Macro to a Button

You can create buttons in Lotus Approach to which you can assign macros. You can then assign a macro to a macro button; when a user clicks on the macro button, the macro runs.

Tip
For users of previous versions of Lotus Approach, macro buttons are the same as push button fields.

You can assign a macro to a button in one of three ways:

- You can create the macro first, then create a button for it and assign the macro to the button.

- You can create the button first and then create a macro to assign to the button.

- You can create a button and attach a previously defined macro to the button.

To create a button for the Switch macro::

1. Switch to Design mode and display the form on which you want to place a button. In the example, display the Background Data Entry form.

2. Display the area on-screen where you want to place the button. In the example, display the bottom of the Background Data Entry form.

3. Click on the Button SmartIcon on the Drawing SmartIcon palette. When you move the insertion point into the screen area, the mouse pointer shape changes to a plus sign.

4. Draw a button by placing the intersection of the plus sign in the location where you want the upper left corner of the button. Then, drag down and to the right. In the example, place the button below the No. of Services field. When you release the mouse button, the Info box appears, displaying the Macros panel (see Fig. 13.8).

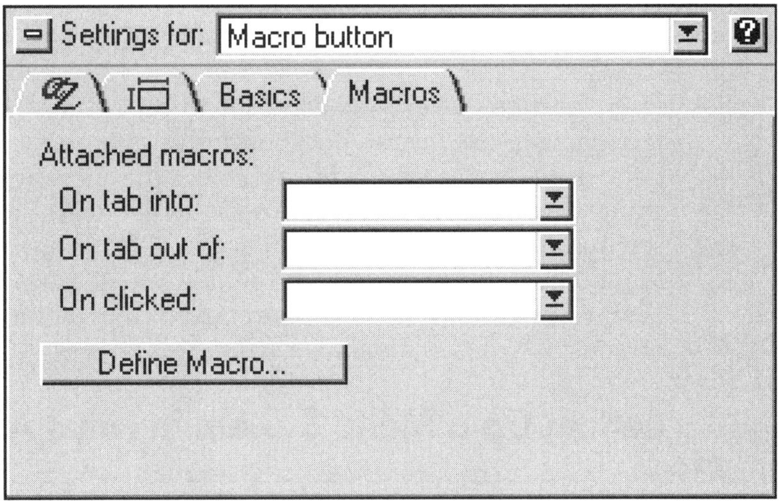

Figure 13.8

The Macros
panel of the
Info box for a
button.

Settings for: Macro button

🖉 \ 🗔 \ Basics \ Macros \

Attached macros:

On tab into:

On tab out of:

On clicked:

Define Macro...

5. Attach a macro using the On clicked list box. In the example, choose the Switch macro.

Tip

If you did not previously define a macro for the button, you can choose the Define Macro command button to open the Macros dialog box and define a macro.

---

6. Switch to the Basics panel to change the text that appears on the button. Use the Button text box to type the word(s) you want to appear on the button. In the example, type **Enter Returns**. Use the Font panel to assign a different font to the button or change the point list of the current font.

In Browse mode, when you click on the Enter Returns button, Lotus Approach displays the Returns Data Entry form.

You can create a button and another macro to switch back to the Background Data Entry form. That way, after completely entering one record, the user will be ready to enter another record. To create the macro, set up the Define Macro dialog box exactly the way you set it up to switch to the Background Data Entry form, but select the Returns Data Entry form from the Options list. Name the macro Switchback. On the Returns Data Entry form, create a button labeled Begin New Record and assign the Switchback macro to it.

Common Uses for Macros

In this section, we explore some common uses for macros. You will learn how to use macros and buttons to create a menu system for a database—that way, users can select the view with which they want to work from a menu. You will also learn how to find and sort records using a macro, and you will learn how to use a macro to renumber records to which Lotus Approach assigned a number. Last, you will learn how to chain macros together to run them continuously.

Setting Up a Menu System in Lotus Approach

You can use buttons and macros that switch between forms to set up a menu system for the forms in your database. Note that these steps only work for form views, report views, form letter views, and mailing label views. You cannot add buttons to worksheets or crosstabs.

To set up a menu system:

1. Open the view file that most often serves as the main database. In the example, open BUSBACK.

2. Switch to Design mode.

3. Open the **C**reate menu and choose the **F**orm command. The Form Assistant dialog box appears (see Fig. 13.9).

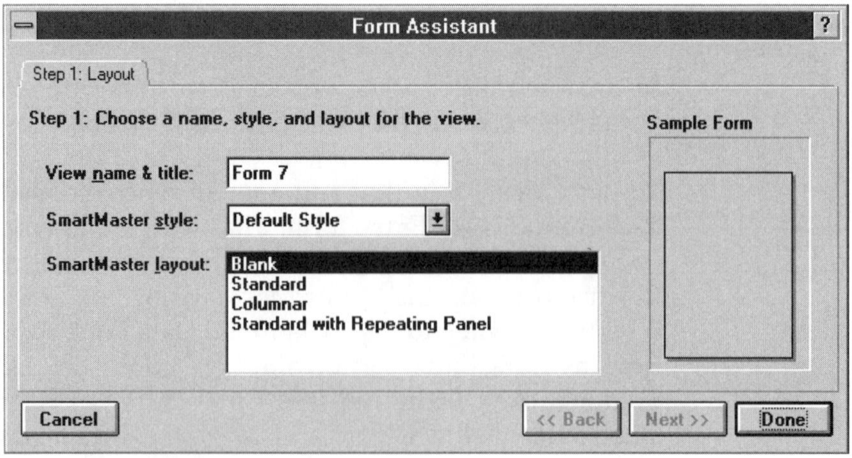

Figure 13.9

The Form Assistant dialog box.

Form Assistant

Step 1: Layout

Step 1: Choose a name, style, and layout for the view.

Sample Form

View **n**ame & title: Form 7

SmartMaster **s**tyle: Default Style

SmartMaster **l**ayout: Blank
Standard
Columnar
Standard with Repeating Panel

Cancel   << Back   Next >>   Done

4. In the View **n**ame & title field, type a name for the menu view. In the example, type **Menu**.

5. From the SmartMaster **s**tyle list box, choose a style for the menu view. In the example, choose 3D Look2.

6. From the SmartMaster **l**ayout list box, choose the Blank layout.

7. Choose the Done command button. If the Define Main Database dialog box appears, select the main database. In the example, choose the BUSBACK database.

You now have a blank form to which you can add buttons and create macros that switch to other form views. On the form views to which you switch, add a button that switches back to the Menu.

To make sure the menu appears when you next open the file, write a macro named **open** and have that macro switch to the menu.

Tip

To create a series of buttons all the same size, create one button as described previously. Then, select the button and press **Ctrl+C** to copy the button to the Clipboard. Click where you want the second button to appear and press **Ctrl+V** to paste the contents of the Clipboard onto the view. You will have two identical buttons on-screen. Double-click the second button to open its Info box, then change its name and the macro assigned to it.

Finding and Sorting Records in a Macro

In Chapter 9, you created the Due Dates for Returns report. To use the report, you needed to find the information and then sort it in due date order.

To write a macro that performs both actions:

1. Open the database in which you want to store the macro. In the example, open BUSBACK.

2. Open the **T**ools menu and choose the **M**acros command. The Macro dialog box appears.

3. Choose the **N**ew command button. The Define Macro dialog box appears (see Fig. 13.10).

Figure 13.10

The Define
Macro dialog
box.

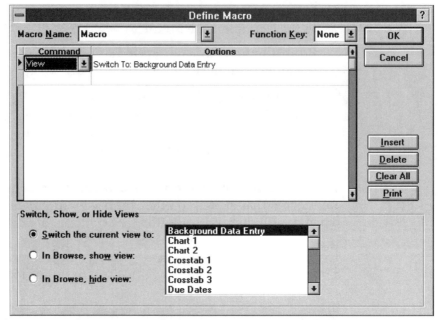

4. In the Macro Name box, type a name for the macro. In the example, type **FindSort**.

5. In the Function Key list box, choose a function key to assign to the macro. In the example, choose F2. (Notice that F3 does not appear in the list because we previously assigned it to a macro.)

6. From the Command list box, choose the View command and select the Due Dates report from the list in the Options box.

7. From the Command list box, choose the Find command and select Show All records.

8. From the Command list box, choose the Sort command; in the Option box, choose the Set sort now and automatically sort the records when the macro is run. Then, from the list boxes, choose the database that contains the field by which you want to sort and the field. In the example, choose the BUSRETS database and the Due Date field. Choose the Add command button and the Ascending option button.

9. From the Commands list, choose the Preview command.

10. Choose the OK command button and the Done command button.

To run the macro, switch to Browse mode and press **F2**.

Using Macros to Renumber Records

When we first set up the database, we told Lotus Approach to assign each new client a sequential ID number; we used the ID number to join all the databases. We set up the field as a required field, and then we created a list field that used database information so that the users would be able to select client names when performing queries without having to remember client numbers.

All of this works fine until you start to enter a record and then change your mind. Lotus Approach assigns the sequential number when you start to create the record; if you press **Esc** to cancel entering a record, Lotus Approach has already used the next ID number. Because you didn't complete the record, no record in your database contains that number; unfortunately, Lotus Approach will not redisplay the number for you to use again. Effectively, you end up with missing numbers in the database.

You can constantly reset the sequential number, but as soon as you delete a record from the database, you have the same problem. In the example database, the ID number serves no purpose other than to act as a join field; you have no reason to maintain the original number assigned to a client. You can use a variable field and three macros to renumber the records in the database automatically.

First, create a variable field on the form in the main database that contains your ID number; in the example, use the Background Data Entry form. Later, if you want to print this form, you can make the field a nonprinting field.

To create a variable field:

1. In Design mode, display the form; in the example, display the Background Data Entry form.

2. Create a new field near the ID number field. Open the **Create** menu and choose the Field **Definition** command to display the Field Definition dialog box (see Fig. 13.11).

3. At the bottom of the list, in the Field name list, type a name for the variable field. In the example, type Variable ID. From the Data Type list box, choose Variable.

Figure 13.11

The Field
Definition
dialog box.

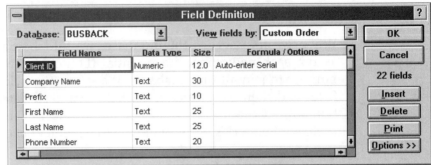

4. Choose the OK command button to close the Field Definition dialog box. The Add Field window appears (see Fig. 13.12).

5. Drag the new field onto the form. In the example, drag the field onto the form just below the Client ID field (see Fig. 13.13).

Next, create three macros. The first macro sets the initial value of the variable field and directs Lotus Approach to display the first record in the file. The second macro sets the value in the ID number field equal to the value in the variable field and then directs Lotus Approach to display the next record. The third macro increases the value in the variable field by 1.

Figure 13.12

The Add Field
window.

Figure 13.13

The Background Data Entry form after adding a variable field.

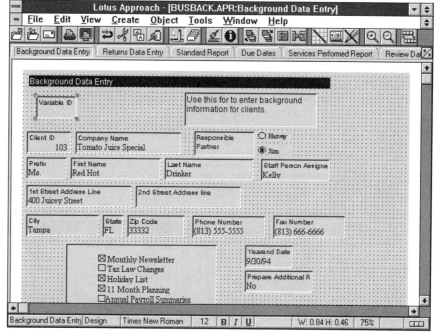

To create these macros:

1. Open the database in which you want to store the macro. In the example, open BUSBACK.

2. Open the **T**ools menu and choose the **M**acros command. The Macro dialog box appears.

3. Choose the **N**ew command button. The Define Macro dialog box appears (see Fig. 13.14).

4. In the Macro **N**ame text box, type a name for the first macro. In the example, type **Renum1**.

5. Define the following commands and options:

   • Choose the View command to switch to the appropriate view. In the example, choose Background Data Entry.

   • Choose the Find command and choose the **S**how All records option button.

   • Choose the Set command. Choose the variable field, and in the To this **v**alue text box, type the initial value you want to appear in the variable field. In the example, choose the Variable ID field and type **101** in the To this **v**alue text box.

Figure 13.14

The Define
Macro dialog
box.

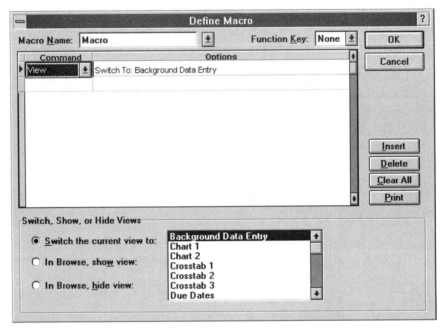

- Choose the Records command and choose the First Record
  option button. Your macro should look like the one in Figure
  13.15.

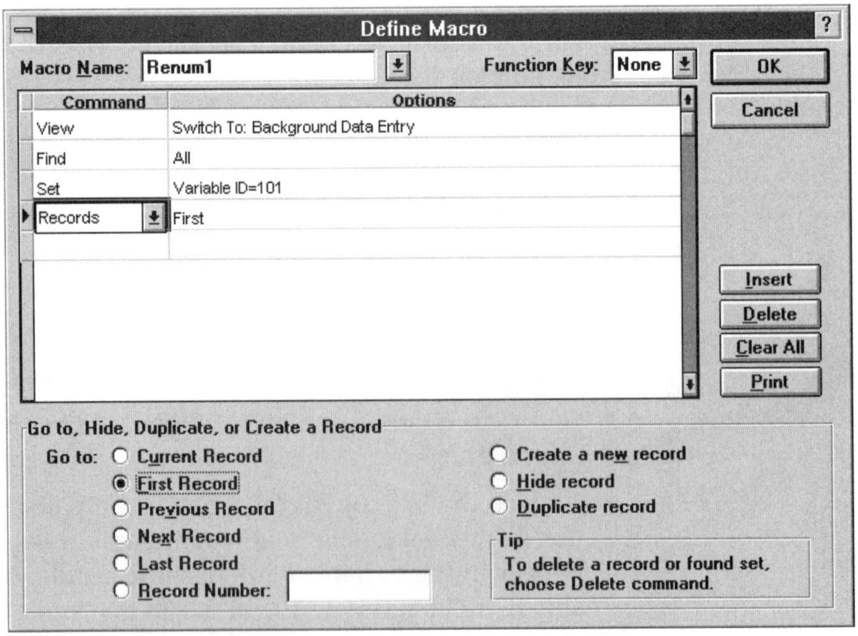

Figure 13.15

The first
renumbering
macro.

6. Choose the OK command button to save the macro.

7. Choose the **New** command button to create the second macro.

8. In the Macro **Name** text box, type a name for the second macro. In the example, type **Renum2**.

9. Define the following commands and options:

   • Choose the Set command, choose the ID number field, and click on the **Formula** command button. In the Formula dialog box that appears, choose the variable field from the Fields list and choose the OK command button. In the example, choose the Client ID field and, in the Formula dialog box, choose the Variable ID field.

   • Choose the Records command and choose the Next Record option button from the list. Your macro should look like the one in Figure 13.16.

10. Choose the OK command button to save the macro.

11. Choose the **New** command button to create the third macro.

12. In the Macro **Name** text box, type a name for the second macro. In the example, type **Renum3**.

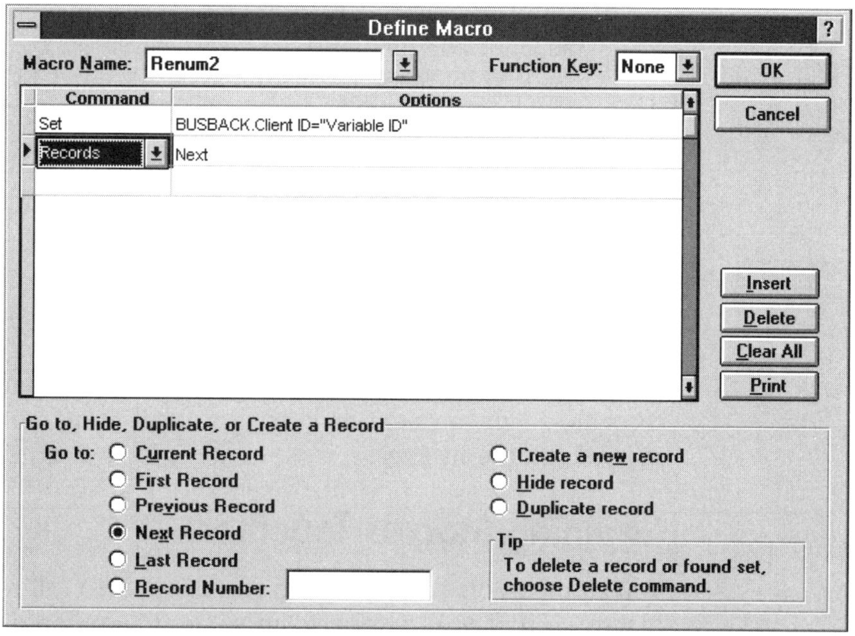

Figure 13.16

The second renumbering macro.

Figure 13.17

The third
renumbering
macro.

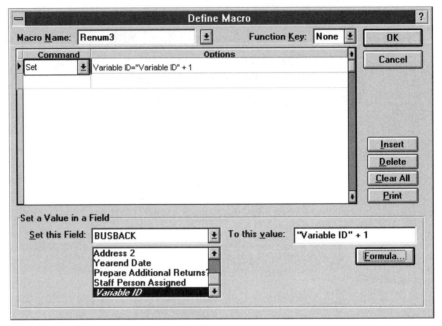

- Increment the value of the variable field by choosing the Set command, choosing the variable field, and clicking on the Formula command button. In the Formula dialog box that appears, choose the variable field from the Fields list, add 1 to it, and choose the OK command button. In the example, choose the Client ID field and, in the Formula dialog box, choose the Variable ID field. The formula should read **"Variable ID"+ 1**. Your macro should look like the one in Figure 13.17.

13. Choose the OK command button to save the macro.

14. Choose the **D**one command to close the Macros dialog box.

To renumber your records, you would run Renum1, Renum2, and Renum3. Then, you would run Renum2 and Renum3 again until all your records were renumbered. Running these macros manually would be as time-consuming as manually renumbering your records, so in the next section, you will learn how to make the macros run themselves.

Chaining Macros Together

You can tell Lotus Approach to run one macro followed by another macro so that you can perform several sequential actions. In the example, we just created three macros that will renumber records. We can chain these macros together so that they will automatically run themselves until all records are renumbered. When we chain them together, Renum1 will run and then start Renum2, and Renum2 will run and then start Renum3. Then, Renum3 will run and then start Renum2 again. Lotus Approach will continuously run Renum2 and then Renum3 until all records are renumbered. Whenever you run macros in a circular fashion similar to the one just described, you are running *loop* macros. If you defined the macros properly, Lotus Approach will simply quit running the macros after cycling through all the records in the database.

To chain macros, first create all the macros you want to chain. Then, follow these steps:

1. Open the database containing the macros you want to chain. In the example, open BUSBACK.

2. Open the **Tools** menu and choose the **Macros** command. The Macros dialog box appears.

3. Highlight the macro you want to run first and choose the **Edit** command. In the example, choose **Renum1**. The Define Macro dialog box appears

4. Move to the bottom of the command list.

5. Add the Run command and choose the **R**un macro option button. Open the list box and choose the macro you want to run second from the list box. In the example, choose Renum2 from the list box (see Fig. 13.18).

6. Choose the OK command button.

7. Repeat steps 3–5, choosing the macros you want to run in order and adding a Run command to run the next macro. In the example, edit Renum2 next and add a run command, selecting Renum3 from the **R**un Macro list box. Then, edit Renum3 and choose Renum2 from the **R**un Macro list box. Don't forget to choose the OK command button after setting up each chain.

8. Choose the Done command button.

To renumber the records in the database, switch to Browse mode, find all the records and move to the first record. Then, open the Tools menu and choose the **R**un Macro command. Choose the first

Figure 13.18

The first macro after adding the command to chain.

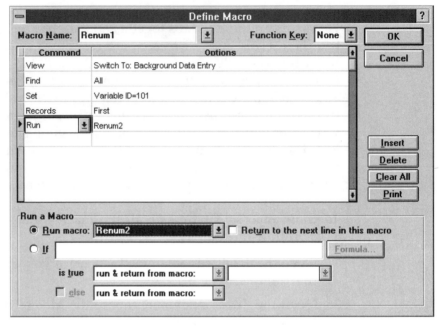

macro in the renumbering series; in the example, choose Renum1. Lotus Approach will renumber the records in the database without skipping any numbers. Since these macros do not reset the serial number for the ID number field in the Field Definition Options dialog box, when you add a new record, it will continue with the next sequential number. You should periodically run the renumbering macros; if you want, you can also reset the serial number for the ID number field immediately after renumbering records.

Setting Database Options

You can change a variety of the default settings in Lotus Approach. For example, if you usually change the font Lotus Approach uses for both field contents and field labels, you can permanently set up your selections as the default. The settings you make will affect *future* views, not views you have already created.

To change options:

1. Open the **Tools** menu and choose the **Preferences** command. The Preferences dialog box appears (see Fig. 13.19).

Figure 13.19

The Preferences dialog box.

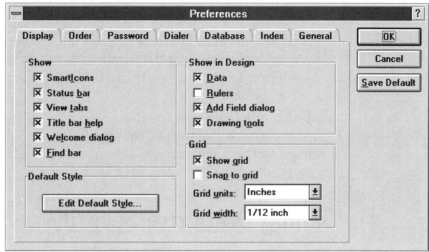

2. Use the panels as follows:

- On the Display panel, you can choose the items that will appear on-screen, such as the SmartIcons and the Welcome dialog box. You also can edit the default named style to change its characteristics permanently.

- On the Order panel, you can define, for any database, the default sort order you want to maintain.

- On the Password panel, you can assign passwords for the Lotus Approach file, and you can set read/write passwords and read-only passwords for particular databases.

- On the Dialer panel, you can set up your modem settings so that you can have Lotus Approach dial a phone number and connect to a modem.

- On the Database panel, you can stop users from updating a database by making all the fields in a database read-only. You also can choose a character set and compress a dBASE or FoxPro database.

- On the Index panel, you can set up indices for dBASE and FoxPro databases.

- On the General panel, you can decide, for example, what key to use to move between fields in Browse mode, whether to show the Add Field dialog box after adding a new field, and whether to show a Cancel Macro dialog box while macros are running. In addition, network users may want to download data before previewing (to send, to a workstation, a fresh copy of the database) and use optimistic record locking so that two users can update the same record at the same time.

3. To save the settings for the current work session in Lotus Approach, choose the OK command button. To change the settings so that they are available in all view files for all future work sessions, choose the Save Default command button.

Setting Database Security

You can set a password for your database so that only those users who know the password can open or update any view file associated with the database.

To set a database password, you use the Password panel of the Preferences dialog box (see Fig. 13.20).

- If you want to protect the design of the views in the file, place an "X" in the Password for this Approach file check box and type a password. You can also set this password from the Save As dialog box.

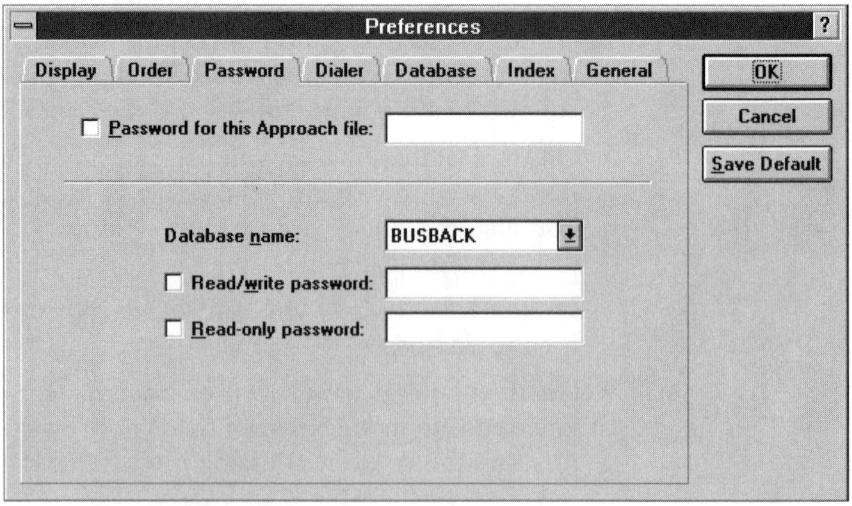

Figure 13.20

The Password panel of the Preferences dialog box.

- Place an "X" in the Read/write password check box and type a password in the text box to give users who know the password complete access to your file.

- If you want to restrict updating of any information in the file, place an "X" in the Read-only password and type a password. If you assign a read-only password, you should also assign a read/write password, so that at least one person can update the file.

The next person who tries to open the view file will be asked for the password.

Customizing the SmartIcon Bar

You can modify the default SmartIcon bar or you can create your own SmartIcon bar to support the way you work. If you create your own SmartIcon bar, it will appear in the SmartIcon bar pop-up list at the right edge of the status bar.

To create a SmartIcon bar or modify an existing SmartIcon bar:

1. Open any view file.

2. Switch to mode for which you want to create or modify a SmartIcon bar.

3. Open the Tools menu and choose the SmartIcons command. The SmartIcons dialog box appears (see Fig. 13.21). The list of SmartIcons on the right displays the current version of the selected SmartIcon bar in the order the SmartIcons appear on the bar.

Tip

If you start from Design mode, you can open the list box at the top of the dialog box and choose either the Label set or the Text set of SmartIcons

---

4. To remove a SmartIcon from the list, drag it from the current set to the Available icons list.

5. To reorder the SmartIcons, drag them within the bar.

Figure 13.21

The SmartIcons dialog box showing the Default Browse SmartIcon bar.

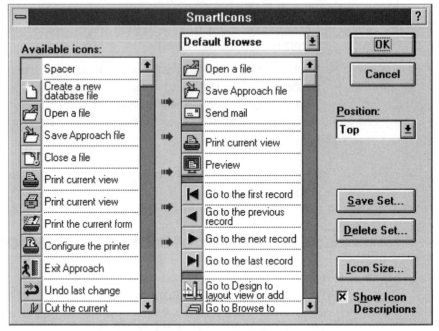

6. To add a SmartIcon, find the SmartIcon you want to add in the list of available icons on the left and drag it to the location you want it to appear in the list on the right.

7. You can change the location on-screen of the SmartIcon bar using the **Position** list box.

8. You can change the size of the SmartIcons using the **Icon Size** command button.

9. You can delete a set of SmartIcons by choosing the **Delete Set** command button.

10. After you finish making adjustments, choose the **Save Set** command button. The Save Set of SmartIcons dialog box appears (see Fig. 13.22).

11. In the **Name** of set text box, type the name you want to appear in the SmartIcons pop-up list on the status bar. To make a set easy to identify, include in its name the mode (Design, Browse, etc.) for which you created it.

12. In the **File** name text box, type a name for the set. Do not include an extension. (Lotus Approach automatically assigns an extension of .SMI to sets of SmartIcons.)

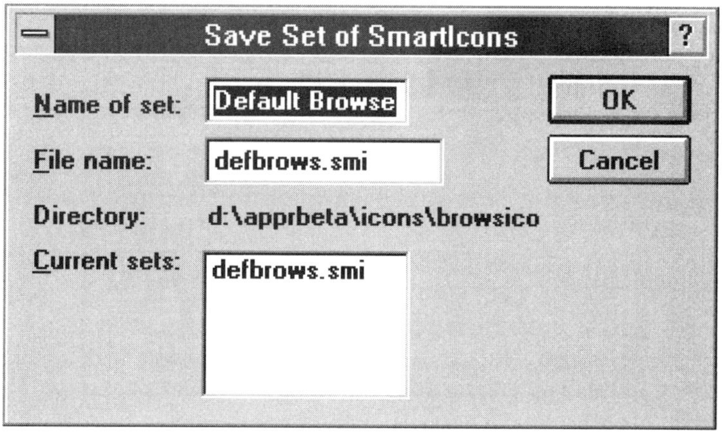

Figure 13.22

The Save Set
of SmartIcons
dialog box.

13. Choose the OK command button. Lotus Approach redisplays the SmartIcons dialog box.

14. Choose the OK command button to activate the select SmartIcon set.

Creating Custom Menus

Lotus Approach comes with a set of short menus you can use if you want, or you can create your own set of menus.

To switch to a different set of menus or to create a new set of menus:

1. Switch to Design mode.

2. Open the **T**ools menu and choose the **C**ustomize Menus command. The Customize Menus dialog box appears (see Fig. 13.23).

3. To switch to a new set of menus, highlight the menu set and choose the **D**one command button. To switch back, repeat steps 1 and 2.

4. To create a new set of menus, choose the **N**ew command button. The Define Custom Menu Bar dialog box appears (see Fig. 13.24).

5. In the **N**ame the custom menu bar text box, type a name for your menu set.

Figure 13.23

The Customize
Menus dialog
box.

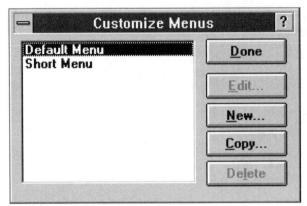

6. Define the first top-level menu (top-level menus appear in the menu bar), by clicking on the first line under the Menu Type heading, opening the list box, and choosing a menu. Next to the menu, in the Menu Name column, type a name for the menu and choose the **Add** menu command button.

7. Repeat step 5 for each top-level menu. You can remove any menus you add by mistake by selecting them and choosing the **Delete** Menu command button. You can change the order of menus by dragging them.

Figure 13.24

The Define
Custom Menu
Bar dialog
box.

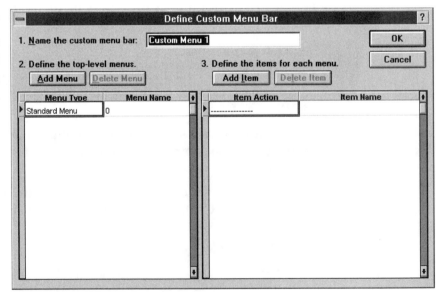

8. Define the items you want to appear on each top-level menu by selecting the top-level menu, clicking in the Item Action column to open the list box, and choosing an item. In the Item Name column, you can change the name that appears on the menu.

9. Repeat Step 7 for each item you want on a particular top-level menu. Then, switch to a different top-level menu and add items to that menu.

10. When you finish creating your custom menu, choose the OK command button.

11. To use your new custom menu, highlight it and then choose the Done command button.

Chapter Summary

In this chapter, you learned how to create macros. You learned how to create a macro to switch from one view to another, and you learned how to run a macro from a menu, using a function key, or by assigning it to a button. You learned how to create a menu system in Lotus Approach using buttons and macros. You learned how to assign find and sort functions to macros, how to use macros to renumber records, and how to chain macros together so that Lotus Approach will automatically run one macro after another. You learned how to set global database options and database security, how to create your own SmartIcon bar or modify an existing SmartIcon bar, and how to create your own set of custom menus.

In the next chapter, you will learn how to exchange information with Lotus Approach and with other applications.

CHAPTER

14

Exchanging Data in Lotus Approach

Because Lotus Approach has no proprietary file format, you can exchange data with a wide variety of database programs. In most cases, you can directly open a database created in another database program, or you can add information from another database to a database in Lotus Approach.

In this chapter, you will learn to copy information in Lotus Approach either within the same view file, to a new view file, or to a new database.

In addition to copying information, you will learn how to import information from another database and how to import views from one Lotus Approach file into another Lotus Approach file. You will also learn how to export information from a Lotus Approach file. Both of these techniques involve mapping fields from one database to another.

You will also learn how to connect Lotus Approach to other applications, using object linking and embedding.

Copying Information in Lotus Approach

As you have seen so far, one view file (.APR file) can contain many views (layouts for forms, reports, form letters, mailing labels, worksheets, and crosstabs). All of the views within a particular view file are available to any user working in that view file. Under certain conditions, you may wish to copy information while in Lotus Approach. You can copy information in Lotus Approach in one of three ways:

- You may want to create a report or form that closely resembles a report or form you already created. Within the same database and view file, you can copy views so that you can use the copies as a foundation to build a new view.

- On occasion, you may want to limit access to certain views within a database; you can do so by creating a separate view file attached to the same database and deleting any forms, reports, and so on that you don't want available.

- You may wish to create a new database that largely resembles an existing database. You can copy the views contained in one view file to an entirely new database and view file. When you copy a database, you can include only the views, or you can include the data as well.

Copying a View

In Chapter 9, you learned to copy a report to use it as the foundation for a new report. You can also copy forms and other views in the same .APR file to create new views using the same basic process.

Tip
Unfortunately, you cannot copy views from one .APR file to another. Instead, you can import the views contained in one .APR file to another .APR file, as you will learn later in this chapter.

In conjunction with the sample databases, Chapter 2 contained a discussion concerning handling individual clients for a CPA firm. One possible method for tracking individual clients is to include them in the same database as the business clients and create a second data entry form in the same view file to enter information for individual clients. Be aware that if you use this method to handle individual clients in the example databases, you will lose control over data entry verification. This issue is discussed in more detail later in this section.

The data entry form you use to enter information about individual clients into the database differs somewhat from the data entry form we created for business clients. Since the two forms will look almost identical, you can copy the Background Data Entry form in the BUSBACK database and then modify the appropriate fields and even add fields as needed.

To copy a form:

1. Switch to the database that contains the form you want to copy and view that form. In the example, switch to the BUSBACK database and make sure you are viewing the Background Data Entry form.

2. Switch to Design mode if necessary.

3. Open the **E**dit menu and choose the **D**uplicate Form command. Lotus Approach makes a copy of the form, giving it the name "Copy of..." and including the original form's name.

4. To rename the form, open the Info box and change the form name on the Basics panel as well as in the Settings for list box. In the example, type **Individual Data Entry**.

If you plan to use this method to handle individual clients in the example database, you need to make some changes to the Individual Data Entry form to make it work better for individual clients:

• Change the title at the top of the screen to reflect the proper data entry form.

• Change the Company Name field so that it is neither unique nor required.

• Remove the Year End field.

• Add a memo field to the Individual Data Entry form to store the names of relatives whose individual tax returns are prepared by the CPA. The tax laws require that taxes be calculated differ-

ently if unearned income of children exceeds an amount specified by the IRS. Therefore, we need to know the names of all
children for a given set of parents and the names of all siblings
for each child. You can store this information in a memo field
that will appear on the Individual Data Entry form only.

Tip

As mentioned earlier in this section and in Chapter 2, you lose
control over data entry verification if you use one view file to
handle both business and individual clients. When you make
changes to the options for a given field, you are not changing the
options in a particular view; you are changing the the options for the
field in *every* view in the view file. When you change the Company
Name field so that its contents don't need to be unique. You want to
be sure that the user is not required to complete the field, Lotus
Approach applies the changes to both the Individual Data Entry form
and the Background Data Entry form that you will continue to use for
business clients. When you enter business records, you would like
Lotus Approach to verify that the Company Name is unique and the
user completed the field. You want to avoid permitting users to enter
records that might be duplicates or missing critical information.
When you enter Individual client records (as opposed to Business
client records), you don't want restrictions on the Company Name
field. Unfortunately, any restrictions you apply to a field apply to all
views within the view file. Therefore, if you handle your individual
clients in the same view file as your business clients, you must remove
restrictions and sacrifice control over data entry.

To change the title at the top of the screen, double-click on the text
object in Design mode and change the title of the form.

You add a memo field to the form the same way you add any other
type of field to a form or report—open the Field Definition dialog
box (from the **Create** menu) and define a memo field. Then, drag
the field from the Add Field window to the location where you
want the memo field to appear.

You change the Company Name field attributes in the Options portion of the Field Definition dialog box. Double-click the field to
open the Info box and choose the Field Definition command button

from the Basics panel. When the Field Definition dialog box appears, choose the **O**ptions command button.

Don't forget to save the new view.

Creating a Second .APR file

For any database, you can create a second view file. Within the second view file, you can create views (forms, reports, form letters, mailing labels, worksheets, or crosstabs) that use the same fields in the database, but are independent of the views in the first view file. Using a second view file is a good way to limit access to a particular form or report, because you can delete views you don't want available and tell a particular user to access the database through the view file that does not contain the specified views. Using multiple view files attached to the same database, you can give different users access to different combinations of views. When you use this method, you create only one actual database, which stores all the information you need.

In the example, using a second view file is a good way to set up a system to handle individual clients. You create a second view file that contains all of the same views you already created. Then, in the second view file, you make modifications to support working with individual clients.

To create a second view file:

1. Set up all the views you want using the first view file that Lotus Approach automatically supplied when you first created the database. Save the views as usual.

2. Open the **F**ile menu and choose the Save **A**s command. The Save Approach File As dialog box appears (see Fig. 14.1).

3. In the File **n**ame text box, type a new view file name. In the example, type **PERBACK.APR**.

4. In the option buttons in the Databases box, choose **.A**PR file only.

5. Choose the OK command button. Lotus Approach creates a new .APR file that contains all the same views as the original view file. Understand that you are also accessing the same database and therefore the data in that database.

Figure 14.1

The Save Approach File As dialog box.

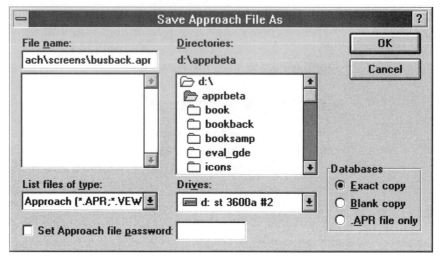

You modify and delete views in the new .APR file as needed. In the example, you can use the Background Data Entry form in PER-BACK, with some modifications, to enter information for individual clients.

First, change the name of the Background Data Entry form in PER-BACK to help users more readily distinguish the view file in which they are working. Display the Background Data Entry form in PERBACK and use the Info box to change the name and title of the form to Individual Data Entry.

Next, you should make some modifications to the Individual Data Entry form:

- Change the Company Name field to Employer Name.
- Change the Last Name field so that it is a required field.
- Change First Name field so that it is both unique and required.
- Add a memo field for children and siblings.

Add the memo field using the Field Definition dialog box (open it from the **Create** menu). To change the the First Name and Last Name fields, highlight each of them and choose the **Options** command button and set their options.

Don't forget to save the new view.

Copying Databases

You may wish to create a database that closely resembles a database you have already created. You can copy a database and all its fields, and you can choose to copy the data in the database or simply create a new, empty database. You might want to use this method to handle individual clients in the CPA system. You could copy each of the databases we have already created without the data in the databases. Then you could join the new databases in the same way we joined the original databases.

When you copy databases, you create a new database file, and Lotus Approach automatically creates a new view file for that database that contains all the same views but *not* the data. The new database is completely separate from the original database.

To handle the individual clients, we could create a database call INDVBACK to store the background information for individual clients. The fields in INDVBACK will be similar to the fields in BUSBACK, but again, some of the fields will be defined a little differently. Again, because of the relational capabilities of Lotus Approach, we can join both BUSBACK and INDVBACK to all the other databases; with this setup, we can use the same views to produce forms and reports for both business and individual clients.

To create the INDVBACK database, copy the BUSBACK database:

1. Open the BUSBACK database.

2. Open the File menu and choose the Save As command. The Save Approach File As dialog box appears (see Fig. 14.2)

3. In the File name text box, type **INDVBACK**.

4. In the Databases option box at the right edge of the dialog box, choose the Blank copy option button to copy the database *without* copying its data. In the previous section, we used the .APR option button to create a second .APR file that uses the same data in the original database; you would use the Exact copy option button to make another copy of both the database *and* its data.

5. Choose the OK command button. The Save Database As dialog box, which closely resembles the Save Approach File As dialog box, appears.

Figure 14.2

The Save
Approach File
As dialog box.

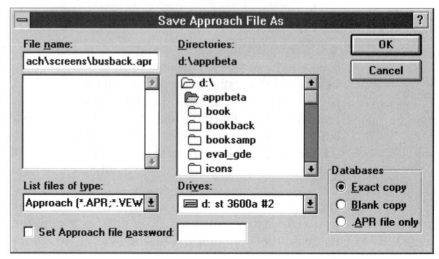

6. In the File **N**ame text box, type **INDVBACK**.

7. (Optional) If you created a file type other than DBASE IV, open the List files of type list box and choose the correct database format.

8. Choose the OK command button. Lotus Approach redisplays the Save Database As dialog box once for each database joined to the original database you are copying (in the example, BUS-BACK). If you rename each of the databases you joined, Lotus Approach creates new database files for them and maintains the joined relationships between the new databases. In the example, rename the joined databases as follows:

BUSMAIL   INDVMAIL

BUSRETS   INDVRETS

BUSSERV   INDVSERV

On-screen, the file you are viewing is now named INDVBACK.APR and looks just like BUSBACK.APR. INDVBACK.APR has not replaced BUSBACK.APR—you just made an empty copy of BUS-BACK.APR and called it INDVBACK.APR. You can still open BUSBACK.APR when needed.

You need to make the same changes to the Background Data Entry form in INDVBACK that we made when we created a second view file. See the previous section for specific information on the changes you should make.

Don't forget to save when you finish working.

Setting Up a Database to Track Estimated Tax Payments

Regardless of the way you choose to handle individual clients, to handle them effectively, you may want to set up an additional database that you will link, as a detail database, to the main background database. The new database will include information to track estimated tax payment amounts and due dates.

In the PMTS database, define the fields shown in Table 14.1 with the associated specifications.

Importing and Exporting

You can import from and export to any database program that can save a file in one of the following file formats:

- dBASE III+

Table 14.1 Fields for the PMTS Database		
Field Name	**Field Type**	**Field Length**
ID	Numeric	12 (set the decimal place to 0)
FORM	Text	10
Payment 1 Date	Date	Not Applicable
Payment 2 Date	Date	Not Applicable
Payment 3 Date	Date	Not Applicable
Payment 4 Date	Date	Not Applicable
Payment 1 Amount	Date	Not Applicable
Payment 2 Amount	Date	Not Applicable
Payment 3 Amount	Date	Not Applicable
Payment 4 Amount	Date	Not Applicable

- dBASE IV
- Paradox 3.5
- FoxPro 2.1
- SQL

In addition, you can import data from Lotus 1-2-3 and Microsoft Excel spreadsheets and data from ASCII-delimited files.

When you want to import data, you place Lotus Approach in Browse mode. Lotus Approach matches fields between the two databases (called *mapping*) and adds the new records to the end of the database. When you want to import views, you place Lotus Approach in Design mode.

Importing Data from Another Database

As long as data in a database is stored in one of the file formats Lotus Approach recognizes, you don't need to import the data into Lotus Approach; you can simply open the file in Lotus Approach. Alternatively, you may need to import data into one database from another database. You can import data from a database created by another database program or from another Lotus Approach database. You can update existing records in the database, or add the data from the import file as new records to the end of the current database. You can even do a combination of the two—update existing records and add new ones.

If you update existing records, Lotus Approach compares data that you specify to determine matches in both databases. If the data match, Lotus Approach updates the existing record in the current database. If the data do not match, Lotus Approach does not update. You can specify that only certain fields be updated.

If you add new records, Lotus Approach simply adds records to your existing database; if you start with 75 records and import (by adding) 25 records, your existing database will contain 100 records after importing (some of which could duplicate others, since Lotus Approach did not compare any information in the two databases).

If you both update existing records and add new records, Lotus Approach performs both operations. If data in the two databases match, Lotus Approach updates records in the existing database; if data do not match, Lotus Approach adds new records to the end of the existing database.

To import data from another database:

1. Open the database (or one of its view files) into which you want to import.

2. Make sure you are in Browse mode.

3. Open the File menu and choose the Import Data command. The Import Data dialog box appears (see Fig. 14.3).

4. If necessary, open the List files of type list box and choose a different file format.

    -   If you chose a Text file type, you see the Text File Options dialog box (see Fig. 14.4), which you use to specify the character that separates the fields in the file.

    -   If you chose Oracle, SQL Server, DB2, or ODBC:dBase files, you see the Connect dialog box (see Fig. 14.5), which you use to specify the connections to the server application.

5. Use the Drives and Directories list boxes to navigate to the appropriate directory.

Figure 14.3

The Import Data dialog box.

	Import Data	?
File name:	**Directories:**	**OK**
*.dbf	d:\apprbeta	**Cancel**
	d:\	**Connect...**
	apprbeta	**Disconnect**
	book	
	bookback	
	booksamp	
	eval_gde	
	icons	
List files of type:	**Drives:**	
dBASE IV [*.DBF]	d: st 3600a #2	
File information:		
Select a file to import.		

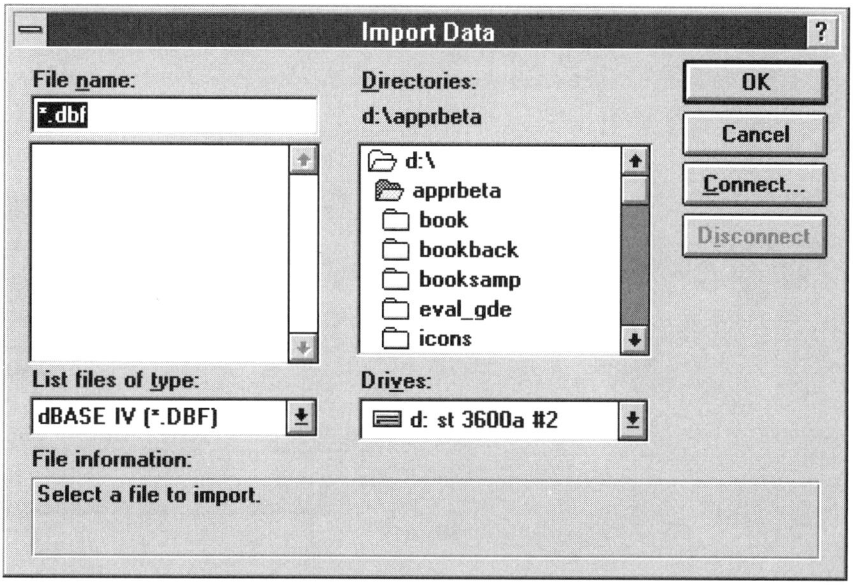

Figure 14.4

The Text File Options dialog box.

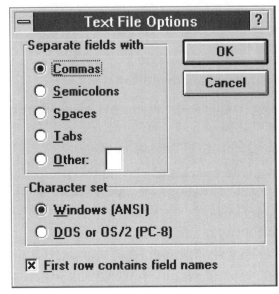

6. In the File name text box, select the database containing the information you want to import.

7. Choose the OK command button. The Import Setup dialog box appears (see Fig. 14.6). The fields on the right side of the dialog box appear in the file you are importing. The fields on the left side of the dialog box appear in the database into which you are importing.

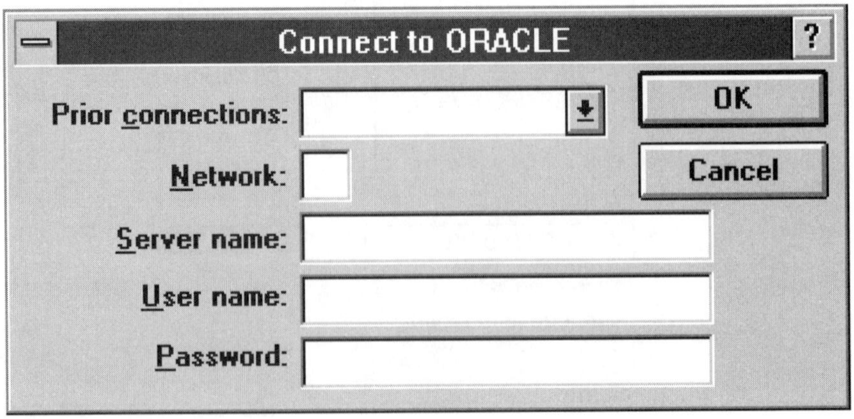

Figure 14.5

The Connect to dialog box.

Figure 14.6

The Import Setup dialog box.

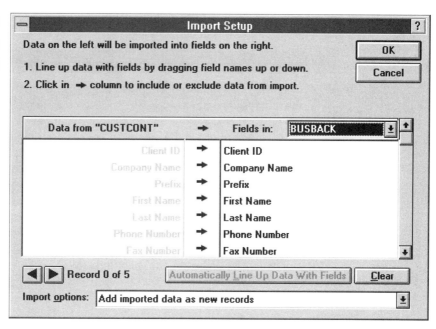

8. If you don't see arrows in the column between the two sets of fields, you must identify for Lotus Approach the fields in the import file that correspond to fields in the current database. Line up the fields on each side of the dialog box by dragging the fields on the right side of the dialog box until they appear alongside the correct field on the left side of the dialog box. Then, click in the column between the two sides of the dialog box to place an arrow in the column. You can exclude a field (and the data in it) from the import by clicking on the arrow that already appears in the column.

Tip

You can map fields in the import file to fields in databases joined to the current database; open the Fields in list box and select a different database.

---

9. Use the Import options list box to specify whether you want to add records to the end of the current database, update existing records, or both.

10. After mapping all the fields, choose the OK command button.

> **Tip**
>
> In Chapter 13, you learned how to create three macros and a variable field to renumber records. You also can use the technique of importing data to maintain an incrementing number field like the Client ID number field in the sample databases. From the database containing the records you want to renumber, open the File menu and choose the Save As command. Save the current database under a new name and choose the Blank copy option button to create a blank copy of your database. In the new database, select the field you want to renumber and open the Field Definition dialog box. Choose the Options command button and reset the starting number for the records. Then, import the data from the original database, but do *not* import the incrementing number field.

Importing Views from Another Approach Database

Earlier in this chapter, you learned how to create a second view file for a database. Sometimes, you need to combine views from multiple view files into one view file.

To import all the views from one view file into another view file:

1. Open the view file into which you want to import views.

2. Switch to Design mode.

3. Open the **F**ile menu and choose the Import Approach File command. The Import Approach File dialog box appears (see Fig. 14.7).

4. In the File **n**ame text box, select the view file you want to import and choose the OK command button. The Import Approach File Setup dialog box appears (see Fig. 14.8), which is very similar to and functions just like the Import Setup dialog box you saw in the previous section. The fields on the left side of the dialog box appear *in* the view file you are importing. The fields on the right side of the dialog box appear in the view file *into which* you are importing.

Figure 14.7

The Import
Approach File
dialog box.

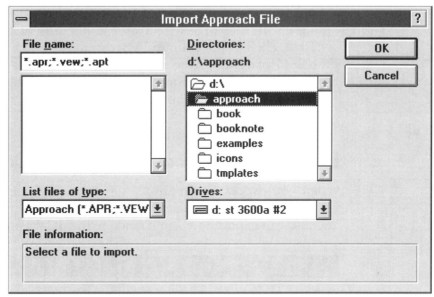

5. If you don't see arrows in the column between the two sets of
    fields, you must identify for Lotus Approach the fields in the
    view file on the left side of the dialog box that correspond to
    fields in the view file on the right side of the dialog box. Line
    up the fields on each side of the dialog box by dragging the

Figure 14.8

The Import
Approach File
Setup dialog
box.

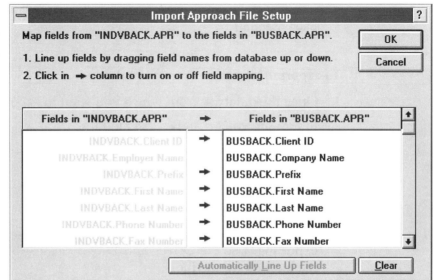

fields on the right side of the dialog box until they appear alongside the correct field on the left side of the dialog box. Then, click in the column between the two sides of the dialog box to place an arrow in the column. You can exclude a field (and the data in it) from the import by clicking on the arrow that already appears in the column.

6. After mapping all the fields, choose the OK command button.

Exporting Data from an Approach Database

When you export information from a Lotus Approach database, you can export all the records in the database or records you select. You also can export only some fields in the database.

Tip

You cannot export variable fields or calculated fields that perform a summary calculation. You can export other types of calculated fields, but Lotus Approach converts their values into a set text, numeric, date, or time value. You can export PicturePlus fields, but only another Lotus Approach database file can read them. You cannot export macros. If you want to keep an existing file intact, complete with calculated fields, PicturePlus fields, and macros, don't export the file. Instead, create a skeleton of the file—a database with no records—and then import data into it. To create the skeleton file, open the File menu and choose the Save As command. In the Save As dialog box, supply a new name and choose the Blank copy option button.

To export information from a database:

1. Open the database from which you want to export information.

2. Make sure you are in Browse mode.

3. (Optional) If you want to export only selected records, create a Find request and locate the records you want to export.

4. Open the File menu and choose the Export Data command. The Export Data dialog box appears (see Fig. 14.9)

5. Use the File name text box to specify the file to which you are exporting. Use the Drives and Directories list boxes to specify the location for the file.

Figure 14.9

The Export Data dialog box.

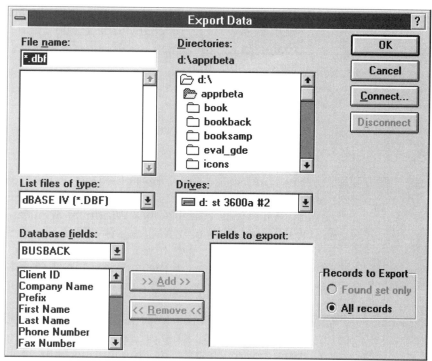

6. From the Database fields list box, select the database containing the fields you want to export.

7. Select each the fields you want to export and choose the **Add** command button.

8. If you used the Find command to locate a specific set of records, choose either the All Records option button or the Found Set Only option button.

9. If necessary, open the List files of type list box and choose a file type.

10. Choose the OK command button. Under most conditions, Lotus Approach simply moves the records you selected from the original file to the new file. If you changed the type of file, you may see another dialog box before the export takes place:

   • If you opened the List files of type list box and chose a text file type, you see the Text File Options dialog box, which you use to specify the character that separates the fields in the file.

- If you opened the List files of type list box and chose Oracle, SQL Server, DB2, or ODBC:dBase Files, you see the Connect dialog box, which you use to specify the connections to the server application.

Connecting to OLE-Capable Applications

You can connect Lotus Approach to other OLE-capable applications in one of two ways: you can link objects or you can embed objects. When you connect two Windows applications, one application is called the *server* and one is called the *container* (you may have seen the term *client* instead of *container*). The server application creates the object and the container application uses the object. Lotus Approach can be either a server or a container application.

When you connect Lotus Approach to another application by linking an object created in the other application, the object is used in an Lotus Approach database but not actually stored in the database; instead, when the object is needed, Lotus Approach calls it.

When you connect Lotus Approach to another application by embedding an object created in the other application, the object is used in an Lotus Approach *and* stored in the Lotus Approach database.

In this section, you will learn how to create an object in Lotus Approach that you can either link or embed in another application; under these conditions, Lotus Approach acts as the server application and the application that uses the object acts as the container application.

You will also learn how to use Lotus Approach as a container application, both linking an object and embedding an object created in some other server application.

Creating an Object in Lotus Approach for Linking or Embedding

You can let your Lotus Approach database act as the server in an OLE connection. If you create an object in Lotus Approach that is then linked to another application, the object will be updated in the container application whenever it changes in your Lotus Approach database.

If you create an object in Lotus Approach that is then embedded in another application, the container application may update the object, but the changes will appear only in the container application; your Lotus Approach database will be unaffected.

You can create objects out of any view.

To create an object in Lotus Approach:

1. Open the Approach file containing the information you want to use to create the object.

2. Switch to Browse mode.

3. Switch to the view you want to use to create the object.

4. Make sure nothing is selected.

5. Open the Edit menu and choose the Copy View command. The Copy View to Clipboard dialog box appears (see Fig. 14.10).

6. If you want to create an object that contains only the current view, choose the Copy current view only option button. Otherwise, choose the Copy all views option button.

7. To include data in the object, place an "X" in the Include data check box and specify how much data: all data in the database, the last found set of records, the current record, or no data (Blank databases).

8. Choose the OK command button. Lotus Approach creates the object and places it on the Clipboard (you can't see it).

Figure 14.10

The Copy View to Clipboard dialog box.

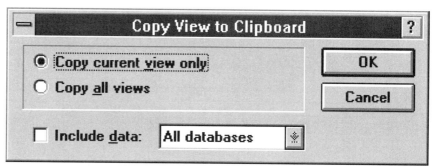

9. Switch to the container application and follow its instructions for linking or embedding.

Linking

You can create an object in any other OLE-capable application and link it to a Lotus Approach database.

To link an object to a Lotus Approach database:

1. In the server application, create the object you want to link to an Lotus Approach database.

2. Copy the object to the Clipboard and then save the file in the server application. Do not close the server application.

3. Switch to Lotus Approach and display the view file and view into which you want to link an object.

4. If you want the object to appear as a Design element in the view, switch to Design mode and click where you want the object to appear. If you want to link the object to a PicturePlus field, switch to Browse mode, go to the record on which you want to place the object, and select the Picture Plus field.

5. Open the Edit menu and choose the Paste Special command. The Paste Special dialog box appears (see Fig. 14.11).

6. Highlight the format for the object you want to link and choose the Paste Link command. Lotus Approach displays the object in the current view. Depending on the server application that

Figure 14.11

The Paste Special dialog box.

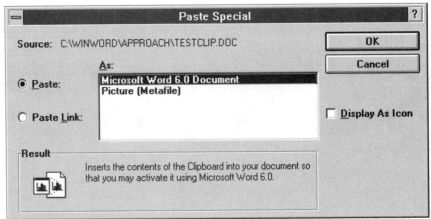

Paste Special

Source: C:\WINWORD\APPROACH\TESTCLIP.DOC

As:
- ○ **Paste:**   Microsoft Word 6.0 Document / Picture (Metafile)
- ○ **Paste Link:**

OK   Cancel

☐ **Display As Icon**

Result
 Inserts the contents of the Clipboard into your document so that you may activate it using Microsoft Word 6.0.

created the object, the object may appear as either an icon or an object.

Tip
To edit a linked object, double-click the object. Depending on the type of server application, either the server application opens or you see the menus from the server application in Lotus Approach; either way, you can edit the object. After modifying the object, choose the Update command from the File menu of the server application and close the server application.

You can modify a link in any of the following ways:

- You can change the way the object is updated from automatic updating to manual updating.
- You can update the object manually.
- You can link the object to a different file.
- You can cancel a link.

To modify a link, open the view file that contains the link. If the object is a design element, switch to Design mode. If the object is a PicturePlus field, find the record containing the object in Browse mode and select the field. Open the Edit menu and choose the Links command. From the Links dialog box, make your changes. If you change a link to manual updating, you must reopen this dialog box to update the existing link.

Embedding

You can create an object in any other OLE-capable application and embed it in a Lotus Approach database.

To embed an object in a Lotus Approach database:

1. In the server application, create the object you want to embed in a Lotus Approach database.

2. Copy the object to the Clipboard and save the file in the server application. Do not close the server application.

3. Switch to Lotus Approach and display the view file and view into which you want to embed an object.

4. If you want the object to appear as a Design element in the view, switch to Design mode and click where you want the object to appear. If you want to embed the object in a Picture-Plus field, switch to Browse mode, go to the record on which you want to place the object, and select the Picture Plus field.

5. Open the Edit menu and choose the Paste Special command. The Paste Special dialog box appears (see Fig. 14.12).

6. Highlight the format for the object you want to link and choose the Paste command. Lotus Approach displays the object in the current view. Depending on the server application that created the object, the object may appear as either an icon or an object.

Tip

To edit an embedded object, double-click the object. Depending on the type of server application, either the server application opens or you see the menus from the server application in Lotus Approach; either way, you can edit the object. After modifying the object, choose the Update command from the File menu of the server application and close the server application.

If you have not yet created the object you want to embed, you can set up the object in Lotus Approach before you create the object in the server application.

Figure 14.12

The Paste Special dialog box.

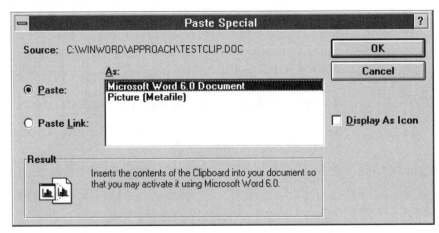

To do this:

1. Open the view file and switch to the view in which you want to embed an object.

2. If you want to embed the object as a Design element, switch to Design mode and click at the location where you want the object to appear. If you want to embed the object in a Picture-Plus field, switch to Browse mode, locate the record in which you want to embed the object, and select the PicturePlus field.

3. Open the **C**reate menu and choose the **O**bject command. The Insert Object dialog box appears (see Fig. 14.13)

4. The Object **T**ype list shows all the types of objects that you can create based on the applications installed on your computer. From the Object **T**ype list box, choose the format for the object. To create an object from a specific file, choose the Create from File option button and type the name of the file. You can use the **B**rowse command button to find the file if you can't remember its name.

5. Choose the OK command button. Depending on the type of server application, either the menus from the application appear in Lotus Approach or the server application opens.

6. Create a new object in the server application and save the object.

7. Open the server application's File menu and choose the Update command.

Figure 14.13

The Insert Object dialog box.

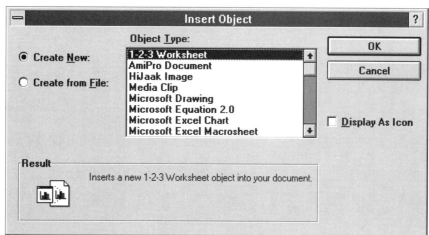

Insert Object

○ **Create New:**
○ **Create from File:**

Object **T**ype:
1-2-3 Worksheet
AmiPro Document
HiJaak Image
Media Clip
Microsoft Drawing
Microsoft Equation 2.0
Microsoft Excel Chart
Microsoft Excel Macrosheet

OK
Cancel

☐ **Display As Icon**

Result
Inserts a new 1-2-3 Worksheet object into your document.

8. Close the server application and return to Lotus Approach. The object appears in your Lotus Approach file.

Chapter Summary

In this chapter, you learned how to copy a view. You also learned how to create a second view file for a database, and you learned how to copy a database. You learned how to import and export information in Lotus Approach, and you learned how to link and embed objects created in other OLE-capable applications.

In the Appendix, you will find samples of the form view for each of the template databases that ship with Lotus Approach.

APPENDIX

Form Views of the Sample Databases

Lotus Approach contains a large series of sample databases that you can use to get ideas for building your own database. You can even use these samples as the foundation for your database. When you first open Lotus Approach, you see the Welcome to Lotus Approach dialog box (see Fig. A.1).

Figure A.1

The Welcome to Lotus Approach dialog box.

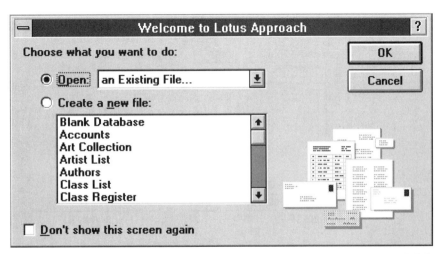

Welcome to Lotus Approach

Choose what you want to do:

OK

Cancel

⦿ **Open:** an Existing File...

○ Create a **new** file:

Blank Database
Accounts
Art Collection
Artist List
Authors
Class List
Class Register

☐ **Don't show this screen again**

If you choose to create a new file, you can select one of the sample databases. Table A.1 contains a list of the available databases and a sample of the kind of information you will find in the database. Use the table and the screen images that follow to help you find a sample database that you can use as a model for your own. Many of the databases were designed expressly to join them with other sample databases; I have tried to note these cases wherever possible.

Once you make a selection from the list in the Welcome to Lotus Approach dialog box, you see the New dialog box (see Fig. A.2).

You can use the name suggested or you can supply a different name. If you think you might want to base another database on the same sample, supply a different name. If you don't supply a different name and later discover that you want to use the same sample database again, Lotus Approach will suggest that you overwrite the first database. If the original database contains data you want to continue to use, do not overwrite the database; supply a different name in the New dialog box for the new database.

Figure A.2

The New dialog box.

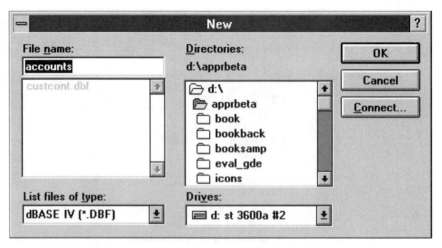

Table A.1 The Sample Databases Available in Lotus Approach

Database Name	Basic Content
Account	Account information, including name, number and type.
Art Collection	Information about artwork, including the title, the artist, the date created, and the medium. Could easily be joined with the Artists database.
Artist List	Information about artists, including name, date and place of birth, and nationality. Could easily be joined with the Art database.
Authors	Information about authors, including name, date and place of birth, and nationality.
Class List	Information about classes taught at an education institution. Fields include items such as the class title, the instructor, meeting day and time, enrollment maximum and current status, and the number of credits.
Class Register	Information about students registered in a class. Could easily be joined with the Class List database.
Collections–Details	Information about items you collect, including a category number and space to store details about the item. Could easily be joined with the Collections–Main database.
Collections–Main	Information about categories of items you collect, including category number and description. Could easily be joined with the Collections–Detail database.
Contacts–Actions	Information about contacts, including name, phone number, action item, and expected closure date. Could easily be joined to Contacts–Meetings and Contacts–Names databases.
Contacts–Meetings	Information about meetings with contacts, including date and subject of meeting. Could easily be joined to Contacts–Actions and Contacts–Names databases.
Contacts–Names	Information about each contact, including name, address, company, and phone number. Could easily be joined to Contacts–Actions and Contacts–Meetings databases.
Contracts	Information about contracts between you and clients, including client name, contract number and type, and project manager. Can be joined easily to the Expenses database.

Continued

Table A.1 The Sample Databases Available in Lotus Approach *(continued)*	
Database Name	**Basic Content**
Customer Contacts	Information about customers, including name, address, and phone number. Very similar to, but not quite as extensive as, the Contacts–Name database.
Customers	Information about customers, including company name, contact, and shipping and billing addresses.
Employees	Information about employees, including name, social security number, manager, department, and salary.
Event List	Information about events, including event name, location, date, planned attendance, actual attendance, and cost.
Expenses	Information to help you track reimbursible expenses in your business, including employee who incurred expense, contract and client to which the expense was charged, date and amount billed to the client, and date employee was reimbursed. Can be joined easily to the Contracts database.
Fixed Assets	Information to help you track the status of fixed assets, including the asset's original value, its depreciation method and rate, and its current value.
Friends and Family	Information about friends, including name, address, phone numbers, birthdays, and nicknames.
Guest List	Information about guests attending an event, including guest name, address, phone numbers, date invited, date invitation confirmed, and number in party.
Household Inventory	Information about items in your home, including their appraised value, their purchase price, and their location in your house.
Inventory	Information about items you stock for resale, including the part name and number, location, quantity on hand, reorder quantity, and quantity on order. Can be joined easily with the Products database.
Invoice–Details	Information found on the line item portion of your invoices, including item number, item description, and quantity purchased. Can be joined easily with the Invoice–Main database.
Invoice–Main	Information found on the top of an invoice, including invoice number, customer number and name, order number, shipping

Continued

Table A.1 The Sample Databases Available in Lotus Approach *(continued)*

Database Name	Basic Content
	information, and terms. Can be joined easily with the Invoice–Details database, the Customer database, and the Orders–Main database.
Letter Tracking	Information about correspondence being exchanged, including the writer, the subject, the responder, the actions promised, and the dates the actions were completed.
Library List	Information about books similar to that found in the card catalog of a library, including the title, author, publisher, ISBN number, and purchase price. Can be joined easily to the Authors database.
Mailing List	Information typically found on a mailing list, including name, address, nickname, company name, phone numbers, and date of last mailing.
Membership List	Information about members of a group, including name, address, phone numbers, and date of last payment of dues.
Musical Groups	Information about musical groups, including the group name, when formed, and number of recordings. Can be joined easily to the Musical Recordings database.
Musical Recordings	Information about recordings, including the title, artist, recording label, and year released. Can be joined easily to the Musical Groups database and the Musicians database.
Musicians	Information about performers, including name, date of birth and death, and group to which they belonged. Can be joined easily to the Musical Groups database.
Orders–Detail	Information found in the body of an order, including the item number and description, the quantity ordered, and the unit price. Can be joined easily to the Orders–Main database and the Invoice–Main database.
Orders–Main	Information found at the top of an order, including order number, customer name, shipping address, and terms. Can be joined easily to the Orders–Detail database, the Invoices–Main database, and the Customers database.
Payments	Information about payments for orders, including the payment date and amount, the invoice number, and the customer paying. Can be joined easily to the Customers database and the Invoices–Main database.

Continued

Table A.1   The Sample Databases Available in Lotus Approach *(continued)*

Database Name	Basic Content
Products	Information about products you carry in inventory, including the product number, name, and description, the supplier, the cost of the product, and the retail price. Can be joined easily to the Inventory database.
Project–List	Information about projects you are working on, including the project name, leader, start date, estimated completion date, and actual completion date. Can be joined easily to the Project–Tasks database.
Project–Tasks	Information about tasks in projects, including the project to which the task belongs, the person responsible, and dates for starting and completing the task.
Receiving Log	Information about shipments that come in, including the date sent, the sender, the recipient, the order number, and the method of shipping. Can be joined easily to the Orders–Main database.
Recipes–Ingredients	Information about ingredients used in recipes, including the recipe that uses the ingredient and the quantity. Can be joined easily with the Recipes–Main database.
Recipes–Main	Information about recipes, including the time to prepare, the number the recipe serves, and the calories contained in the recipe. Can be joined easily with the Recipes–Ingredients database.
Services–Billing	Information that appeared on bills, including the client and project billed, the employee who worked on the project, the number of hours billed, the hourly rate, and the date billed. Can be joined easily with the Customers database and the Project–List database.
Shipping Log	Information about items being shipped, including the customer name, shipping address, method of shipment, and date shipped. Can be joined easily with the Customers database.
Stocks and Bonds	Information about securities, including name, date purchased, and date sold.
Student List	Information about students, including name, address, parents' names and addresses, and major and minor areas of study. Can be joined easily with the Class Register database.

Continued

Table A.1   The Sample Databases Available in Lotus Approach *(continued)*

Database Name	Basic Content
Student Records	Information about students enrolled in classes, including the student name and the class name.
Suppliers	Information about suppliers, including name, contact, address, and phone number. Can be joined easily with the Products database.
Transactions	Information about transactions made, including the amount, the account against which the transaction was made, and whether the transaction is taxable. Can be joined easily with the Stocks and Bonds database and the Accounts database. Could also be joined to the Contact Name database if you add an Account ID Number field to that database.
Video Library	Information about VCR tapes, including the title, lead actor and actress, producer, director, year released, and length.
Weight Training	Information about weight training, including name, workout number, number of sets, and repetitions per set. Can be joined easily with the Workout Log database.
Wine List	Information about wines, including the name, the vineyard from which it came, the variety, vintage, and country of origin.
Workout Log	Information about workouts, including name, exercise activity, and workout duration. Can be joined easily with the Weight Training database.

Figure A.3

The Account default form view.

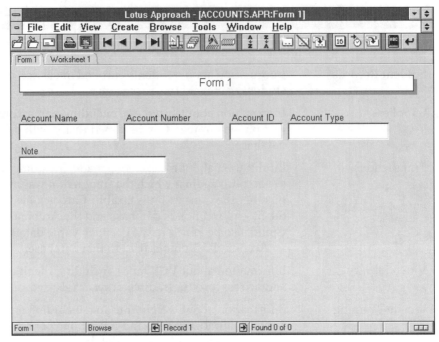

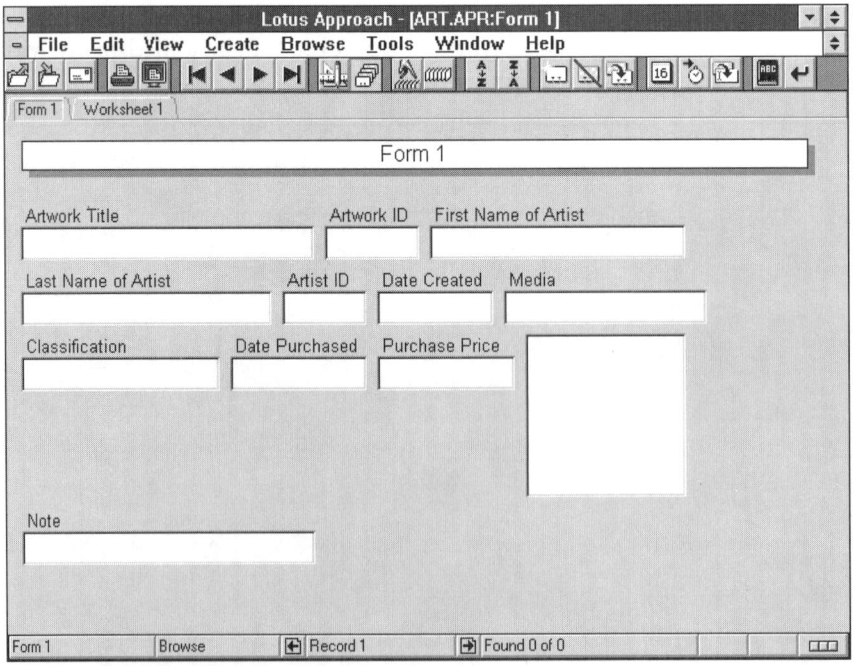

Figure A.4

The Art Collection default form view.

Figure A.5

The Artist List default form view.

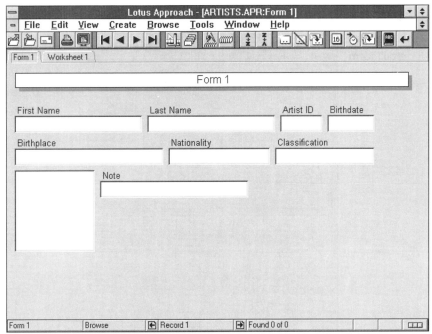

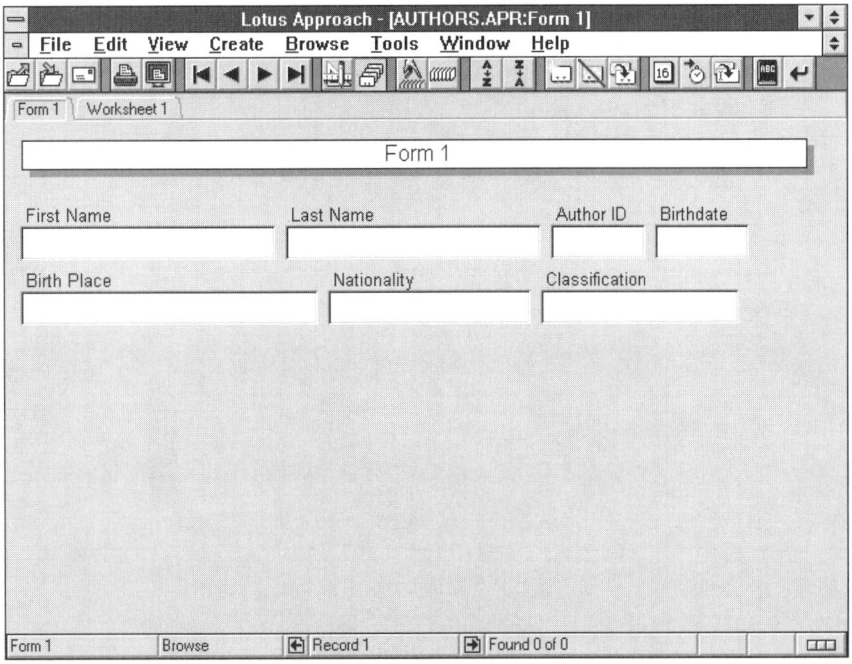

Figure A.6

The Authors default form view.

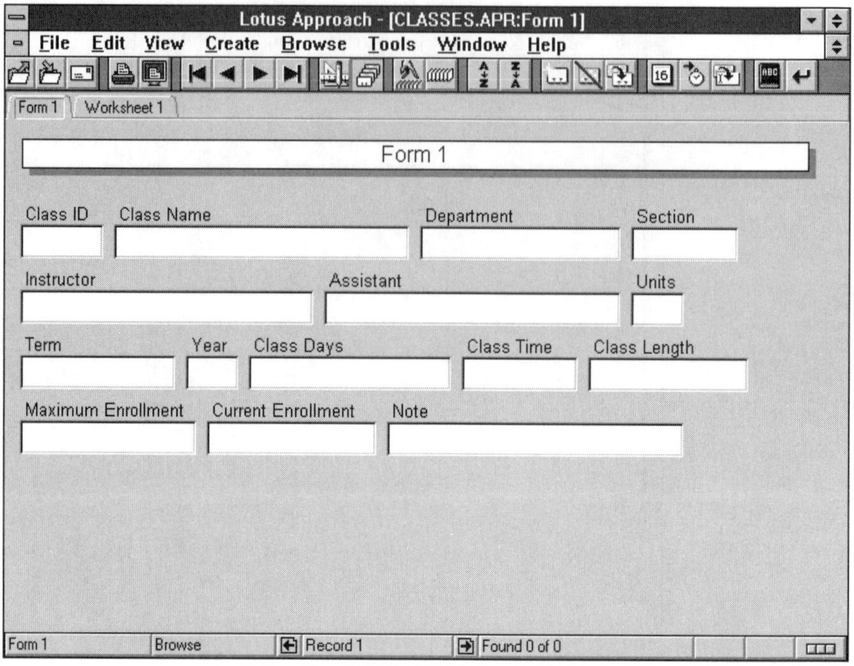

Figure A.7

The Class List default form view.

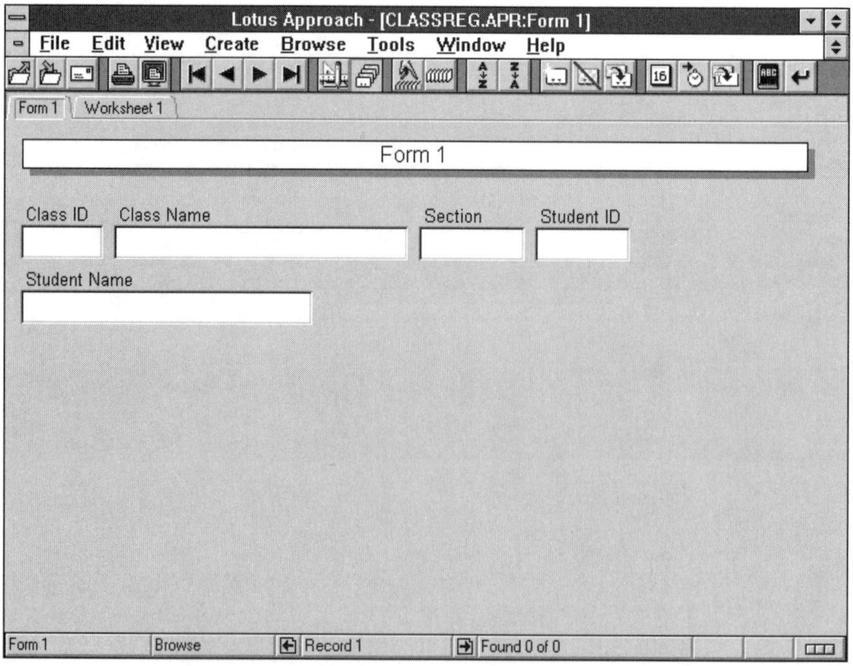

Figure A.8

The Class Register default form view.

Figure A.9

The
Collections–
Detail default
form view.

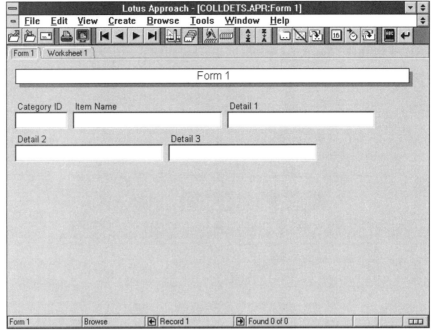

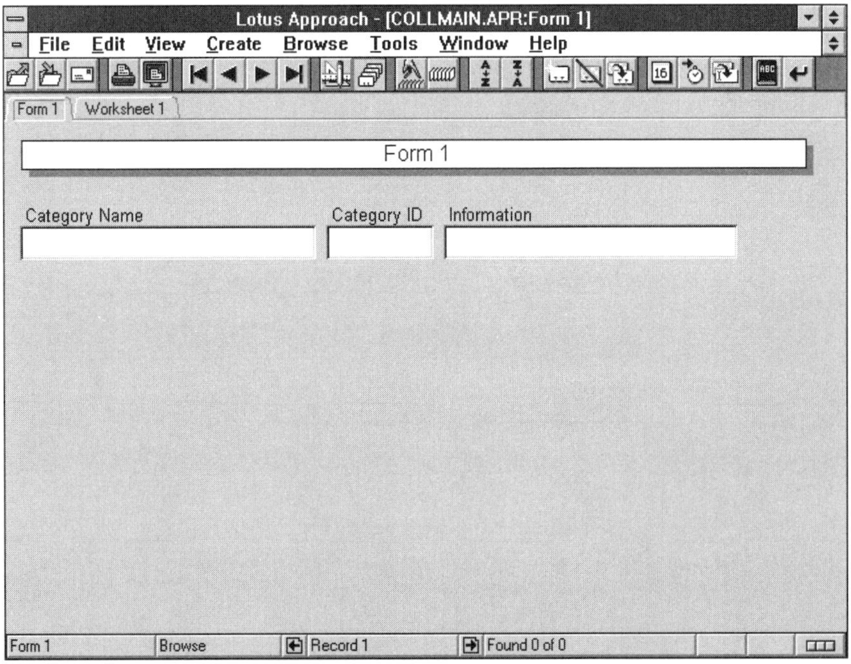

Figure A.10

The
Collections–
Main default
form view.

Figure A.11

The Contacts–
Actions default
form view.

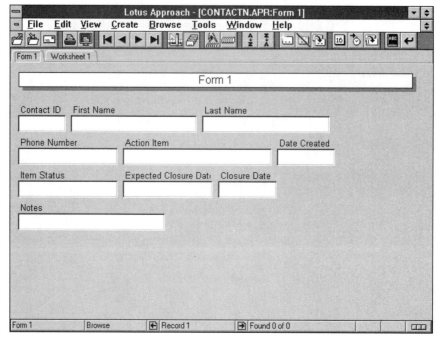

Figure A.12

The Contacts–
Meetings
default form
view.

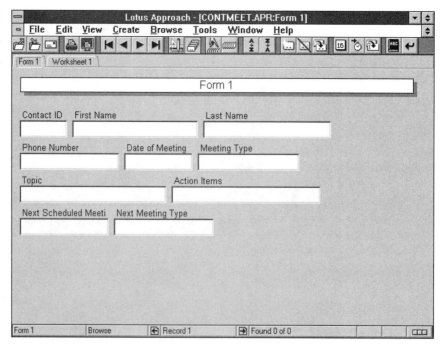

Figure A.13

The Contacts–
Names default
form view.

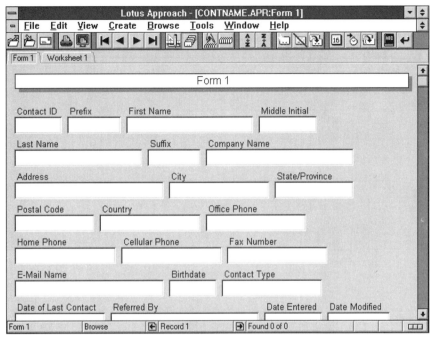

Figure A.14

The Contracts
default form
view.

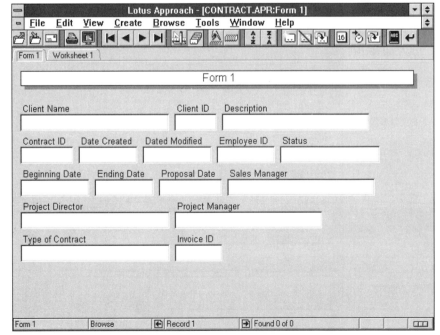

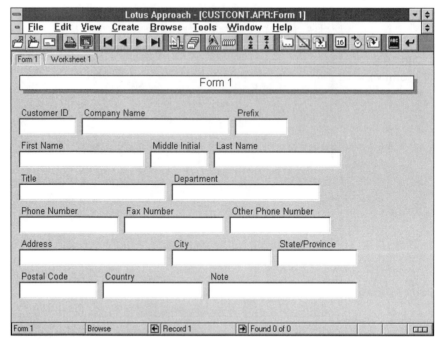

Figure A.17

The Employees default form view.

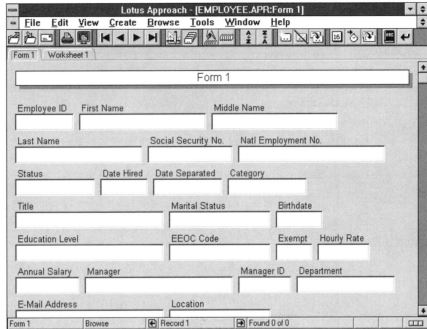

Figure A.18

The Event List default form view.

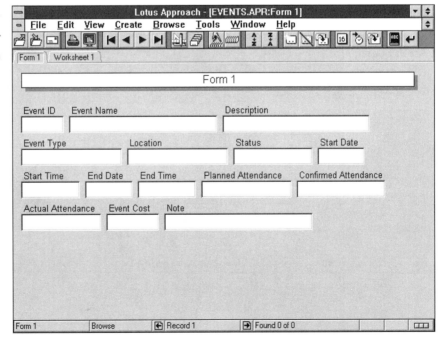

Figure A.19

The Expenses default form view.

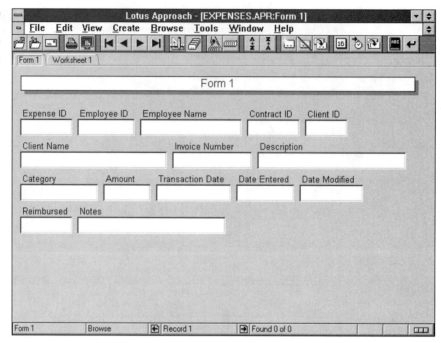

Figure A.20

The Fixed Assets default form view.

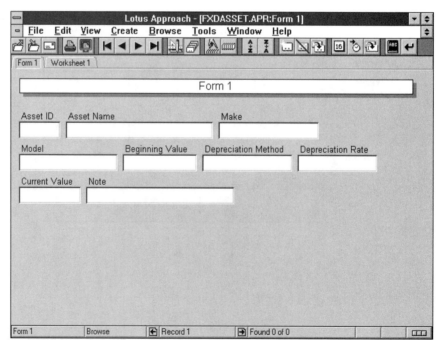

Figure A.21

The Friends and Family default form view.

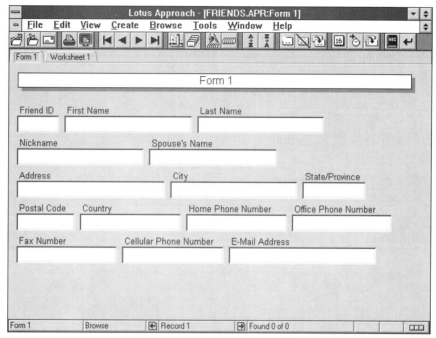

Figure A.22

The Guest List default form view.

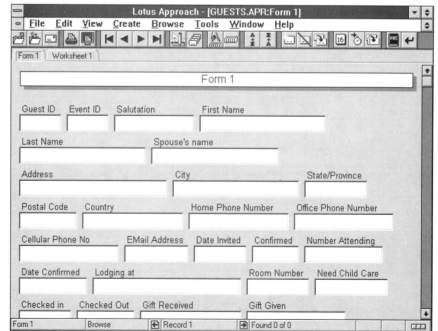

Figure A.23

The Household Inventory default form view.

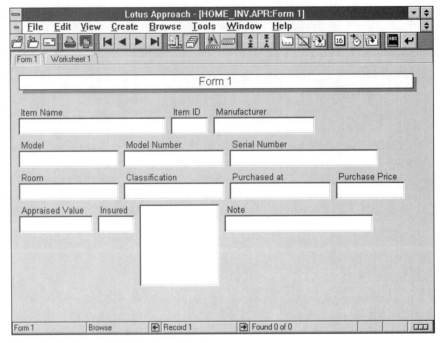

Figure A.24

The Inventory default form view.

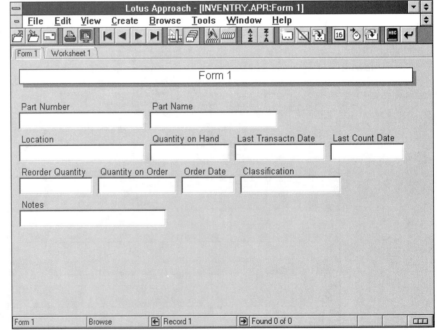

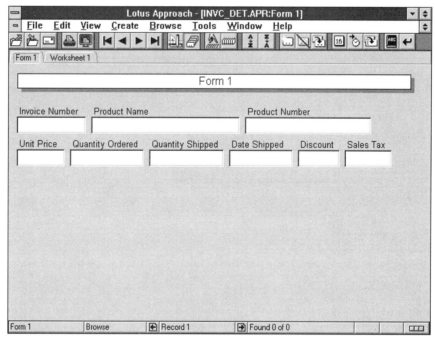

Figure A.25

The Invoice–Details default form view.

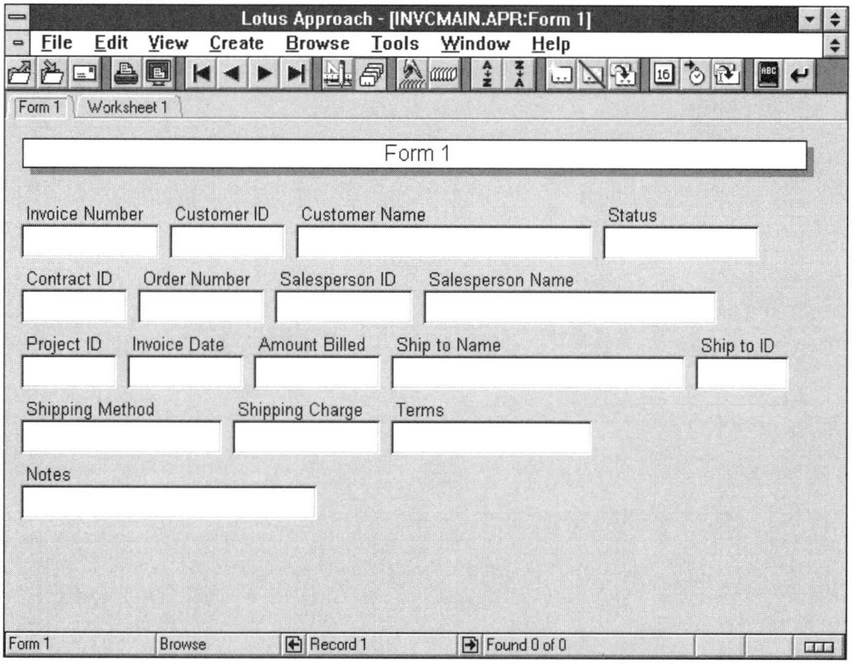

Figure A.26

The Invoice–Main default form view.

Figure A.27

The Letter Tracking default form view.

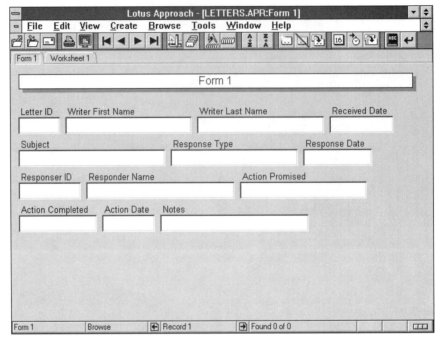

Figure A.29

The Mailing List default form view.

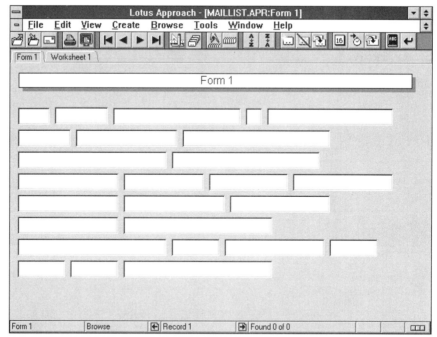

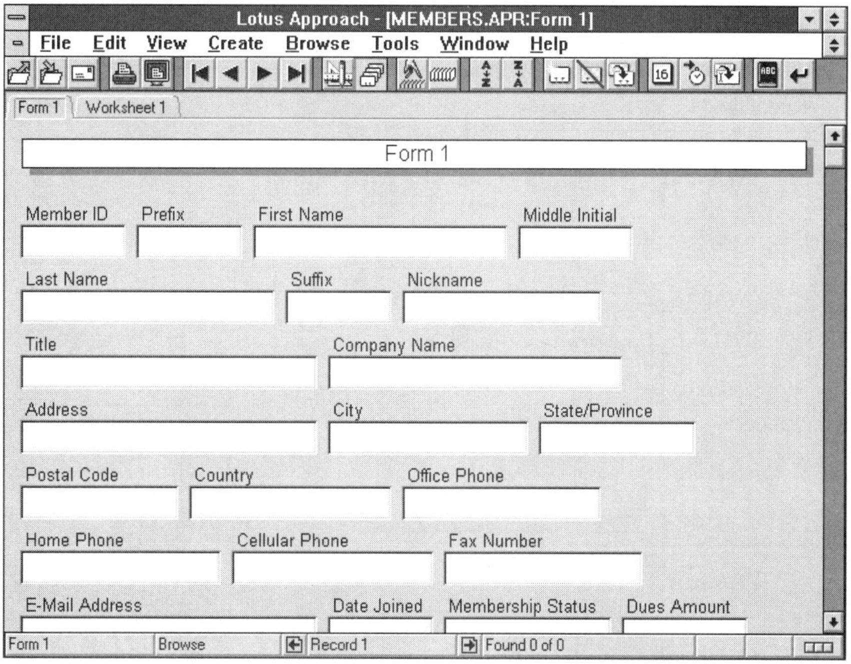

Figure A.30

The Membership List default form view.

Figure A.31

The Musical Groups default form view.

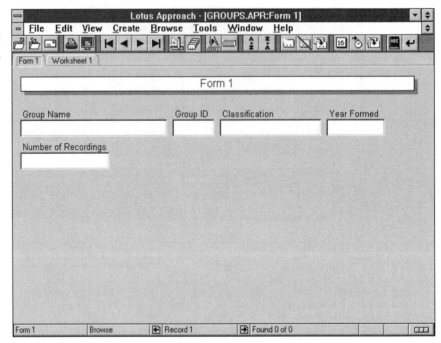

Figure A.32

The Musical Recordings default form view.

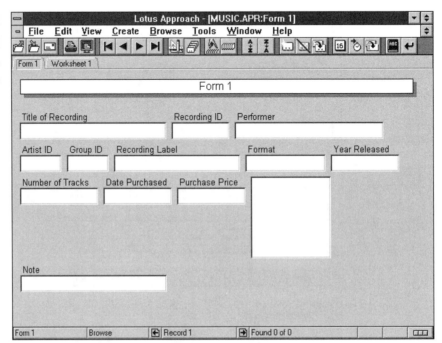

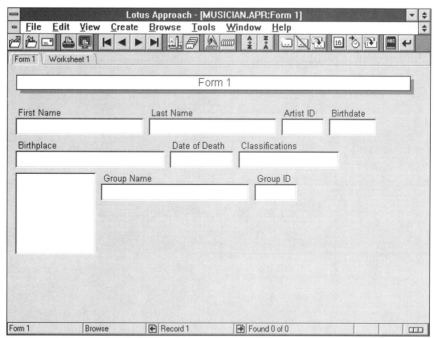

Figure A.35

The Orders–Main default form view.

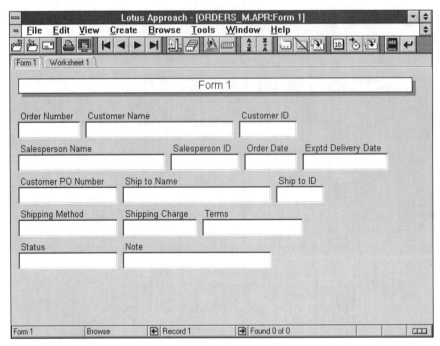

Figure A.36

The Payments default form view.

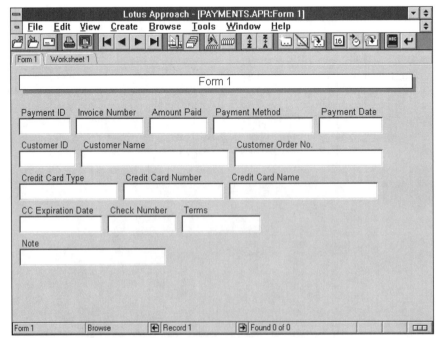

Figure A.37

The Products default form view.

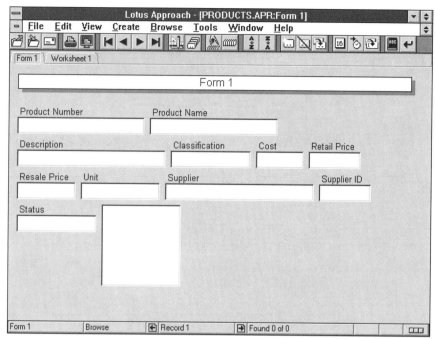

Figure A.38

The Project–List default form view.

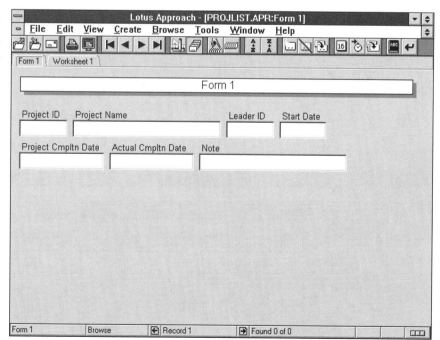

Figure A.39

The Project–Tasks default form view.

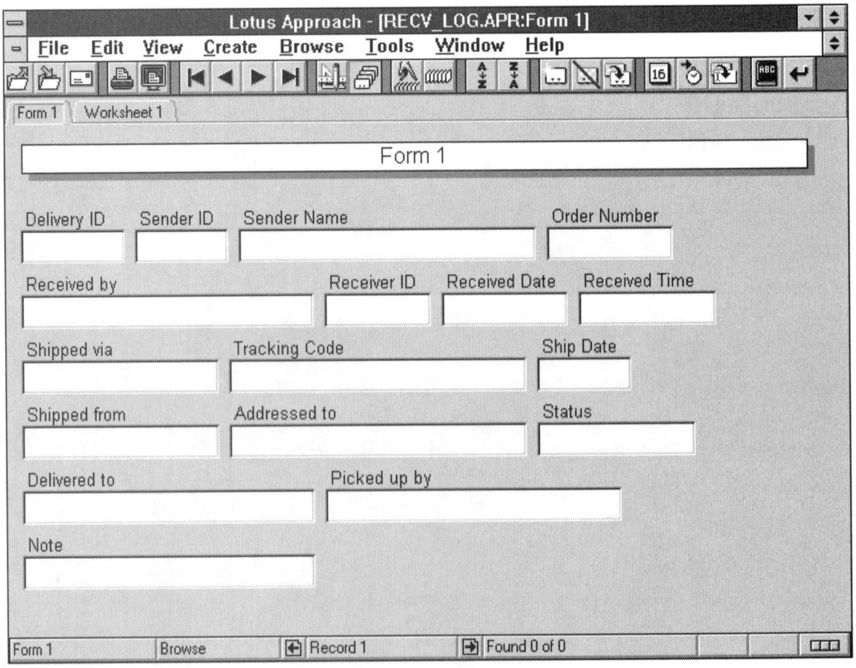

Figure A.40

The Receiving Log default form view.

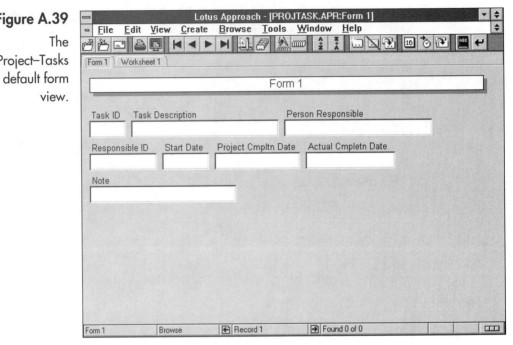

Figure A.41

The Recipes–Ingredients default form view.

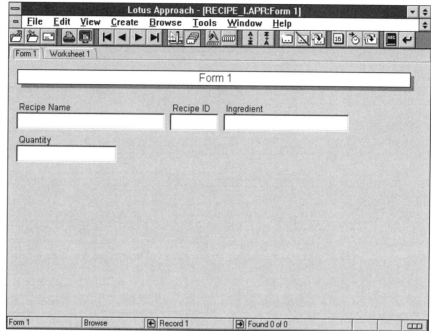

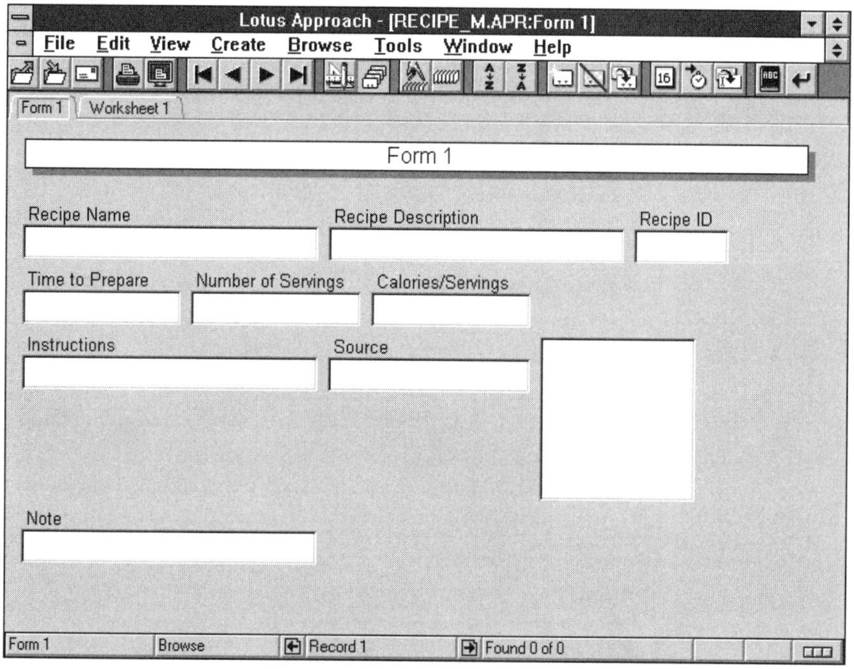

Figure A.42

The Recipes–Main default form view.

Figure A.43

The Services–
Billing default
form view.

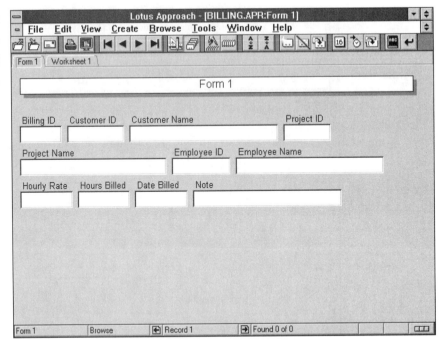

Figure A.44

The Shipping
Log default
form view.

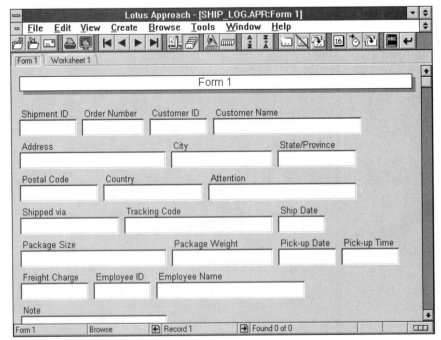

Figure A.45

The Stocks and Bonds default form view.

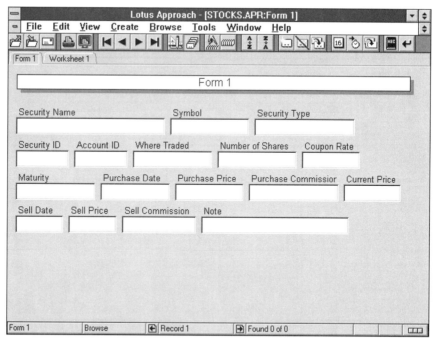

Figure A.46

The Student List default form view.

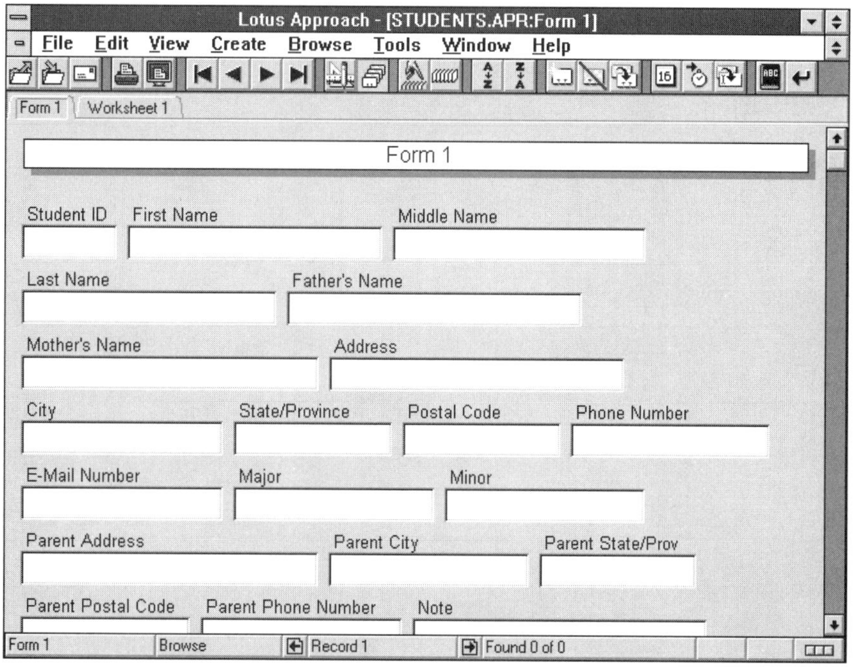

Figure A.47

The Student
Records
default form
view.

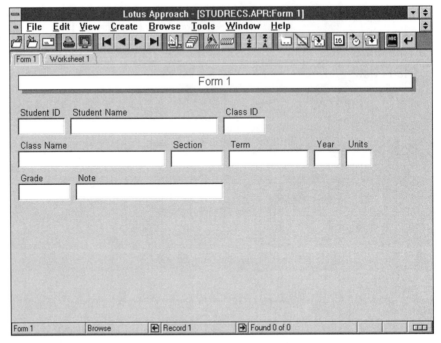

Figure A.47

The Student Records default form view.

Figure A.48

The Suppliers
default form
view.

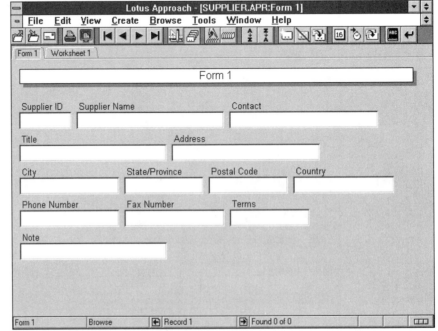

Figure A.48

The Suppliers default form view.

Figure A.49

The Transactions default form view.

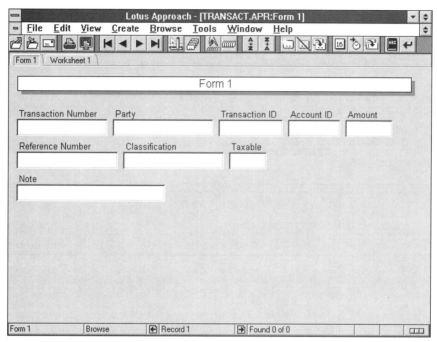

Figure A.50

The Video Library default form view.

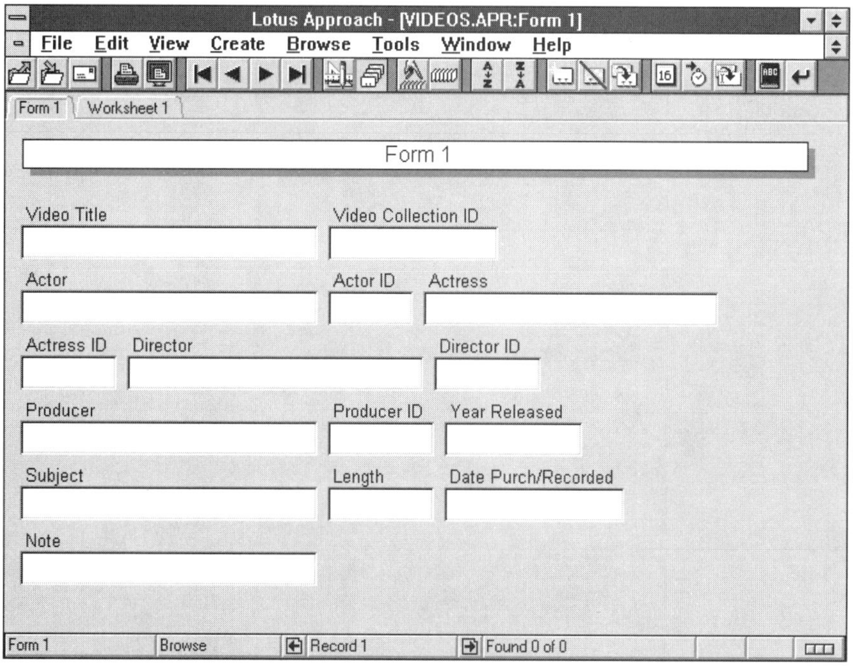

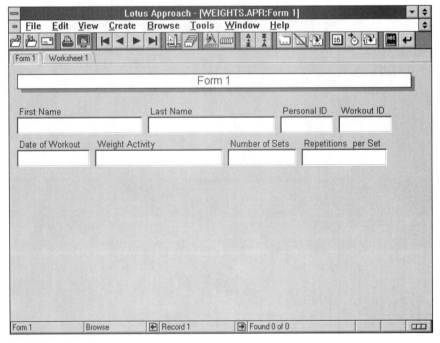

Figure A.53

The Workout
Log default
form view.

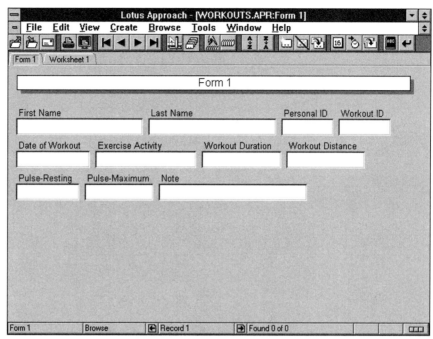

Index